CHILDREN

OF A

FARAWAY WAR

CHILDREN

OF A

FARAWAY WAR

WENDY GRUNER

IGUANA

Publisher: Meghan Behse
Editors: Diana Fitzgerald Bryden, Jane Warren, and Lee Parpart
Cover design: Meghan Behse
Cover image – Lancaster aircrafts: courtesy of Shutterstock.com
Cover image – F/Sgt. Arthur Plowman's diary entry (August 4, 1943):
courtesy of Wendy Gruner

ISBN 978-1-77180-369-4 (paperback)
ISBN 978-1-77180-370-0 (epub)
ISBN 978-1-77180-371-7 (Kindle)

This is an original print edition of *Children of a Faraway War*.

Because if you do not plunder the past, the absence feeds on you.

—Michael Ondaatje

For Robbie, my sister and my friend

Losing

She is sitting on the front verandah shelling peas when a young man in uniform crosses the ramp at the end of the driveway and begins walking through the orchard — his orchard — toward the small green and white bungalow. He seems in no hurry as he makes his way up the dirt road with its centre of raised grass, moving steadily toward her. The apple and pear trees in their neat rows on either side are thick with snowy blossoms. She stops what she is doing and watches his progress. "I'll go to him in a minute," she thinks. She will leave the verandah, scattering the carefully shelled peas, run through the trees and into his arms. "Soon," she thinks, "I'll be with him soon."

And then she wakes and is instantly flooded with regret.

"Even now," my mother tells me, nearly twenty-one years later, "I am sorry I didn't go to him. It's silly, of course. It was just a dream, but now it seems like my last opportunity wasted."

It is the summer of 1965, we are in a restaurant on the Ponte Vecchio in Florence being charmed by the waiters and the food, leaning into each other across the table, talking in a way mothers and daughters rarely do — as if just friends, equals. The candle on the table flickers in the silky breeze of this very Italian evening, its shadows permitting unaccustomed intimacies. Beyond the parapet the Arno slides by, silent and mysterious. I have told her things about my life in Europe. And now she has told me this.

We have been travelling together for a week, having met in Naples, she arriving on a cruise ship from Australia, me after leaving my hitchhiking companions and travelling from Greece. I have just enough Italian to smooth our path and I am now, after two years away from home, a seasoned adventurer, while for her, this is her first trip to Europe. Our roles are suddenly reversed; I am now the caretaker. Perhaps that explains the ease with which we talk. Perhaps that is why she has chosen to enter the seldom-broached world of her husband and my father to tell me of her long ago dream. A dream she had on the night he died.

At the time she told me this story I was not far from my twenty-fourth birthday. She would have been just twenty-six when she had that dream. Within days of the dream a telegram would arrive and she would be a widow with two small daughters, one three, the other nearly five. The regret that washed over her as she woke would be a permanent ache. It is only now, when I am so very much older — by nearly fifty years — than she was when we sat together by the Arno, that I am asking myself why I did not take that moment to ask about my father.

November 11, 1944
RAF Spilsby, Lincolnshire, UK

This is how it is, the night he dies.

By 4:30 the light is fading. By six, as the trucks begin to pick up the crews and head for the airfield in the thickening dark, a waist-high mist blankets the flat fields of Lincolnshire, swirling across the base, softening and obscuring the convoy of utility trucks with their canvas canopies. Their slotted headlights send squinting beams into the murk. Ahead, in Dispersal, the Lancasters wait, a scattered pod of noble whales, their bulbous noses poking out above the mist.

It is two weeks since a full moon dangerously bathed the bombers in its cold light, making them easy pickings. Now, with just four days from a moonless night, there is a slim melon rind of a moon — a good night for flying.

The line of trucks breaks up as it approaches the scattered planes. Bumping across the grass, a truck halts beside one of the planes. The WAAF driver, young, pretty, and smartly capable, stands by the tailgate wishing each of the seven men a cheerful "Good Luck," as they clamber out, awkward in their bulky flying gear. When Arthur, the wireless operator, climbs down she smiles broadly and says, with deliberate emphasis, "Good luck ... SIR. And congratulations."

"Thanks," he says, grinning.

He has been at this base for four months — a long time. She knows him. He's a likeable man, quiet, always smiling, and, two days ago he got his Commission: "Sir" to her now.

The ground crew clusters together under the wings, smoking and watching as the air crew approaches. These are their boys. They want them safe. The plane behind them is serviced with all the care they can muster. It is fuelled, the bomb bays are full. They want these men to get back. They will be at the airfield in the early hours of the next morning, waiting and hoping for them to return.

Seven young men walk awkwardly toward their Lancaster, calling their thanks for the ride to the pretty WAAF. They are weighed down by flying suits and Mae Wests, carrying their parachutes.

Cigarettes are stubbed out as they move in under the wings. Arthur takes one last drag of his, standing for a moment, staring out into the mist, listening. There is the retreating growl and rattle of empty trucks returning to base, and the fog-muffled voices of other crew as they head toward their aircraft. And then, in the far distance, he hears a farm dog bark. Smiling, his shoulders relax a little, he drops his cigarette, grinds it under his heel, and turns to join his fellows.

Already it has been a long day. The time spent waiting for an Operation is often the hardest. And this day has offered two doses of waiting. A daylight raid had been scheduled but it was scrubbed. He feels the familiar tangled emotions when a raid is cancelled: relief (no flying and no flak) and irritation (no chance to get one more raid on his record). The more he ticks off, the sooner he'll be done.

He and his mates relax and amble off to the Mess with an appetite. It will be just another day. And then, just as they are commencing lunch, the news comes in: night Ops are on again. And the food has lost its appeal. They are back to the churning stomachs; back to the fear they all feel but cannot show.

Arthur leaves the Mess and joins the crowd headed for the briefing hut. They move into the long room, calling greetings, making jokes, loud and cheery. He finds his crew and they settle into the rows of chairs, eyes on the shrouded Ops board: a red ribbon from base to the target hidden there. Glowing cigarette ends wink in the dim light as they wait, chatting about anything but ... They stand, like school kids, when the base commander and the squadron commander enter, are told to relax — irony unintended — and then the sheet draped across the Ops board is pulled aside, the mission unveiled: Harburg, just south of Hamburg, oil refineries their target.

The usual warnings are issued: watch for fighters, there will be flak, mind your times, stick together. Section leaders distribute details on headings, bomb loads, target times, wireless frequencies. The men at the front with their pointers and their advice are careful to avoid saying "we" about any of this. Catcalls and shouts of "We???" would follow. The line between those being sent and those doing the sending is clear.

They are wished good luck, stand again as the brass leave, and turn their minds to the task ahead: the navigators to their charts, the engineers to their fuel logs, the bomb aimers to their target maps, and the wireless operators, Arthur among them, to their codes for the night. These last are distributed on "flimsies" — messages typed onto very thin paper designed to be eaten rather than to fall into enemy hands.

In the morning Arthur and his crew had pedalled to their plane on their bikes. Checked her out, run her up, spoken to the ground crew. They don't need to repeat that, so the long afternoon stretches ahead. This is the hardest time, these empty hours between briefing and Ops. Some catch an hour's sleep in the corrugated Nissen huts. Arthur is tempted; he enjoys his sleep. But it is early November, damp and cold in these living spaces with their rows of bunks and a coal-burning stove, and he also enjoys being warm. Any thought of hopping on a bike and heading for a pub is a no go before Ops. Now that the target has been revealed, telephones are sealed, so the local boys cannot call home. But they and the others write letters, get things in order. Arthur wanders into the Mess where men sprawl in armchairs reading or dozing, their lives scrolling behind closed lids. Some play cards. Anything to still the twisting gut. Anything to avoid the "what if?" He finds a chair. The gramophone spills music into the room: "Tristesse," a favourite pre-Op tune. *So deep is the night/ No moon tonight/ No friendly star to guide me with its light.* They are so young, many in their teens; they have so much to lose. Wives and sweethearts on their minds, they sink into the armchairs around the fire, allowing melancholy to wash over them. *In my dream our lips are blending/ Will our dream be never-ending?*

While these men wait, the base is humming. It takes three people on the ground for every man in the air to keep these missions running. Parachutes are packed and checked. Sometimes, more often than any man likes to dwell on, they don't open or they become hopelessly tangled. Then there is a long silent fall to the unforgiving earth. Or they snag on the aircraft, trapping the man desperately bailing out through flame and disintegration, condemning him to the pure agony of death by fire.

The WAAFs, those young women of the Women's Auxiliary Air Force, who pack the parachutes, also put together a flight ration package for each airman: a flask of coffee, sandwiches, Fry's chocolate, boiled sweets, Horlicks malted milk tablets. And they make up the escape kits that each man will be given as he climbs into battle gear in the locker room: silk maps of the area they will cross, local currency of the countries they pass over, useful phrases in the languages of the territories where they may find themselves, wakey

wakey pills, water purifying tablets. In their lapels their escape pictures are sewn ready to be glued into (one hopes) convincing documents should they be lucky enough to stumble onto a Resistance group after bailing out. In the sole of their flying boots is a razor to hack off the boot tops giving them a more civilian look. One of their buttons is a tiny compass.

It is time to head to the locker room to kit up. Arthur joins the line to pick up his parachute. A jolly WAAF trots out the tired: "If it doesn't open, file a complaint." He smiles on cue, no point in being rude, she is only trying to lighten the mood. He collects his Mae West, a bulky, and, yes, bosomy life jacket to keep him bobbing in the North Sea should it come to that. Then they climb into the layers necessary for a long ride above the clouds in a cold metal tube. The gunners wear the most layers, topped off with bulky, electrically wired suits. They will spend the next six hours freezing in their turrets, eyes scanning for enemy fighters. But for all, over silk underwear (and sometimes added pyjamas), there is the battle dress uniform, the heavy white roll-neck sweater, the Irvin flying jacket of fleece-lined leather, the socks, the boots, the gloves, the scarf, the flying helmet, the Mae West. Then lugging their parachutes they lumber outside to wait for the trucks driven by the WAAFs.

Under the wings of the giant bomber they stop for a brief word with the ground crew. Anything more we should know? Any problems with the servicing? Reassured, they turn to the plane. One by one the seven clamber up the ladder to the entry door, crawl in and make their way to their positions. After the last man is in, one of the ground crew slams the door and pulls the ladder away. The gunners hoist themselves into their turrets. The others make their way forward, some climbing over the spar that runs across the plane between the wings. It is the often fatal flaw in this otherwise magnificent war machine. Should things go wrong, getting out safely is made doubly difficult by having to negotiate this awkward barrier. Perhaps they think of this each time they swing their legs over it. But perhaps not, for now that they are aboard and the familiar tasks are taking over, now that they have something to do, the clenched guts relax a little. There is a purpose; they have a job.

The gunners in their Perspex turrets hook up their electrical suits and test the gun mounts. The pilot and the flight engineer move to the front and stow their parachutes. The pilot sits on his, an unyielding lump under his bum for however long this will take. The bomb aimer goes with them. He will sit on the floor, or stand, peering ahead, until he must take his position, lying on his belly in the nose, over the target. Then he becomes the most important person aboard for that run up to the dropping of the bomb load. This is why they are going. This is the job they must do. Behind the pilot sits the navigator in his curtained "office," laying out his charts, testing his equipment. He must have light at all times and it must not be visible either to impair his skipper's night vision, or to alert an enemy fighter, hence his curtain. All wear headsets through which they communicate. Oxygen masks hang from their necks.

The wireless operator's position is behind the navigator's table. Arthur settles in to test his set and await the skipper's check in. He is twenty-seven, an old man to the teens who crew so many of these planes. He is married with two small daughters. He is more than halfway through a tour. When it is over, he will apply to instruct. There will be no more raids into Germany for him after that. There may be some small regret at this: the end of such a terrifying and intense time in his still young life. But he knows he needs to think of the family he has left behind. Another tour would be, quite literally, suicidal and so unfair to them. But, for now, he thinks, let's get through this one. Let's not think of what might get in the way of that.

Radio headset on, he listens for his skipper's checks. The roll is called. Each man responds. They are ready. One by one the engines turn over, the ground crew pulls the chocks away, their bomber lumbers down the narrow perimeter paths, part of a line of Lancasters each following the white tail light of the plane ahead, moving toward the runway threshold. There, a crowd of WAAFs, ground crew, fellow airmen, and base personnel have gathered to wave them off as they do every night of operations. They cheer as their boys lift up into the air.

The plane judders and shrieks, gaining power. Then the green Aldis lamp flashes for take-off. Four huge Merlin engines scream, the pilot fights the controls. The giant, fully fuelled, bomb-laden death machine must claw its way from the runway and into the air. Hearts tick in throats, sweat pours, mouths dry up. Any error and they are incinerated in a blaze of exploding bombs and flaming fuel.

And then, with a final lurch, they are airborne. They gain altitude, soar over the flat farmland and blacked out villages of Lincolnshire, their engines rattling the windows of families at supper, as they head for the coast. Another operation has begun. Another night hoping to beat the odds. But tonight, the seven men on this plane will not be lucky. They are not going to land safely, debrief, and enjoy the post-Ops bacon and eggs. Of course they do not know it, but this, for all of them, not just for the man at the centre of this story, is their last raid.

***

I have no memory of him. I cannot conjure up his face, his voice, the warmth of his presence. But there is one scrap: a shred of our life while he was still alive, although far away at war, a memory from when I was two.

My mother is scrubbing the linoleum kitchen floor and would rather I keep out of her way. She sets me up with paper and crayons on the wood box in the back porch. "Write Daddy a letter," she tells me before returning to her task. I remember obediently wielding the crayon in the way of a toddler. But I became a cynic early. "This isn't real writing," I think to myself. "It isn't what Robbie does." This single memory, one of failure to connect, is all I have.

As a child, I had only the sketchiest idea of how he died. Some of my notions were simply invented. When my mother remarried, some five years after his death, I worried my eight-year-old head that he would suddenly reappear and be horrified to find this stranger running his orchard, living in his house, sleeping in his bed. I'd somehow embraced the romantic notion that he had been shot down over Germany and could miraculously have survived to return to us. I confided none of this to her that night, decades later, as we dined together in the Italian dusk. I let the moment slide. Over the years we, my sister and I, have let many such moments slip by.

My sister, Robbie, eighteen months my senior, has also been told of our mother's dream. We have both read of women who have similar dreams at the time of the death of husbands and lovers. We are not inclined to believe in divine portents. At best we might keep a wary open mind. Mummy, in particular was suspicious of the fanciful, the non-practical. She would purse her lips and let out a skeptical puff of air. But this dream, for us, is different. It is, I suppose, so vivid it is hard to discount. And it did predict or suggest something real.

If only she had started up, spilling her apron full of shells, letting the colander roll along the verandah scattering her dream peas, if she had run across the lawn through the dream trees toward her dream husband coming up the driveway, would he have dropped the kit bag slung over his shoulder and run to her in his turn? Would he have reached out and pulled her close and would she for a glorious moment have felt his solid reality? If she had done this, acted as she knew she should in her dream of his return, would this somehow have changed what happened that night?

Our mother, permanently wounded by her loss, struggling to run our little orchard and raise her two daughters, had remarried for convenience rather than love. It seemed impolite to speak of our dead father in this new family. This was so much her story, her grief, a subject never expressly forbidden, but also not nurtured. And, anyway, how would our stepfather, much older and with bad feet that kept him out of combat, feel if we paraded our war hero around the dinner table?

This stepfather (and for all the years he held this role we never referred to him as anything else; he was never "Dad," certainly not "Daddy") lived in the shadow of the man whose orchard he had taken over. In the shed, where we graded and packed the apples, pears, plums, and cherries, was a large ink pad and an equally large stamp to label the wooden cases of fruit. "A. L. Plowman Orchardist" it proclaimed: our father's name. It was never replaced by a stamp declaring "A. A. Chiswell Orchardist" to acknowledge the fellow actually growing, picking, and packing the fruit. I think my stepfather knew enough to leave this alone, although I do recall a moment in the shed as he stood, arms folded, gazing at the stacks of packed fruit bearing his predecessor's name, when he muttered glumly, acknowledging this erosion of his identity, "I might as well be the bugger."

And so years passed and questions were not asked. We felt it inappropriate. Mummy confided to a friend that she thought we did not care. To even think that, let alone write it, causes me pain. How could three people who loved each other, my sister, my mother and I, have been so unable to speak of this hole in our lives? Off we went, Robbie and I, to get an education, to see the world, to marry, have children, and then grandchildren, make lives apart from her. I married a Canadian and lived in Canada, depriving her of closeness to my three daughters who knew her only through rare visits, letters, and carefully chosen gifts. My sister, having lived in England, eventually returned to Australia and saw our mother often. Now this sister and attentive daughter wonders, to her growing bewilderment, why she never sat her down and said, "Tell me about Daddy."

Memory is important; it needs tending. It is the only immortality I can cling to: the hope that those we have lost will live on in the stories told by the people who loved them. We have so little of our father. For a long time he was not given that chance of immortality. Not that he was forgotten, but we did not work at finding the memories and passing them on. We did not bring him into our world, my sister Robbie and I.

Until we decided to fix that.

Seeking

Suddenly, at the age of seventy, our tiny mother, who had lost her soulmate and never fully healed, was gripped by an aching depression. She had, I believe, never allowed herself to mourn her loss, never faced it down, and now it engulfed her. Everything was an effort; she could barely get out of bed, was not eating, hardly spoke. I knew she was struggling. Married and living in Canada, I was not very helpful as a daughter. "It's like a rat gnawing in my chest," she told me in one of her rare calls. Miserable and guilty at being so far away from her, I arranged to take a leave from teaching to go back to Australia. I would, I promised myself, take care of her, ask about her life, find her and my father perhaps. But, before I could get there, she died.

The staff of the senior's home to which she had retreated found her on the floor of her room with her arms stretched toward the light spilling in from the passage. The mixed message in this — a will to live and a need to be free of her dark shawl of depression — undid me. I fell into bed and wept for three days. My family gathered: a perplexed and hovering husband, three daughters, anxious moths to my sobbing flame, miserable in their inability to comfort me.

This engulfing grief surprised me as much as it did them. I was guilty, bereft, orphaned. It would be many years before I would give myself the gift of exploring these feelings.

My sister and brother arranged her funeral and it was not easy. Our mother, hugging her privacy to her, had specified in her will that she be buried before a death announcement was made, that she be cremated and that "nothing" be done with her ashes. People in the town who loved her, and there were many, bristled indignantly at being deprived of a chance to pay their respects. My poor siblings felt their considerable wrath. The ashes, in a utilitarian plastic box, languished on the funeral home shelves. "Nothing" was clearly not an option.

I travelled home. My sister and I embarked on a pilgrimage around New South Wales visiting friends and family who had known her. After carrying the sealed box of ashes about for an awkward amount of time we scattered her ashes from a pimple of a hill, ambitiously named The Pinnacle. From its modest summit it is possible see every place she ever lived. It felt right. We could only hope she would have approved.

Some time before Mummy died she told Robbie that she had our father's wartime diary and, with some reluctance, gave it to her to read. An unexpected door to him opened. Robbie read it and wrote that I must too, and soon. Bill, my half-brother (and that is another puzzle: why this label? Why not just brother?) photocopied my father's diary for me. Robbie, being the elder, is the keeper of this neat journal with its maroon cover, brown spine, and lined pages full of our father's elegant cursive script, a record of his adventures overseas. Now I had my copy.

He was not an effusive diarist and there were lengthy periods when he made no entries. But, through descriptions of his day-to-day life as he left his home and family and travelled by troopship to the UK, to train and serve there during the war, with careful reading and attention we believed he could be known better. He could become a reality in our lives.

On one of his leaves in London, he had bought two volumes of *The Pickwick Papers* and shipped them home to his Nooney. That was his pet, and exclusive, name for her. Although his name was Arthur, she called him "Paddy." Nooney and Paddy — I love that. Before he left for the war, after a day of hard work on their orchard, after tucking us into bed, they read to each other by the kerosene lamp in the kitchen of their little farmhouse. Dickens was a favourite. From the diary we know that he bought those two volumes in London and mailed them from there on September 29, 1943, and that he got a cable from Nooney telling him of their arrival on January 7, 1944. That was a journey of over three months.

I have a second book, *A Tale of Two Cities*. It is inscribed, "To Nooney from her ever adoring Paddy" and dated October 4th, 1944. He mailed it from Edinburgh a little over five weeks before his death. This volume, with its loving message, would have arrived around two months after the "Deeply regret to inform you..." telegram. I tried to imagine how this must have felt for her. The reality of what had happened to her, to all of us, blazing anew.

I typed out the contents of the diary to give to Joanne, Megan, and Marion, my three daughters, now young women with children of their own and a growing curiosity about this missing grandfather. I began to untangle the arcane references that stud his wartime prose. I suggested to Robbie that we go to the UK, journal in hand, and visit all the places it mentions. It would, I said, be a small homage to the man we never had the chance to know. On a selfish level it would give us a trip together, allow us to be sisters again after years of being apart.

November 11, 2010

On Remembrance Day of 2010, I phoned Robbie. To be totally accurate, I made the call on November 10, wanting to catch her, in northern New South Wales, on the actual anniversary of his death: Armistice Day, November 11, 1944.

After an exchange of family news I reminded her of the date. "Gosh, I didn't even realize." We laughed, acknowledging that this will happen, that the present so often trumps the past, and then I reminded her of our trip. "What do you think? Perhaps some time next year?"

I could hear apologetic panic in her voice. She and her partner share a macadamia nut farm requiring much cosseting. In addition she has forty steers, every one of which is named, a beloved friend, and can only be left with much trepidation. There are the hens as well, and a cat. She frequently is out of the house by dawn to plant native tree saplings, creating a safe corridor for endangered koalas. *And* she has a son, a daughter, three grandchildren and numerous friends and family who must be visited and loved. She is a woman of large heart and the calls on that heart would fell the average ox.

I had, by this time, been retired for a number of years and, apart from a little light gardening and a gentle social life delightfully punctuated by boisterous family gatherings, my world was not nearly as crowded as hers.

"OK," I said, "just think about it."

The next day she called, voice firm with determination, "This is just silly. All that stuff can wait. We're doing it."

And so it began.

In the months of preparation before Robbie and I set off on our journey, the fickleness of facts almost drove us mad. As we ferreted about in the events and lives of people, now mostly dead, who engaged in the ghastly adventure of World War II, we no sooner established one thing, before being told by another source that we were wrong. We became smugly convinced that we had unravelled a mystery only to have this victory snatched away by some piece of the puzzle that simply did not fit. More than once I despaired. My sister, 12,000 miles away, and on the same quest, did not succumb to the same despondency. We are different, she and I. She was enjoying the search, collecting each little shred and holding it dear. She was wise enough to know that we, however much we might want to, cannot know everything. The dead keep their secrets. And although we have both kicked ourselves black and blue for waiting to do this search until the dead, apparently, were our only source, she was more resigned to the reality. I needed to follow her lead in this. All my life I have wished I were more like her and, as we searched, this longing only intensified.

Despite our differences, we were both consumed by this need to know. In my house dishes and laundry languished. There was quite a bit of slapdash cooking. The bedroom I had turned into an office was a shambles: papers, books, piles of notes. My husband, Tony, was researching his family tree at the same time, a far neater and more organized process than mine. We met at lunch and supper to share what we had learned in our different explorations. A bit of a war buff, he gently corrected some of my wilder theories and glaring inaccuracies. "Look," I cried triumphantly, as he poured me a pre-dinner glass of wine, "I've printed a really good picture of a Lancaster."

"Wendy," he was trying not to smile, "that isn't a Lancaster. That only has two engines. A Lancaster has four."

"Oh." Steep learning curve.

All those miles apart, Robbie and I continued furiously researching, making lists, consulting maps, reading and rereading the diary. Back and forth our emails flew: "Did you know..." "I just found out..." "There is a wonderful article..." "The most amazing pictures popped up..." "I am reading such a good book..." Robbie's spotty rural internet service made her mildly homicidal. Mine offered up a juicy fact only to suck it back, refusing to release it ever again. We both honed our skills as our obsession grew.

We had entered a new world, its jargon quickly becoming ours, slipping effortlessly off the tongue. "Harwell Boxes," "Pathfinder Force," "Oboe," "Window," "Group Command," "Exodus," "ENSA." Slowly we fleshed out the diary, building for ourselves the world he inhabited.

Bald facts — names, places, dates — were fairly easy to come by. As a start, and quite quickly, we knew a something of the men who had died with him. On that plane were three Brits, two Canadians and two Aussies. A fine representative Bomber Command crew. The details of only one have remained elusive: the mid-upper gunner, a Scot whose homeland seemed more reluctant to give up his story. Of the others we know that their ages ranged from nineteen to twenty-seven. They were, on average, an older crew. For the youngest, the nineteen-year-old rear gunner crouched in his Perspex bubble, I can only hope that the giant optimism of youth shielded him from the worst of the terrors. Three of the men were married: our father and two others. We do not know if they also had children. All crew members are buried in Britain, their remains enfolded in a variety of cemeteries, beautiful Portland stone markers at their heads, in graves lovingly tended by the Commonwealth Graves Commission. I have visited only two of them: my father and the bomb aimer who lie side by side in the Cambridge Borough Cemetery.

What we do not know, and may never know, is how often our father flew with this group of men. His original crew, much more powerfully connected, had been split up a couple of months before and there was a frustrating time for him as "spare bod" before he was assigned to this second crew. They could never be the friends his first crew became, but they died with him; he is buried beside one of them. It would help to know more. How did those two other widows cope? Were there children? Did the baby of the crew, the rear gunner, piss on the rear wheel for luck just before climbing aboard for a mission? Did he have brothers and sisters? Did his family ever recover?

Now that we had gone looking for our father, we were greedy for any scrap, any detail. "Do you have any memories of him?" I asked my far away sister during one of our many long-distance calls. That she might have had never occurred to me until that moment and I was stunned when she answered.

"Yes, I have four really good ones."

I was silent, filled with envy and respect. For me he is just a series of photos; for her he is real. I recovered enough to ask her a question that had nibbled at me since we began: "What colour were his eyes?" It seemed to me a simple and necessary thing that every child should know about their father. She didn't remember but even without this detail she has a larger claim. She remembers his face, his voice, his nearness. That it had taken me decades to discover this marvellous fact about my sister was yet another puzzle. It was also a gift.

What we wanted, and will want for the rest of our lives, is to know who this man was, a man who could have been a part of us.

All those young men in Bomber Command were tested in ways we cannot imagine. How did he do? We are prepared for frailties. In fact we long for them. We are not looking for a superhero, just the man who was our father.

Offering

By the time our father left for England, he and Nooney had bought a small orchard and built their own little house, a two-bedroom cottage that sat at the bottom of a fairly steep slope on which most of the older apples and pears grew. We called this simply "the hill." On the top of the hill was an area for grazing our cow, a caramel Jersey, supplier of milk, butter and cream, and our draught horse, Toby, who worked on the orchard pulling the various drays and a spray cart. Our parents had dreamed of one day building a larger house up there in an open field against a row of tall pines; the view across the valley was glorious. As they began this life it all seemed possible, achievable, and right. Nobody plans to have their dreams interrupted by a war, and for a while theirs weren't.

My father did not need to involve himself in this conflict far from home. As a fruit grower and a family man, he was seen as a valuable asset to his country. His was a Reserved Occupation: he and others like him were exempted, and in some cases barred, from serving. He was also older than many of the eager young men who rushed to volunteer. He had a wife and children; there was more to lose.

As I grew up I frequently wondered why he went. But whom could I ask? He was often on my mind. In fact, my long held fantasy — that he'd been shot down over Germany and might suddenly come home — was a reality for more men than you'd expect. Men who parachuted out of planes and landed in German territory were, if they survived, often caught, and spent the rest of their war in POW camps. A surprising number, the Evaders as they were known, cunningly made their way through Europe and finally got themselves home to their squadrons. They arrived back at camp irritated to find that all their possessions had been packed up and shipped off to a grieving family. It's a good thing I did not know these stories at the time; my imaginings were vivid enough, if a little vague on geography and logistics. The horrifying scenario that I'd developed, of a father returning to find that we had callously moved on, explains my eight-year-old self's noisy objection to our mother's second marriage. I didn't explain my fears during this incoherent weeping fit; I just knew that this stepfather in waiting shouldn't live with us in our house and made the sensible suggestion that he should live in the packing shed.

I did wonder if our mother was angry that Daddy had joined up and left us. Then I found some notes she had made for a "Life Album" my half-brother, Bill, had given her on her sixty-ninth birthday. A great idea, even if she did begin by complaining that she had so much else to do and that her arthritis would make her handwriting hard to read.

I am grateful that she persisted, reluctant as she was. We have so little else. In this brief and grudging memoir, she speaks with great affection of her childhood. We know that her mother was less than loving, vain and spoilt, but Mummy learned to find the positive. "Life on the land is wonderful," she writes. "I married an orchardist. Paddy and I had a terrific few years together, working on our property. Every day a holiday. Not much money and many ups and downs but so good ... Then we had two little girls, Robyn Dunia and Wendy Patricia..."

It touches me that she wrote, "Every day a holiday," of a life of hard work dragging a much neglected old orchard into productivity, living without electricity or indoor plumbing, milking a cow each day, killing, plucking and cooking their own chickens, two little kids so close together — to her, there is no hardship, it is just "so good."

And oh, my most blest of sisters has a tiny portal into that time: she saw them, absorbed, working as a team, weaving a life together.

She remembers them in the dog pen behind the tall tank stand. They are kneeling together, all their attention on Julie, one of their bulldogs, who is whelping, and things are going off the rails. The first pup is refusing to be born. Robbie sees her parents, heads together, in anxious discussion. She hears the worry in their voices. She doesn't like being excluded.

They love their dogs, but breeding bulldogs is also a way to make money; there is an investment on the line. Earnestly they discuss what needs to be done. They are not in the mood for an importunate child looking for attention. "They got cross," Robbie recalls with an affectionate absence of rancour. "I think I wasn't used to being brushed off. Maybe that's why I remember this moment."

Mummy remembers that time, before he went away, the teamwork and the love, as the happiest period of her life. And then this scant explanation of what came next: "When the war started Paddy stood it for a couple of years, seeing his friends join up. One was killed. I really felt that if I'd been him I'd have wanted to go so didn't stand in his way."

***

It is Sunday evening at Mount Pleasant, Nooney's family home, the one from which she has so recently escaped and the family tea has been interrupted. Nooney and Paddy stand in front of the wireless console in Mount Pleasant's infrequently used lounge room. Nooney's parents are seated in the comfortless armchairs, leaning forward, listening intently. Nooney's two young brothers stand in the doorway, excited and frightened. It is September 3, 1939, and Prime Minister Menzies is speaking to the Australian people. "Fellow Australians, it is my melancholy duty to inform you officially that in consequence of a persistence by Germany in her invasion of Poland, Great Britain has declared war upon her and that, as a result, Australia is also at war."

Paddy reaches for Nooney's hand. Everything has changed. Already he knows, and so does she, that he will eventually need to go. She is five months pregnant.

My mother tells me, in a rare discussion about my father, that they really did believe in King and Country. Paddy's own sisters speak longingly of "going home" as they imagine trips to the British Isles, a place where they were not born and which they have never seen. The roots run deep. Our father believes it a matter of honour to sign up and head off to protect the Empire. These loyalties, now frayed to gossamer, were sturdy and compelling for their generation.

Even for our generation, Robbie's and mine, the ties to Britain were real. We listened to the Queen's Speech at Christmas, lit bonfires on the hill to celebrate her coronation, and longed to visit England as our own sort of going home. When I stood for the first time in Piccadilly Circus, gazing up at Eros, his arrow ready to fly, I burst into tears. I felt I had returned to my Spiritual Centre. Embarrassing, but true. I did not, as I gave in to my twenty-one-year-old paroxysm of patriotic fervour, wonder if Daddy felt a similar thrill under Eros's gaze. After all, he had gone to war, in large part, because of his ties to Empire.

Our parents' generation was born at the tail end of the Great War, into a world tinted with the mythology spun out of its bloody history. It was, they believed, fought for the honour of the Empire; Australians answered the call and died nobly with a smile on their lips. The young men of this new generation were expected to do the same. The careless massacre of Gallipoli was, by most, sanitized. Australian youth were used as cannon fodder in a war that had little to do with them, or anyone, really. And here they were being groomed to do it all over again.

Motherland, in this young country, was revered: that which was English seen as superior. Gardens displayed English blooms; Australia's native flowers stayed in the bush where they belonged. In choking heat, Sunday roast dinners and British puddings were served in stuffy dining rooms, the men in shirt and tie. Children read Shelley

and Keats and Dickens and it was only apologetically that the odd
Australian poet sidled into the curriculum.

Each morning at the school assembly an oath was taken to love
God, serve the King, obey Parents, Teachers, and the Law. Obedience
underpinned much of life. This is not to portray the famously
iconoclastic Aussie as a meek sheep-like fellow; it was simply a
different time. And change comes slowly.

As kids, Robbie and I continued to be subjected to midday roast
turkey and plum pudding at Christmas, the sun beating down on the
corrugated iron roof. Wearing shorts was permitted, we had not
completely lost our minds, but we were a long way from the current
Aussie Yuletide of cold prawns under a backyard gum tree. Our
Christmas tree, cut from the hill was ridiculously decorated with
homemade snow. Our Christmas cards featured robins perched on
snow-laden trees or jolly gatherings around blazing fires. My
classroom had a framed portrait of Elizabeth Regina above the
blackboard. When the dewy young Queen visited Australia, my
royalty besotted eleven-year-old self cheerfully travelled miles to
stand in the blistering sun for the most fleeting of glimpses.

This adoration has faded. The majority of Australians would be
happy to be rid of the monarchy, a long road from our parents who,
in their early twenties, could not imagine a future where Mother
England would let her loyal subjects down. They believed their duty
lay in defending the Empire. Knowing this, our father's motives for
going are not so hard to understand.

As a seemingly unstoppable German machine poured across
Europe it was clear that a way of life was in peril. The brutality that
was Nazi Germany was no secret. In September of 1941, when I was
just two weeks old and my little family was safe on its little orchard,
the people of France were about to experience the full brutality of a
German occupation. A Code of Hostages was published and imposed.
To discourage acts of resistance, the Germans rounded up hostages,
innocent French citizens, and held them as reprisals for civilian acts

against occupying Germans, summarily executing them as retribution for the death or injury of German soldiers. The ratio was anything from fifty French lives for one injured German to one hundred French lives for one killed German. Anyone who read the papers could clearly see the barbarity of this enemy. And everyone knew about the concentration camps; they did not know their full horror, but they knew enough. To sit at home protected by the ability to grow apples and pears while his friends died was humiliating to my father. My mother understood Paddy's need to go.

***

"And you slept through the whole thing?" My mother was laughing at the other end of the phone. Calling from my college, first year Uni and still in need of a frequent Mummy fix, I had stimulating news. The night before, a prowler had been spotted in my women's residence. The young women were hustled from their beds to sit in solidarity on the staircase, many armed with tennis racquets and hockey sticks, waiting for the police to track the felon down. I, however, was not there. I slept through the entire drama.

Mummy found this more riveting than the notion that a prowler could gain access to the dorms of the young and nubile. "You must take after your father," she told me. "He was a good sleeper. He managed to sleep through the attack on Sydney Harbour."

"Really? He was in Sydney when that happened?"

"Yes, he was staying with Uncle George and Aunty Flo. I'm amazed he was able to fall asleep in the first place — Uncle George keeps half the street awake with his snoring."

When one of the three miniature Japanese subs that entered Sydney Harbour got stuck in the net strung between the Heads, the submariners on board realized the end was upon them. In true kamikaze style, they blew themselves up. A Keystone Cops of a battle followed, with torpedoes zooming about the harbour, battleships firing on subs, visible or not, and the sky lit up with exploding shells. During this mayhem, the Sydney Harbour ferries continued to run serenely. And then a torpedo, aimed at the USS *Chicago*, missed and slammed into HMS *Kuttabul*, killing nineteen Australian and two British sailors. It was dangerous, dramatic, tragic, and noisy. The whole city was awake and terrified. Well, not the whole city. My father slumbered on, with no idea that, at home in Orange, his Nooney, her ear glued to the radio, feared for his safety.

So, that is where I get my gift of sleep.

"Why was he there?"

There is the tiniest pause, "He went down to join the Air Force."

The sub attack was June 3, 1942. He formally volunteered five days later.

I, Arthur Leslie Plowman, swear that I will well and truly serve Our Sovereign Lord the King as a member of the Air Force Reserve of the Commonwealth of Australia, and that I will resist His Majesty's enemies and cause His Majesty's Peace to be kept and maintained, and that I will in all matters appertaining to my service faithfully discharge my duty according to law. So help me God! June 8, '42, age 25 years and 4 months.

"Was there a Morse code set in the cupboard in the kitchen when we were little, or did I make that up?" I ask Robbie during another of our phone calls.

"No, I remember that too. We used to play with it. I wonder what happened to it."

It sat at the very bottom of the big pantry cupboard in among balls of string and a stack of preserving bottles. We knew it belonged to our father and that it had something to do with war. At some point it disappeared. And now it has popped into my head.

"I expect Mummy got rid of it. Too hard for her to have it around. Do you think he had it there to practise his Morse when he was on leave?"

"Yes, I suppose so."

Home Training

Some months later he was called up. He came by train to Sydney to report to the ITS, the Initial Training School, at Bradfield Park. His younger daughter was just over a year old, her sister two and a half. He left Nooney in charge of the orchard and his two young children — both, possibly, still in nappies. She was alone, running a house that seems fearfully primitive by my twenty-first century standards. Laundry was accomplished in a giant copper-lined cauldron heated by a fire underneath. Wielding a large wooden pole, she hauled out the boiled sheets and towels, dumping the steaming piles in the laundry tub. She fed them through the hand wringer, piled them into a basket and carried them to the clothesline beyond the tank stand.

Each morning, she was up early to feed the chickens, milk the cow and carry the brimming bucket up from the barn. The milk was then separated, turned into cream and made into butter. She weeded the vegetable garden, cleaned the house, cooked the meals, and ironed the clothes (with a series of solid, black irons heated on the stove). And all this before there was even the tiniest blow struck at keeping the orchard running. But she understood why he had to do this, why he was in training that would take him to the other side of the world.

He had chosen to volunteer for the Air Force. Time and again those who chose this path are described as "the cream of the crop." Pretentious perhaps, and slightly insulting to the Army and Navy. But there it is. A life in the air appealed to these independent-minded men. Most had never flown, but barnstormers who travelled the country between the wars offered a glimpse of this new world. And there were daring flights from the UK and the US. Australian aviators Charles Kingsford Smith and Bert Hinkler defied these unimaginable distances, followed with breathless awe by the Australian people, our parents among them. Then Amy Johnson, an aviatrix no less, stormed the skies, breaking records and conquering hearts. Our mother, at age twelve, had a dog who rejoiced in the name Amy Johnson Higman Hawke.

The Air Force had other inducements. Discipline for the fly boys was less stringent than in the Army or Navy. Death would be quick and clean; no drowning in icy waters surrounded by blazing debris, no bayonet twisting the entrails. There was little to tempt in the stories of the choking mud of the trenches of the last and not-so-distant Great War. Only the Air Force promised the freedom to "slip the surly bonds of earth." There was honour and adventure in flying with the RAF and, as war took to the skies, there was also the promise of getting the job done.

George, Nooney's uncle, is at Sydney's Central Station to meet the train from Orange. He is a short bulldog of a man who could easily stand in for Churchill. He claps Arthur on the back, insists on carrying his suitcase, and marches proudly beside him revelling in the smart RAF uniform of his niece's valiant husband. He is honoured to drive him to Bradfield Park.

Arthur trots beside him, smiling a little sheepishly at the fuss. "Good for you, mate," George tells him. "Tough on young Neen and the kiddies. But it's the right thing."

It isn't a long drive from Central Station, through the city and onto the Harbour Bridge. Arthur rolls his window down and sticks his face into the wind, smelling the salt air and taking in the great expanse of harbour. ITS, Initial Training School, Bradfield Park, nestles under the northern bridge approach. Acres of parade grounds, line upon line of dormitory style wooden huts, surrounded by daunting barbwire fences ... it is an impressive and efficient training ground for future airmen.

All in all, for young Arthur, Sydney in spring is not a hardship posting. Dusty silver grey eucalypts are in blossom, there are flashes of red banksia. The base is bordered on one side by the Lane Cove River, mangroves crowding its banks, the thick muddy smell mingling with the fresh scent of gum trees. On the other side is the harbour, a freshly laundered blue sky touching its polished cobalt where small boats heel and tack. A steady breeze holds the city's heat at bay. For a country boy from Central New South Wales, where bodies of water of any kind are a rare thing, it is a marvel: a glorious day to go to war. For, although the roar of guns and the screams of the dying are far away, this is his first step on an uncertain road.

Uncle George deposits him at the gate, shakes his hand with alarming vigour and tells him he is welcome any time. "Come for tea, mate. We all want to see you. Flo is a good cook. You'll need a break from camp food." Arthur promises to visit, says his thanks for the ride and the support, waves as George drives off, and squares his shoulders for what lies ahead.

Now officially an aircrew trainee, he is entitled to wear the "white flash," a snowy piece of fabric tucked into his forage cap. It is worn proudly. And it gets attention. Innocent young men fresh from the Australian bush suddenly find themselves objects of female admiration, even, dare we say, desire. Those local girls have seen the recruiting poster featuring a handsome young airman staring heroically into the skies. "RAAF," it trumpets, "This is a Man's Job." The white flash signifies that these young men are Aircraftsmen 2, the lowest possible rank, but a rank nonetheless. They are part of the romantically charged world of flight; arm candy of the most desirable sort. Not everyone is pleased by this set-up. The men of the ground crew do not have a white flash. They attempt to even the odds by spreading the story that the white flash, like the black cross on the door of a plague-infested house, serves as a warning: the men into whose caps it is stuffed have VD. Clever ruse but no hard feelings; the men gifted with this potent sign turned the joke on themselves by christening it "Kotex."

Officially in uniform, the scratchy blues, the Air Force owns Arthur now. Volunteer or not, from here in he is bound to do what he is told, when he is told, and to have very little opinion about the matter. There is drilling, shoe polishing, saluting, potato peeling, sentry duty ... whatever seems necessary to build men who will be mentally and physically prepared to take orders no matter how foolish, misguided, or counterintuitive they seem.

He will be here a month. For Nooney, left to fend for herself, this is a rehearsal for what is to come. She is on his mind that first night in barracks as he waits for sleep, trying for comfort on his thin straw paillasse, and listening sympathetically to the muffled choking sobs of homesick teenagers. These volunteers with stars in their eyes are, after all, mostly just kids, away from family for the first time, harangued and bullied by superiors, sleeping in crowded conditions, deprived of privacy, fed unappetizing slop, desperately missing home.

The next day finds them all mustered in a lecture hall where dire warnings about venereal disease are on the menu. A crisp, no nonsense WAAF proceeds, without hint of vulgarity, to tell these squirming young men to keep their sexual equipment firmly zipped. "Syphilis and gonorrhoea, unless properly treated, can lead to blindness, insanity, and premature death. Eighty percent of prostitutes are infected and just because a 'nice girl' you might meet looks clean, does not mean she is. The best choice is to remain pure. You owe it to your family and your country. If you contract VD you are not much use in the war against Hitler. If you cannot control your urges, use a contraceptive, urinate immediately after the act, wash your private parts with soap and water, and see the medic."

A series of nightmare-inducing, hectically painted, plaster models of suppurating genitalia cinches the deal. Condoms are distributed. Many of these young men, fresh from the farm, have no clue what to do with them, filling them with water to turn them into hilarious bombs. At twenty-five, married, and with two small children, Arthur may appear to these eighteen-year-olds to be an elder statesman but even he is still an innocent at heart. What can he have made of those dire warnings?

After all the health issues have been taken care of, these shocked young men, in between the drilling and polishing and preparing vegetables, are in class getting some serious upgrading: Maths, Physics, English, electrical technology, basic fitting, engineering, drawing, aircraft metal work, welding, carpentry, blacksmithing, metal machine work, general service training, and character guidance. Phew!

The siren song of big city Sydney, a short bus or ferry ride away, calls the trainees from camp on free evenings. Local boys can go home for Mum's cooking. One fellow, on night sentry duty, hides his rifle under a bush, climbs through a hole in the fence, skips off home for a kip in his own comfy bed, and is back on duty the next morning. He is never caught.

Arthur accepts Uncle George's invitation to come to tea. Auntie Flo does not disappoint; she lavishes her best efforts upon him. And she is an exceptional cook. When she dies, years after the war, my mother's tribute to her — "She was a wonderful woman, always kind to her neighbours and always had cakes in her tins" — finds Robbie and me, women who do not even have tins, squirming with inadequacy.

Each weekend provides a leave. Arthur gets himself to Central Station on Friday evening after one of these packed days. He climbs aboard the Orange-bound train and tries to snooze through the night as they cross the coastal plain to the Blue Mountains, climb up and over, and chug across the Central West, stopping at Katoomba, Lithgow, Bathurst, and Lucknow, rolling into Orange in the early morning. Kit bag over his shoulder, he walks the five miles home to Nooney, cutting across the country through the morning dew, his back warmed by the early rising sun.

They are in each other's arms. Words tumble from them. He wants to hear every detail of her week on the orchard, how she has coped, what the kids have done. She is fascinated by his new life. How is the food? What are you learning? Any new friends? Oh, and all that stuff about sex and VD, tell me everything.

Her eyes widen in sympathetic horror as he tells her about the short arm inspection where he is required to drop his trousers, take himself in hand and give a firm squeeze so doctors can check for any telltale oozing.

His Presbyterian prudery has been sorely challenged; he now bathes in open showers. He entertains a giggling Nooney with his observations, telling her he believes there is a correlation between nose size and the generosity of the male member. As he is endowed with a respectably ample nose, and has included himself in this informal, and surely covert, survey, here is more fodder for marital mirth. Two days and one night and then back to camp by the Sunday night train, every moment precious.

For each of these men in training, when the month ends, a decision has to be made. In what capacity will they serve? Most see themselves as pilots. The daring of the glamorous fighters, high above burning London, blasting the Luftwaffe out of the sky, shines luminously in the mind of each volunteer. Although the Battle of Britain is over, fighter pilots are being trained to fly with and protect the bomber streams as they flow into the perilous skies over occupied Europe. And the Battle of the Pacific is well underway; Australia is now firmly and geographically in the gun-sights of this part of this war. Throughout 1942 and into 1943 Japanese bombs have dropped not only on Darwin but on a number of other northern towns. Airports are being built. Air raid shelters are being dug. Road signs are removed to confuse the enemy. Fighter pilots are needed. Failing that, being a pilot in Bomber Command has its own glamour and authority. It is, however, completely out of the hands of these embryonic airmen. They are slotted into a spot driven by supply and demand and the convenience of the administration, no arguments allowed. Poor quivering nobodies that they were, they must accept whatever role they are assigned.

At the time Arthur's future is being decided there is an abundance of pilots, closing that option for him. He has left no record of his preference. Maybe he longed to be a wireless operator. Many years on, his two daughters hope so, but if not, we hope he is not disappointed when that becomes his lot. The more we come to know him, the more we doubt that he would have sulked and pouted. After reading the diary, my husband, Tony, who recognizes a kindred spirit, says, "He seemed like an easygoing fellow."

On his graduation from ITS the obligatory photo is taken. He sports the white flash and a broad and open smile showing a set of even white teeth that I wish he had bestowed on me. His hair is very short, having been treated to a fierce buzz cut on arrival a month before. He also looks about seventeen; perhaps he is not so out of place among all those young boys in Bradfield Park. This photo is taken on November 7, 1942. He is about to start his wireless operator training, one more step closer to war.

A few hours west of Orange is a dusty farm town called Parkes, a town that we had grown to know well as kids. After Daddy's death, Mummy became friends with a family there and we visited often. They ran cattle and sheep on a sprawling property outside of town. I remember the heat, and the little dust devils, whipped up by the wind, as they danced about the yard picking up empty, rusting kerosene tins and tossing them about. One year we were there during a plague of grasshoppers. They landed in masses, blanketing the wide verandah that ran around the house. We rode our bikes through them listening to the satisfying crunch, and leaving a sticky trail of mangled bodies. This is where Arthur is headed next: Parkes No. 2 Wireless and Gunnery School, and he is there, as we were, in the summer. It is easy for us to imagine him in that same dust and heat.

Some nights trainees spray their corrugated iron huts with water, hoping for sleep. When one poor chap decides to haul his cot outside to get some rest in the cool night air, his fellow hut-mates sneak out and pick up this cot, in which he slumbers, and carefully place it on the hut roof. It is here that he finds himself when he awakens next morning. Daddy is not the only one who can sleep through anything.

Another fellow develops a clever method of getting to his bunk, the farthest from the door in a line of twenty army cots. He runs into the hut, gallops from bed to bed, mussing each one as he goes, often flattening a fellow attempting to read or get some rest, and lands with a triumphant smack on his own. He grins; his hut-mates grouse. But not for long. As all the beds are bolted to the floor it is the work of a moment to remove said bolts on the bed belonging to the annoying idiot and replace them with twigs. They will hold the bed in place but not resist the momentum of a flying leap. Then the men in the hut sit about waiting, concealing their anticipatory smirks. In due time, with a howl of joy, our fool does his party trick. As expected when his final leap lands him on his far away bed it parts company with the floor and careens into the wall carrying him with it. Ha! Job well done.

There are sixteen drinking establishments in Parkes and they are well patronized by most of the lads. Arthur, product of a strict Presbyterian home, doesn't drink much ... yet. He will smoke more and drink more as time passes. The fact that he drinks at all, and that he has taken up smoking, is a source of pain to his prim elderly mother who strongly disapproves. Her influence shows: most nights when the lads are out seeing how many of the sixteen pubs they can hit in a night and exploring the charms of the local girls, Arthur is at camp.

Often he plays draughts with a fellow trainee, young Tony Adams, only eighteen and not a drinker. He enjoys our father's company and clearly admires him. They remain good friends and correspond throughout the war. He meets my sister and me when we arrive in Parkes with our mother to visit Daddy. The world of little kids is a mystery to him and, luckily, he finds us enchanting. He is devastated to hear of Daddy's death. When he returns, marries, and has a daughter, she is named Robyn. His children grow up hearing our story: two little girls whose father died in the war and didn't come home. We are part of this family's folklore.

This friend, Tony, is one of the lucky ones, living into his nineties. And he has an interesting war. What he and his crew do is very hush-

hush: their task is to air-drop supplies to the French Resistance. They must fly low with great accuracy and nobody can know they are coming; their lives and the lives of the men and women on the ground, appearing in forest clearings to scoop up the packages falling from the sky, depend on it. A war spent in bringing life rather than taking it is, for these crews, a gift.

One hundred and eleven men are enrolled in the wireless course, Course 32. Our father counts many of them as his friends, keeps in touch with them as they, too, go to war. One in particular becomes one of his closest mates: Dutchy. His name is also Arthur, Arthur Dutch, and he too is known as Paddy, a fact that will visibly unhinge our mother when he visits her after the war.

The members of Course 32 spend five months in this hot and dusty camp taking the first steps to becoming fully trained Wireless Operators. They practise on the ground and in the air, flying in Wacketts: a two-seater Australian-made trainer plane, pilot in the front, embryonic wireless operator in the seat behind, receiving and transmitting while trying not to be sick. Many are, and the results provide a handy punishment for any trainee overstepping base rules. "Three nights on Wacketts" for such offences as clandestine drinking means three nights cleaning out the planes ready for the next day of training, three night of swabbing vomit from the seats and the ceiling, three nights of wondering if sneaky drinking is worth it.

We have a photo of Arthur in his flying gear. It is taken on leave; our bulldog is standing by him. "Want to see me in my flying suit? Let's get a picture. Come on Kitchener old boy, you can be in the photo too." It may or may not be significant that all our bulldogs, and we had a series, were named after military heroes: Caesar, Nelson, Kitchener.

After a leave, Daddy and his classmates set off for Port Pirie, just north of Adelaide in South Australia, two states away. This is the Bombing and Gunnery School. More skills to master. Officially designated as WAGS, they are wireless operators and air gunners expected to be proficient in both capacities.

Our dear Arthur could have ended up as an air gunner. He was trained for it and if he had failed to measure up as a wireless operator the embroidered wings on the left breast of his uniform would have been a simple AG for Air Gunner, not WAG for Wireless Air Gunner. The w/op training was the longest of any other crew member. But even as a fully qualified w/op he is subject to supply and demand; his arse belongs to the RAF and if they want that arse in a gun turret, then that is where it will land. Only once while in the UK does he record occupying the gunner's seat, and that is during training. What kind of a war would he have had if it had turned out differently? It might have been more interesting; it might have been shorter. The last line of Randall Jarrell's gut-punching poem, "The Death of the Ball Turret Gunner," says all that needs to be said: "When I died they washed me out of the turret with a hose."

Air gunners have a reputation for gallantry and carry a heady whiff of danger. They are also, as a rule, tiny men. In their electrically wired gear, bulky, awkward, and necessary to keep them from freezing to death, as they climb into their cramped turrets, starting off pocket-size is a distinct advantage. The space is so limited that many need to take their boots off and carry them in to the turret, struggling back into them once they are seated. As is the case for many small men, what they lack in stature is offset by giant personalities. They are often the scallywags of the crew, always up to mischief. They love a prank, a party, a boozy night, and a chance to chase the girls. To be fair, this could describe great swathes of the men in Bomber Command, but the AGs seem to go at it more energetically than most.

Given an air gunner's life in the sky, looking for fun on the ground seems a sensible path. Theirs is an intense and lonely job, constantly on high alert for attack, making snap judgements as an enemy craft is sighted. Has he seen us? Foolhardy to blaze away if he hasn't; perilous to hold fire if he has. So, wait and watch in the freezing turret, eyebrows and cheeks caked with ice, feet and hands numb with cold, eyes burning from looking, looking. There is no respite; even as they turn from the target toward base, they cannot relax. All the way home, across the North Sea, and over the welcoming fields of England, these small gutsy men are on watch to keep their crew from harm.

Daddy was not particularly tall at five foot eight; had he lived his younger daughter would, in high heels, have overtopped him. But he would have been one of the taller gunners had that role fallen to him. I am glad that it didn't. He hated the cold and also had a hard time staying awake. Better to be in the w/op cubby wearing the lightest outfit of all the crew. His seat, next to the heating for the aircraft, is often uncomfortably warm, his left boot wrinkled and deformed from contact with the heat duct. Not too pleasant, but a better spot for an Aussie than freezing in a gun turret.

At Port Pirie, as Arthur climbs into the gunner's seat and practises shooting down balloons dragged by aircraft, I doubt he ever contemplated a future as an air gunner. This is just a fun interlude in the long grind of home training. There are endless lectures and there is so much to learn. During operations every member of the crew is expected to keep a tally of downed planes. Every man aboard needs to be proficient in aircraft recognition. The more I read the more astonished I am at the staggering variety of aircraft used during the war. They have to know them all and in an instant pick friend from foe. I am very impressed by my clever Dad.

Once the Air Gunner training is over, his Australian training is too. The next chapter is about to open and it is time to say goodbye. As Nooney holds her Paddy on their last night, is there revisionism, spoken or not, of the unwavering support she has given him for this path he has chosen? Of course, there is no going back whatever either of them may feel. He has his orders: off to a second Embarkation Depot in Ascot Vale, near Melbourne. Twelve days later he is in Adelaide, marching aboard the troopship that will take him to the UK. The logistics of all this seem random and bizarre. The hurry up and wait of military life has him in thrall. He serves at His Majesty's pleasure.

From the time he sails until his death is just fifteen months — not a long time in the average life but the opening of an abyss for her. "It was lonely on the orchard but, with many good friends and much work, time flew. Lived for the mail. He was a great letter writer."

On the top shelf of a bedroom closet was a box filled with those letters, the writing scored with black bars by the censors. I am hazy about Mummy's reaction when my snooping ten-year-old self found them: she wasn't angry; I don't remember what she said apart from telling me what they were. And then they were gone. It was clear that they were not meant for me. At some point she destroyed them; they were, in her mind, like his diary, "too personal," not for sharing. Such a loss for us. So many things we could have known and don't.

We wonder about their parting. We don't know how he leaves Orange. Does he fly to Victoria where he will embark? Does she drive him to the little local airport? Are we, his two infant daughters, taken to see him off, stuffed into the cab of our utility truck? Do we stand on the tarmac and wave him goodbye? Or do we drive him to the station to wait on a platform dusky with smoke, shouting farewells over the grinding acceleration of the great black steam engine? Is it a troop train, packed with men being moved about the country? Do they hang out and wave to us, thinking of their own families left behind? It is a world offering room for rich imaginings.

Travelling Daughters

May 2011

I have taken the red-eye from Toronto, the cheapest and possibly the only way to get myself to Glasgow. But certainly not the most direct route; I have to go to Holland first.

I am groggy, eyes gritty, mouth dry and gluey, body stiff and cramped in my cabin-class seat. I pride myself on my ability to sleep on a plane, but not this flight, my mind a hamster wheel packed with all I have learned in the last months and all that lies ahead. I am facing a four hour layover in Amsterdam. I miss my home, my comfortable bed, and Tony.

On the cusp of turning seventy, I am aware of a small voice in my mind wondering if I am still up for such adventures.

My plane slides in toward Schiphol Airport, gently losing altitude. As we tilt toward the east I can see the wrinkled sea studded with freighters; I count ten of them under the dipping wing, waiting to move in to the docks of Amsterdam. We have just been treated to a scarlet sunrise, splashed across the eastern sky. It is a relief to see the dawn, to know that this part of the journey is almost over.

Below, closer every second, the neat-as-a-pin Dutch countryside slips underneath us: ruler-straight canals lined with Van Gogh poplars, peak-roofed red barns, scrubbed farmhouses in their green, fenced fields. I long for windmills and tulips, but even without them, the ordered prosperity is balm for the soul.

For the last four or five months I have read obsessively about a time when this country, this continent, wondered if order of any sort would ever be restored. As part of my preparation I reread Anne Frank's diary. She is on my mind as I look down on her city. Hers is one of those books you feel you know but find revelation in a new reading. Perhaps coming back to this story as an adult, a senior citizen — oh horrible designation — makes it new. Anne, prickly and tough, is not the limpid-eyed philosopher we have canonized. I like this Anne better. Her strength serves her well. As the allied bombs rain down on Nazi installations in neighbourhoods populated by terrified, occupied, and at the same time grateful, Dutch, the wise child writes, in April of 1944, "If the invasion comes, and bombs with it, then it is every man for himself, but in this case the fear was also for our poor innocent protectors. 'We are saved, go on saving us!' That is all we can say."

I am happy that she sees Bomber Command that way: "poor innocent protectors" and that others share that view. Even, I hope, a good friend of ours who recently, and quite casually, revealed that his mother had been killed in Holland while waiting in a line at a grocer's. Stray fire from a bombing raid. "Unintended consequences," "friendly fire," such tidy euphemisms for a life gone, a family bereft.

Sometimes, as they thundered over Holland headed for the flak and fighter planes of Germany, those young men in the crews of Halifaxes, Lancasters, Stirlings and Whimpeys took the chocolate bars given as flying rations and tossed them down the bomb chutes. Years afterward, the starving Dutch who found these precious treats remembered them with gratitude and amazement. After the war when Holland was liberated, a woman who had suffered five years of German occupation wrote from her home in Arnhem to the RAF: "During the occupation, the throb of your bombers overhead at night sounded like music to our ears," something to cling to "in the dark days." That little story is something for me, and my sister, to cling to as well. It will not always be enough.

***

"Mind the step. Mind the step. Mind the step," the detached electronic voice warns continuously. It is beginning to grate but I do not have the energy to abandon my spot next to the moving walkway. I've found a table and chair to plunk down my weary body, my carry-on luggage, my laptop, and my giant handbag bulging with the precious binder. This now unwieldy pile just crept in under the baggage allowance but I am determined to entrust nothing to the hold. Certainly not the binder, and even my suitcase needs to flow seamlessly off the plane in Glasgow, firmly attached to me. We have just two weeks for this mission and I cannot risk a day hanging about waiting for errant luggage to catch up.

With two hours to kill before my flight to Glasgow, I have dutifully trudged the shops and foolishly eaten some pricy airport food. Now I feel vaguely ill and an attempt to nap is a failure. I pull out the binder, stroke the face of the handsome fellow in the photo slipped into the cover sleeve and, for the thousandth time, flip through the documents, photos, printouts, lists, and scribbles it contains. I am looking for one item in particular.

The photo is black and white, as they mostly were at that time. It is a little battered, peeling away from its backing, a crack across the upper third. It is much travelled, frequently and lovingly looked at. Perhaps it went with its owner, stuffed into a flying suit pocket.

In it, two little girls, around two and four years old, stand side by side on the flatbed of a utility truck. The tailgate is down and you can see that the sides of the interior are faced with wooden slats. This is a working truck; behind the children two hand-mowers lie neatly side by side on its floor. To one side of the tailgate, front paws on its edge, is a bulldog, head up, anxious to be part of the action. But the children, my sister and I, ignore him. We are intent on posing for the photo. Somebody must have told us to put our hands behind our backs. Robbie, the four-year-old, has hers obediently out of sight. I'm doing my two-year-old best, my right arm tucked away while the left one, having escaped, hangs by my side, doll in hand. We are smiling, not those awful grimaces kids often make when told to smile; we look genuinely pleased to be there. We're wearing our best. Robbie's sleeves are lace-trimmed and a row of buttons marches down her front. My dress appears to be knitted and has decorative ribbon threaded through the bodice ending in a couple of bows. We both have little black shoes and white socks, but the laces of my shoes seem to be missing and my socks are scrunched around my ankles, not neatly pulled up like my sister's. Robbie stands closer to the edge, one toe overhanging. She seems sturdier, her head much bigger than mine, her larger feet planted firmly. I am further back, weight on one leg, slightly off-balance as if ready to fly. I am also much the tinier of the two, coming barely to my sister's shoulder although there is only a year and a half between us. We are not particularly alike except for the funny little bags under our eyes. We have them still. But she is certainly the prettier, with the sweetest smile and curly hair pulled back from her forehead, her eyes directed at the photographer. My hair, very blonde, is cut in a miniature haystack and I'm smiling cheerfully, but not at the camera.

It is tempting to read a future into this. Perhaps we arrive with a blueprint. But of course, life reshapes us. Robbie, who had longed for a roses-round-the-door, children-underfoot kind of future found herself committed to a marriage that led her to travel, sail the world, raise two kids and grow her gently formidable strength. There is truth in those firmly planted feet. I grew taller, eventually reaching five foot seven, overtopping my now littler sister. I flew away from home and never came back. I am the less tranquil of the two. That slightly unbalanced stance, those laceless shoes point to something real.

It is a long time ago, the day of that photo: mid-1944. And for many years we sisters, separated by half a world, saw little of each other. While we waited for the time when we could reconnect we pored over the photos we exchanged, searching for each other in the faces of our children.

The photo was taken at our grandparents' farm. In the background I can see their packing shed and the octagonal cement tank that supplied the house with water. Our father knew this setting well and would enjoy this picture even more because it framed us. On the back, in a firm hand, the ink still remarkably fresh, our mother has written: "To Dear Daddy, smiles for you from Bobs and Wendy." I'm sure we were told to "Smile for Daddy" as we posed. We could not have known that we were smiling for a man we would never see again.

This carefully posed keepsake was processed at the only photographic studio in our hometown. On the back, along with our mother's message, is a stamp: "La Doré Studio, Orange, NSW." I remember that studio. Its large window always displayed the hand-tinted photos of the latest weddings. They must have taken a long time to be coloured and processed because, by the time they were on show, the local gossips could tell which of the brides has been hastily bundled to the altar due to pre-marital indiscretion. As a small child I loved to gaze at the array of happy couples in the window. Behind me I could hear the whispering, "She's due in May; they were married in January and her a good Catholic girl. Oh my." I was, for a very long time, puzzled by this prurient math.

Our parents were never displayed for scrutiny in this window. They eloped and married in Bathurst, a town thirty miles down the road toward Sydney. My mother's mother, a possessive killjoy, had opposed the marriage, even feigning heart attacks to sabotage any planned union. I don't think this had anything to do with my mother's choice of partner; any marriage that would deprive our grandmother of the free labour her oldest child provided would have brought on, at the very least, an attack of the vapours.

So away they ran. Both were twenty-one. They'd had to wait until they were free and clear, needing no consent. Determined to marry in spite of faux hysterics, they took the first step on April 1, 1939, when they drove to Bathurst, thirty miles to the east, and got themselves a licence. Arthur Leslie Keith Plowman, Orchardist and Bachelor, and Enid Ruby Hawke, Home Duties and Spinster, declared themselves free of impediment to marriage. Licence in hand, excited, scared, defiant, they returned to Orange, to announce a non-negotiable plan of action: in three days they would drive back to Bathurst and become man and wife.

Our father's family raised no objection. This son of theirs was possessed of a level head and had chosen a woman of good fruit-growing stock. These parents were also older, and perhaps wiser. His mother was a startling forty-nine when he was born, the last of seven children. This would make her seventy at the time of this marriage. A fuss-free elopement must have looked very tempting to her. They agreed to a wedding on April 4 in Bathurst — "we'll be there on the day, congratulations you two" — and went back to whatever they'd been doing before the excited couple burst in with the news.

A very different drama unfolded at Mount Pleasant, the inaptly named family home my mother was about to flee. There these two young people, who would become our parents, licence in hand, stubbornly faced whatever howlings and screamings and how-can-you-do-this-to-me's reverberated through the house. Finally, with an eye on how a rebellious elopement would play out in her social circle, my grandmother caved. She withdrew her objections, recovered from her ailments, relented, capitulated, and agreed to come to this hastily organized union. So, both sets of parents would attend the wedding. There would be no fanfare, no proud mother-of-the-bride, but there would be no scandal either. She could claim some control, even ensuring that her signature was on the Marriage Certificate.

We would not be human, we two sisters, if we had not done a little La Doré Studio math of our own. Counting on our fingers from April 4, the day of their marriage, to January 16, the day of Robbie's birth, we came up with a respectable nine months and twelve days. No fodder for the gossips there. Of course, no wedding pictures in the window either. I doubt they cared. They just wanted to be together.

I take one last look at the picture before returning it to the binder. It was carefully cropped, processed and inscribed before its journey to England and to Dear Daddy to enjoy those smiles and a glimpse of home. It was among his meagre possession collected from his hut and packed up the night he died.

That parcel did not arrive until July of 1945, eight months after his death. There was a war on; things did not speed across the world. I can only imagine the pain involved as our mother picked up the cardboard box from the Post Office, stowed it carefully in the back of the ute and drove home with us in the cabin beside her. After she'd fed us and tucked us into bed, she retrieved the package, placed it on the kitchen table, cut the string and took out, one by one, the few things he left behind, holding and gently touching each one. This is how I think it would have been but I cannot know. There are so many things we will never know but yearn to, Robbie and I, two sisters who once, long ago, stood so companionably side by side on the back of a truck.

Once more I stroke the face of the long dead airman slipped into the plastic cover on the front of my binder and begin to pack and tally my belongings. It is time to board for Glasgow.

As we fly across the Channel and over the coast, headed for Scotland, I think of those bombers going over in waves, limping home in pieces. Hard to imagine that this clear and peaceful sky is the same airspace.

And then we are down and I clear customs and emerge through the doors and onto the raised ramp like a diva bursting onto the stage. Those waiting scan the arrivals. Little shrieks of recognition fill the air. Robbie and I stagger into each other's arms, delighted to have pulled this off.

She'd flown in the night before and checked into a hotel close to the airport, so she could meet me in the morning. Fears of delayed or cancelled flights, lost luggage, missed connections, bad weather, obstreperous passengers, and aborted flights have plagued us both. We are uncomfortably aware that we are both travelling in airplanes to search for a man who has been killed in such a machine. If fate were looking for a moment of irony, this would surely be it. On top of which, days before we left the safety of solid ground, the United States had sent a parcel of Navy Seals into Pakistan to assassinate Osama Bin Laden. The world of aircraft travel is in the crosshairs of an army of cranky jihadists. But here we are, unscathed, laughing and crying, each exclaiming how well the other looks, which isn't particularly true but we'll improve as the jet lag wanes. First goal accomplished. We are together.

We need a cup of tea. We need to talk. Words pour from us like the tea from our pots.

"I practically force-fed Melatonin to my seat mate. She was Muslim, head scarf, very little English and intent on sleeping. She asked me if it had any sugar. 'No, no,' I assured her, having no clue really if it did. She took one and then her meal arrived, special order — she was a diabetic. What is the matter with me? I was terrified she'd go into a coma or something."

"But did she sleep?" Robbie wants to know.

"Like a log. Me, not so much. How about you?"

"I did a bit but Peter insisted I go through Seoul. It was nice to have a night in a hotel but really I didn't particularly want to see Korea"

"God, what a knob. Why did he do that?"

"Oh, you know what he's like," she sighs.

We haven't drawn breath since we met, talking over each other while rifling through our binders. Yes, of course she has one. Her printouts are carefully annotated with quotes from the diary. She was, in a former life, a librarian, and is far and away more organized than I will ever be. I am impressed and covetous; I want every one of her observations. I pull out the picture of us on the back of the truck. "I love that photo," I tell her. "I sat and gazed at in for ages in Schiphol Airport."

"Yes, I love it, too," she says. "We look so happy and hopeful."

"Still are."

We get a refill for our pot of tea. I am feeling my lack sleep. Robbie is more rested after a night in a hotel in Glasgow as well as a night in

Seoul. Perhaps her bossy husband had a point after all. But just being here together pumps some energy into me. On we babble. The pent up news of the two years since we've last seen each other flows across our table. Back and forth we go from family news to the fascinating details of the Daddy Project. We weep and laugh by turns. "Oh," Robbie cries, "even if we just had this it would be worth it." And I think it would.

But we cannot spend all morning in an airport Starbucks. Outside, a slightly damp day and a fairly long drive await. We pack up our belongings and head for the hire car office where papers have to be signed and a GPS arranged. The perky Glaswegian lass at the counter tells us we look a couple of rogues, with much arch winking at two male employees who are flirting with her. To our increasing horror, we have become two little old dears, harmless and quaint.

Later Robbie admits that she was quite nervous about this trip. Not that the lovely UK daunts her: she lived here once, drives on their side of the road, and tilts at more windmills than most. It is that she was unsure how we would do it — find what we are seeking, that is. I, of less vivid imagination, have decided that we will blunder about and see what turns up; I have very little in the way of expectations. We will simply be bearing witness. There is, I admit, the occasional fantasy that we will stumble on somebody who actually knew our father, some doddering old chap, in a pub perhaps, who will shed radiant light. But I also know this is unlikely, having left this search so late that any first hand witnesses are probably dead.

We have rented a compact car, a stick shift, our eyes on economy. It is small but it will be very crowded — not by us, we are careful packers and travel light — but by the cast of characters accumulated in these fourteen crucial months of our father's life: all the men he trained with, went on leave with, and fought alongside — men who became his family. And we will also carry the family he left behind: his Nooney, his six brothers and sister, his parents, Nooney's family and, of course, us. Those two children in that photo, caught in a moment in 1944 while there was still a hope that he would come home, they travel with us too.

One step at a time. First, we have to get out of the airport parking lot. We stow our luggage but keep our binders of research jealously at hand. I plug in the GPS and start fiddling with it. "Shit," I mutter. These things are not my forte, but if Robbie is to do the driving, I must at least control this beast and get us where we need to go. I cannot hear anything and for a horrible moment think we have been given a machine that won't talk to us. Then I detect a faint voice like a tiny Scot whispering at the bottom of a well. We have no instruction manual and I cannot find a way to increase the volume. I leave Robbie to conduct her exploration of the gears and gallop to a nearby hut/office. They do not happen to be the organization we rented from but are happy to solve my problem. I already love the Scots.

Robbie stalls three times just attempting to back out of the parking space. I'm no help here. I have not driven on the left for over forty years, am seriously spatially challenged, and at that precise moment a groggy mess. "Oh, it's fine," she cries, all undaunted enthusiasm. "I love driving, I really do. Damn, stalled again. Perhaps we should circle the lot few times."

We do this, going the wrong way at first and giving other drivers a scare. Finally it seems to be going more smoothly and our GPS appears to know where we are going and how to get us there. We're off, lurching triumphantly onto the highway and negotiating our first roundabout.

Travelling Father

August 4, 1943

By dusk we were out of sight of land.

There should be ribbons, streamers, a band — preferably playing "Waltzing Matilda." The dock should be packed with women, tears spilling onto their cheeks, bravely lifting children up to wave goodbye, elderly parents, holding hands, proud and frightened. Men should line the rails as the ship moves away, calling last messages, blowing kisses. That's what I want for him, for all of them. But for those slipping away in the dusk, there is nothing.

It is all very secretive, perhaps because "Loose Lips Sink Ships." They are moved by tender from the Embarkation Depot. And there, before their alarmed eyes, she is: the *Denbyshire*. Dutch-built, of the Bibby Line, and credited *as having a sister ship concerned in the sinking of the Sydney at the time of the fall of Singapore*, Daddy records in his newly begun diary. Such provenance is a consolation to the men about to sail on this vessel, their home in hostile waters for the next five weeks. It gives her some heft, some gravitas, helpful for morale because, on first acquaintance, she is not a thing to inspire confidence. *How my heart sank*, my poor father writes of his first glimpse of the *Denbyshire*, a *puny thing with her well deck only reaching to the level of the wharf, the cramped deck space and the motley crew, which crowded the rails.*

Three hundred or so men assemble on the dock in Adelaide, jostling together, kit bags slung over shoulders, about to leave home, glumly wondering what they've signed up for. How many of these fellows have ever been to sea? How many can even swim? If they have consulted an atlas or a globe in the days or weeks before embarkation, that stretch of Pacific Ocean, now worm-holed with Japanese submarines and, after Panama, the Atlantic teeming with Germans longing to torpedo them, must seem vast and terrifying. Even the least imaginative would have spent a night or two curled up in a foetal ball of misery and doubt. But maybe not: these young men, many still in their teens, may be homesick, but they are up for adventure. The new and the unimaginable lie ahead.

Once aboard, Arthur and his mates survey their quarters in the hold: *our dormitory, living room, dining room, games room, concert hall for the duration of the voyage. After sorting ourselves out our little clique Dutchy, Pearson, Baldwin, Elger and myself found ourselves sharing a table with ten others.* A pep talk followed. *We were issued with life jackets (to be worn at all times), a hammock and blankets. Then we were free to inspect the ship.* They are issued blankets but no sheets, his concerned daughters note. Each night they will sling their hammocks and crawl in to rock with the sea.

On first inspection they are more concerned with the *Denbyshire*'s ability to get them safely to Mother England than with the comfortless living quarters. Much is made of her armour: *6 inch aft guns, Orlicon guns at various points, a Beaufor gun amidships, Balloon Barrages, minesweeping apparatus, and she had been Degaused.* Of course we look them up, those exotically named armaments. Weapons are not of huge interest to us, Arthur's now elderly daughters, more worried about how their twenty-six-year-old father is eating and if he can survive without sheets, but we have to know. It turns out that he misspelled "Bofors," "Oerlikon" and "Degaussed." I like that these things are part of their vocabulary, spoken of with familiarity and ease, but perhaps never seen written down. "Degaussing" means that the hull of this steel ship had been demagnetized to foil the Germans' magnetic mines. Perhaps the level of the well decks is less disturbing knowing that they are armed and prepared to pass through dangerous waters.

They leave, seen off by *some air force brass and a couple of disinterested wharfies at seven bells. Our last glimpse of fair Australia was an endless stretch of flat sandy waste. By dusk we are out of sight of land.* In less than four days they are passing through Cook Straight between New Zealand's North and South Islands on this hastily and roughly converted troop carrier. A routine is established, resignation over living conditions reached.

On the front page of the diary he has written his name, his rank, and his serial number. He gives the date of departure as the beginning of the adventure — ignoring the months of training already accomplished. *THE DIARY OF (AUS) 424880 F/SGT. PLOWMAN FROM AUGUST 4TH 1943 UNTIL....* This last is the saddest word of all. It implies survival. It implies going home. He also numbers all the pages in this small book and many of those numbered pages are blank. I find this desperately sad. Robbie finds it hopeful; at least when he starts the diary he thinks it will come to a neat ending, and then he can go back to his life as an orchardist, back to Nooney and his two little girls.

Of course he knows that going to war could mean that this will not happen. His diary's first words, rather formal and solemn, in the distant second person, acknowledge this: *Today began for all something in the nature of a great adventure — leaving one's own home for the first time for an unknown destination, knowing that you have seen, perhaps for the last time, all those whom you love and in whom your whole existence is bound up.*

But he does not dwell; that is not his nature. His next reflection is on the food. First meal, and they have not even left the wharf, bully beef: *can't be much worse than this we said. Poor blind Nell it couldn't.* Apart from one surprisingly delicious chicken lunch in the middle of the Pacific, they are fed an unappetizing, and often unrecognizable, mess. Smoke frequently billows from the galley heralding the next disappointment.

The first few days are rainy and cold. *Nobody very happy,* he reports. He has the flu and aches all over. *Life doesn't look so good. Home and Nooney very far away.* But he manages to get a bit of a laugh out of *all the chaps sitting on the patent latrines four feet off the ground like a lot of pensive hens.* These conveniences are on deck, unprotected from the elements, facing the sea. Privacy is neither expected nor provided.

But there are compensations. He sees his first albatross and is awed by its majesty. Porpoises frolic around the bow of the ship and flying fish spray out of the water, some even landing on deck. He spends much time gazing over the ship's rails. *Never grow tired of watching the sea, only cold drives me below.* He comes to know and respect its moods. *Very oily sea today. Most unnatural.* His two daughters, products of the same inland country town, in a dry land, have also grown to love the sea. We find pleasure in this shared passion.

Just out of New Zealand somebody is caught smoking on deck after lights out. *The C.O. goes to town* our father notes approvingly. Nobody relishes a glowing cigarette end attracting enemy attention just because some fool needs his nicotine fix.

Evening entertainment cheers them up. The route march round the deck less so — only ten percent stagger to the end. Our father is not in that number. There is a padre on board and I feel a little sorry for him. On the one hand there is praise for a quiz night he arranges; on the other his attempts to organize an evening of hymn singing are rejected in favour of card playing and letter writing. *The padre,* our father notes drily, *has a nice solo voice.*

His friendships strengthen even as they are tested. Pearson, one of his mates, is sadly prone to seasickness. He is a spry little fellow, full of mischief, instigator of many of the pranks at the base in Parkes, and certainly an avid patron of the sixteen pubs and an admirer of the local girls. Now his bravado is gone as he pukes with horrible intensity, vigour, and persistence. He cannot shake it. His plight is reported with less sympathy than it probably deserves. Daddy notes, perhaps a little proudly, his one and only "perk" on day two, but Pearson is going like a fountain all day. From then on the poor man pops up regularly in each entry.

Day 3: Pearson perking.

Day 4: Pearson bubbling over as usual.

Day 5: Pearson still perking.

Day 6: (as they cross the International Dateline and gain an extra day for Pearson to pass in misery): *Fed Pearson our oranges today but they followed the usual route. He is letting it get him down and I am losing patience.*

Day 7: Pearson still going strong.

Poor Pearson. The *Denbyshire*, wallowing through the swells, once carried other cargo; its hold had been packed with meat and the stench of fat and congealed blood lingers. When his mates, all now over their wobblies, sensibly plan to keep some food supplies with them in their hammocks in case they are torpedoed in the night, Pearson declines. He actually longs to be torpedoed and has no desire to survive. Being prone to seasickness myself, I know how it can rob one of the will to live. You often wish everyone in the vicinity dead as well.

It isn't until day ten that there is a sigh of relief: *Pearson improving.*

This digestively challenged chap, forever known as "Perking Pearson," firmly believes that the application of the precious oranges most likely saved his life. If it were really that dire, Daddy seems fairly unmoved. He is, as Australians often are, intolerant of moaning. "Go on, have a whinge," they say derisively to those unwilling to suck it up.

He expresses more concern for the well-being of his other friend, Dutchy, keeping a faithful log of any illness. In two entries, Dutchy is the sole subject. He has been put in the ship's hospital *for gastric problems* (the vile food no doubt); two days later *he is much better.*

As they approach the equator and the weather warms, a canvas pool is erected on the deck. Swimming, sun bathing, deck tennis use up some time. It is too hot to sleep below, so they move to the deck. There is a tour of the engine room and, later, crossing the line ceremonies.

The voyage has begun to take on a cruise-like tinge. They have been allowed to remove their life jackets until they reach Panama. So, it is not all misery; even a few days of heavy weather and a raft overboard at least add interest. Finally they are close to Panama: last posting of letters before docking. He has a stack, written throughout the voyage, most to Nooney who will be waiting anxiously for news.

They sight land three weeks from embarkation and are soon in the thick of the excitement of the canal. Returning from shore leave they are told that a middy has knifed a fellow crew member: *a Chinaman.* The Chinese members of the crew go on strike, the Chinese Consul comes on board. Peace is made. A British aircraft carrier steams by, band playing. Then they are passing through the canal, lock No. 1, in the early morning. Arthur and his mates lean on the ship's rails, fascinated by the powerful inrush of water raising them thirty feet in six minutes. A second and third lock follow before they move slowly through the level canal. In the mid-afternoon they heave to, allowing the men overboard for a swim. *Very refreshing and novel.*

Finally they are through Cristóbal and into the Atlantic, a much more dangerous place. *No leave but straight out into the quickly gathering darkness ... Life jackets on again. Running a zigzag course. Guards have been posted on the deck.* On the way out they pass a British timber ship and give her a cheer. Later they hear she was torpedoed. *How lucky we are,* he writes as they approach England unscathed. There is a party atmosphere on board with a concert and beer flowing. *Even felt merry myself.*

They make their way across the top of Ireland, then south into the Irish Sea. As the Irish coast comes into sight our farm-boy father reports it *rather rocky but with patches of green and brown farmland to quicken the pulse.* Later, steaming up the Bristol Channel he sees *the beautiful fields of Devon.* He aches with homesickness as they make their way into the Severn Estuary.

The farms of southern England are not so different from those he has left behind. His and Nooney's families farm in Orange's Canobolas

District, named for the sweet curve at the base of Mount Canobolas whose long-distant volcanic past supplies rich red soil. It is just high enough to persuade passing clouds to drop their life-giving loads. Orchards flourish and livings can be made on small acreages, edged by very English hawthorn hedges. It is lovely country. He is proud of it and speaks of it often. He is quickly nicknamed the "Canobolas Kid" or, as a dig at his advanced age, "Old Man Canobolas," names he enjoys.

They wake, tied up to a rather depressing dock in Avonmouth, in a country at war. Aircraft buzz overhead and, while waiting to disembark, they are *'shot up' by a Beaufighter — quite thrilling*. The ship has been packed up and they are dressed and ready to be transported to their billets in Brighton. Already workmen have boarded to dismantle the troopship fittings. It is time to say goodbye to the *Denbyshire* and they find themselves, *although heartily glad to be on land once more, a little sad to part from her*; she has delivered them safely and been their home for the last five weeks. *Most of us had become, in a small way, attached to and quite proud of her.*

From Avonmouth they are moved to Brighton to be billeted in a large seaside hotel to await the next step. Spirits are high on the train ride to Brighton. They wind through the countryside of the south, glimpsing quaint villages threaded together by narrow country roads. It is all so succulently green, so unlike the land they have left, let alone the Spartan world of a troop ship. A bus meets them at Brighton station; they heave their kit bags on board and head for the Grand Hotel on the sea front. And grand it is, even in the steady English rain. From the hold of the *Denbyshire*, where each night they sling their hammocks and try to sleep swinging with the swell, serenaded by groaning engines, inhaling the stink of carcasses past, fearful of attack, they are transported to a world of relative luxury. Daddy is pleasantly surprised by the food, having feared privation and shortage. They are fed, allotted rooms, issued blankets and, joy of joys, sheets.

When Robbie and I arrive in Brighton much later in our Odyssey, rain is sheeting down. The town is slick under a dull sky. The traffic is horrendous but we score a rare and convenient parking spot next to the Grand, still standing and only a little changed in the decades that separate us from our father's time here. This, in itself, is a bit of a miracle. Sitting on the south coast, looking across the Channel to occupied France, Brighton was a juicy target for Germany's Luftwaffe and was bombed many times, even having its own Brighton Blitz. However, the Grand, elegant and noble old lady that she is, survives the War unscathed. It is a much later bomb, courtesy of the IRA and directed at Thatcher and her cabinet, which does damage in 1984, leaving a ragged hole in the centre of the building. The hotel is defiantly rebuilt and, apart from modifications to the entry to improve security, it is much the same as in September of 1943 when our father enjoyed its opulence and its laundered linens.

For us, the ghosts of these young men are everywhere. We imagine them, eager for adventure, set apart by their uniforms, strolling the halls and reception rooms, taking the stairs, two at a time, up the wrought iron spiral that winds its way around the open stairwell all the way to the seventh floor.

The foyer is relatively modest in size. We like this intimate scale. Its praises are sung by an enthusiastic young woman who has been produced for us. She can point out all that is still here, unchanged, since it was requisitioned to house young men at war: the slender Corinthian columns of veined green marble that support the ceiling, the creamy grey marble floor and the sparkling chandelier. Our guide points this last out with great pride: "It would have been hanging here just as it is now. He would have walked under it each day coming and going from the hotel." We stare open-mouthed. The staircase is as it was; no change there. The ghosts continue to come and go. "And you must see this." She takes us to one of the columns, and points. At eye level, on the inside, facing the wall, scratched in the marble are three tiny letters: "RAF."

It is such a human longing, this need to make a mark. Megan, my middle daughter, wrote her name everywhere. I would find it engraved on bananas, scratched on the underside of furniture, or the inside of drawers. Every book she ever owned was inscribed. There was no doubt that she had passed by. I hope she got all that out of her system by marking up our house. I've always scorned the confessionals of public bathroom stalls. They offer secrecy for those who malign, spread rumours, indulge in pornography, or boast. But once in Wales, I found this enchanting confession inside a carefully inscribed heart: "Glenda loves Olwen — true very true." Heartfelt graffiti. Glenda wants this known. All of us need a record that we have been here, that we exist, that we matter.

So who was the young airman who carved "RAF" into the soft marble in the lobby of the Grand? He did not carve his name. This is not the clumpy message splashed on rocks and overpasses and tired buildings: "Joe was here," desperate assertion of substance in an indifferent world. This modest little vandalism speaks of quiet pride at being part of this bigger thing. Yes, they are young, and yes, they are quite likely to die — of every hundred who serve, forty-five will be killed — but they feel the honour and importance of what they are about to do. One of them needs to leave his seal. If he were Megan, he might find it enough to carve it into a piece of fruit. But fruit is scarce in this rationed island. And I, for one, am glad to find his message in the green marble.

Daddy and his mates spend ten days in the Grand. Leave is dangled as a possibility, but not a certainty. There are forms to be filled. They parade to Princess Hall for pep talks. *Usual thing*, he notes, already jaded. He manages to skip a couple of church parades. One truancy is spent under a tree on a park bench, smoking and reading while the church bells chime in the distance.

These chillier climes require different gear. One morning they turn in their overalls and khaki goods in exchange for battle dress. Gas masks are distributed. The complicated webbing straps create some hilarity in the assembling. A chap called Ikeringill is the most comically creative; our father sends him *to the top of the class*.

There is time to mooch about exploring the town. Brighton, then and now, exists as a tourist destination. Generations of pasty Brits have flocked here to emulate Royalty's discovery of the joy of "taking the waters." Before he became George IV, for a short reign remarkable only for extravagance and scandal, the Prince Regent, as these poor monarchs in waiting frequently do, had time and money to spare. His uncle, Prince Henry, was fond of Brighton and introduced his young nephew to its pleasures and, bonus, the seawater was considered good for his gout. There was also George III, his batty and difficult dad to consider. Heading as far south as possible seemed a smart move. And so the Pavilion was built to accommodate these needs. John Nash designed a colonial-Indian inspired fantasy of decorated onion domes sprouting elaborate finials, minarets, scalloped arches, lace fretwork ... well, you get the picture. It makes the Taj Mahal look suburban. It is Brighton's joy. But we are happy to learn that the shell-shocked, gassed, and wounded of World War I were tended to in this glorious place: as a military hospital it found a higher calling.

After being confined in a small and malodorous troop ship for many weeks, these embryonic airmen are hungry for activity. Ocean swimming is out. Brighton's beaches, those pebbled strands dismissed by our father — *did I say beaches?* — are mined and draped with coiled barbed wire. Both piers have been split in half. These precautions against German landings scar Britain's coast from end to end. Public baths stand in for the sea — *all right, too.* Swimming parades and P.T. are organized and welcome. Daddy enjoys watching a soccer match and ice hockey, both novelties. On one walk about town they find a tennis court and plan to go back. There are nights at the pictures and hikes on Falmouth Downs.

Every night there are alerts but no bombs are dropped. Overhead streams of bombers head for Germany and Spitfires do acrobatic manoeuvres. It is stirring, of course, but a reminder of what is to come. He will not get mail for several weeks but he sends a cable home to let us know he has arrived and is safe.

Running About on the Dunes

From Glasgow Airport, Robbie, now pretty much in control of the gears, gets us safely on the road to Whitley Bay. On the east coast, in Tyneside country, a place new to both Robbie and me, it is the site of our father's first UK training. It isn't far; nothing is on this compact island. From huge and sprawling lands, we find these distances less than daunting even though the roads are narrow and winding and journeys often take longer than estimated. Dilly-dallying through the countryside, as we drive away from Glasgow, we are enchanted by its gently rolling green fields, divided by neat hedges, with clusters of whitewashed farm houses tucked into their folds. Robbie, who loves cows, exclaims happily at the calmly munching bovines we pass. These old cottages, these tranquil fields would not have changed so much in the sixty-six years since our father travelled through them. It is early May for us and, to my surprise, the daffodils are already fading, well ahead of the Canada I left with just the first hint of spring in the tiny rocket tops of my hostas poking through the soil. Our dad was here in a different season but, faded clumps of daffodils aside, what we are seeing on this softly overcast day must have been very much the autumn landscape he saw all those years ago. That is what we tell each other. We have begun the hopeful process of finding him and sometimes we do not let actual facts get in the way.

We are also not sterling navigators and rely far too heavily on the wee Scot in our rented machine prone to telling us, with quiet confidence to, "Tak the round-a-boot, fust luft" while leading us precisely nowhere. We call him "Fred," a careless label for somebody who is a bystander in life. Big mistake. This Fred will be very important for the next two weeks. We should have called him the Laird of the Fens and held a formal Christening complete with a bevy of gift-bestowing fairies. We will need, but not always get, his goodwill.

As we speed along the A69 guided by Fred's wavering hand, we see tempting signs indicating we are travelling just south of Hadrian's Wall, a marvel neither of us has seen and we are, we tell ourselves, also on a holiday. We turn north and quickly end up surrounded by walls. Which one is Hadrian's?

When we finally blunder into the real thing there is no mistaking it; Hadrian knew how to build a wall. Started in 122 AD, it snakes its way across seventy-three miles of lowland. It is ten feet wide at the base and stands fifteen feet high. It was built, we are told, to keep the barbarous Picts from straying over the border into Roman Britain. It must have been effectively daunting. Even now, much depleted after having been scavenged for building material for centuries, it is impressive. At the time, it is believed, it was daubed with stucco and painted white, a startling barrier in this wild area. I imagine the Picts giving it a wide berth.

As we tramp about the wall with the other tourists it is hard not to admire the workmanship in those neatly squared off stones still here after nearly nineteen centuries. When driven to conquer, or avoid being conquered, we do seem to rise to some sort of greatness. Under this pressure we become our most inventive, creative, and indomitable selves. Why do I find that actually rather depressing?

The United Kingdom is a lovely shape: an eccentric lady in a large hat, riding a pig. Around her slender neck, just below the Scottish border, Hadrian's Wall rests like an iron chain. It isn't the Scottish border, but perhaps it should be. A reminder of the foolishness it represents might be helpful, for this is a wall dedicated to hanging on to real estate. Robbie and I, two daughters of a dead airman, marvel at the energy and money spent to preserve and celebrate this particular monument to war and power. How much energy, we wonder, has been devoted to honouring men like our father?

***

As we slip out of bucolic rural Northumberland into Tyneside it begins to rain in earnest. Having driven through an unchanging and uncluttered corner of this antique land, gently rolling fields stretching in all directions, every so often a church spire, marking some little village, poking its head above the trees off the highway, Newcastle is a cold, hard slap in the face. Negotiating her grim outer suburbs, we are plunged into the soot and misery of twenty-first century northern Britain. The North has suffered in the recession: shops are boarded up, houses decaying; there is little sign of hope. We trust Fred to get us through as fast as possible. Whitley Bay calls: rain belts down. Ah, England in May!

Hunger drives us to a café on the waterfront, the Rendezvous, a building that, to our delight, dates back to the war. Our father and his mates may well have enjoyed a cuppa in this tea room, which seems to have worked hard to avoid any vulgar updating. It feels like a good start. Standing at the window of this café, unchanged, it seems, for decades, looking out across the wide deserted beach through a veil of spring rain, we are seeing, surely, very much what he saw in early October of 1943. For a moment there he is, a young man in uniform, wandering across the sand, stooping occasionally to pick up some treasure tossed in by the sea. He and his mates joke, chat, and smoke their interminable cigarettes, gazing eastward over the water. One day soon, when they have finished training, they will fly across that grey expanse and head for the waiting enemy. But not yet. Not just yet.

The rain lets up as we leave the café. Robbie is wandering around the parking lot, lost in thought. She is smiling. I pause for a moment to enjoy my lovely sister. Although actually quite well off, she buys all her clothes in Op Shops, Australia's thrift stores. She believes passionately in conservation, abhors waste, and is meticulous about recycling. I've come in standard travelling gear — a selection of rather boring tops, jeans, a windbreaker and the inevitable running shoes, add a camera slung over my shoulder and I might as well wear a sign saying "tourist." Robbie, by contrast, wears natty but practical leather flats, a series of shabby-elegant buttoned and laced-trimmed tops, a brown wool coat, a burnt orange hat and matching scarf. The scarf often trails and is a little tattered, having been gently mangled in the rollers at the airport. The hat is frequently askew, sitting in a way never designed for a hat to sit. Her only nod to tourist common sense is her elastic-waist jeans. But, as I fondly watch her drifting toward our car, I see a sense of style delightful for its eccentricity. She could have stepped right out of a Miss Marple village.

We need to book a room for the night. Nobody seems to know where the tourist centre can be found and with the rain again bucketing down we set off toward St Mary's lighthouse after our waitress suggests we might find it there. As the lighthouse is reached by a tidal causeway, under water at that precise moment, this advice is of minimal help. In the far corner of the abandoned, rain-swept parking lot is a caravan serving tea and fried objects. I hop out, run through the rain and wait as the fellow behind the counter prepares steaming drinks for two chaps in orange city gear. They listen in as I ask for the Tourist Information Centre. "Oh," one cries, "we know where that is."

"Right," the other chimes in, "hop in your car and follow us. We'll take you there."

"You'd do that for us?"

They nod enthusiastically.

"Follow that truck," I cry as I clamber in beside my startled sister.

Tourist Information, it turns out, is a minimalist office attached to the Library where a polite young fellow suggests a guesthouse called Sunholme: it is close, clean, reasonable, and available, and we like its optimistic name given the unrelenting rain. We have some hours before we need to be there so decide to see what the library, so conveniently next door, has to tell us about the RAF in Whitley Bay.

Very little, as it turns out. Although many men came here to train, there is no trace of them. It is a small library and close to empty but not lacking enthusiasm. The staff and several customers leave what they are doing and get stuck into our search, so that, even though it yields little, we enjoy the process. We ask about the Spanish City, an impressive folly along the waterfront. It features a huge dome and was, at one time, a pleasure palace for dining, dancing, fun and games. It has sagged into disrepair and is now boarded off to be refurbished at some future date. It will, the town hopes, revitalize the strand and lure tourists. Somewhere I have read that it housed troops during the war but now I am wondering which war. The cluster of interested natives eager to fill in our considerable gaps is of little help. Nobody recalls troops being housed there. Nobody recall troops at all.

When Arthur and his fellow trainees arrive at Whitley Bay they are billeted in private homes: *we six*, he says: himself, Ern, Dutchy, Pearson, Jacky Ware, Murphy. He is fond of them, staying up late to talk. *We have great old yarns, Murph and I, he's a good chap.* He also sits up having *a natter* with Jackie Ware: *a very ingenuous youngster*, whatever that means. To be fair, when I look over my own scrappy diary keeping and wonder what some distant ancestor might make of it, I can understand the problem. Just as I never feel the need to fill in the back story of any friend or acquaintance — I know them, after all, and I am writing this for me — he has no call to flesh these men out. It is enough to record that they end up in the same house, that it was very nice, even if there is no hot water.

He takes what comes cheerfully. This two weeks of training and getting physically fit is not too taxing and fun in its way. It is also completely unnecessary. They are involved in what can only be described as busy work. Some kind of bottleneck in the system has meant that there is no spot for them in an Advanced Flying Unit. A challenge for the higher ups:

"Well, that's that. No place for these chaps. What to do?"

"Not healthy to have them hanging about in Brighton for too long."

"No. Ghastly place. Too many pubs.

"Quite."

"There's always Whitley Bay for ground training."

"Spot on. Running about on the dunes. Getting fit. That's the ticket."

So they learn to push guns long distances and to fire them, to use fixed bayonets and heave grenades, to scramble over assault courses and fight mock battles, to practise guard duty on the golf links. Dinghy drill lectures have some relevance; the rest is just busy work.

If Arthur has questions about the point of what he describes as a *Commando Course* he does not express them. He simply gets stuck into it. He gets a chuckle out of Paddy's wet behind as he misses the water jump on the assault course. I love how he then makes the point that the water jump is, after all, difficult. He may laugh at their blunders but he gives friends their due. And he is frankly amused at his own clumsy attempts to fire guns and fling grenades. His grenade falls apart when tossed and he ruefully confesses *I'm not very good with the rifle I'm afraid*. It doesn't seem to worry him. His ego is not involved and, anyway, he will not carry a rifle where he plans to go.

It isn't all watercourses and cross-country; they have some free time to explore. They play bad golf with no shame. Daddy and Murphy give the local caddies *a few frights*; ditto for the local golfers when he and Dutchy play. There is a rugger match in the sands of Whitley Bay's vast beach. When it is cold and wet, Tea Rooms (the Rendezvous perhaps) provide a haven. There are fish and chip shops. The food is not too bad. The Sergeant's Mess, Prudhoe Hall, is a converted rest home whose anteroom provides darts and a place to hang out. Mail has caught up with them and he is happy hearing news of Nooney and his girls. A couple of evenings of discussion and debate are organized: "The power of the press for good or evil," and "Australia's immigration policy."

We leave the library with only one gem: we have seen a photo of Prudhoe Hall and believe it will be easy to track down; we will explore on my laptop tonight and go to see it tomorrow.

So we set off for Sunholme, fantasizing that it may be the very house in which he was billeted. No harm in such optimism. When we booked, the helpful chap in information had one small *caveat*: we will be sharing the house with a group of hens. Even Robbie, who loves her chickens, finds this a bit of a stretch. An explanation is hastily provided. Whitley Bay is a Mecca, perhaps *the* Mecca of Hen Weekends: a last Bacchanal of freedom before the chains of marriage tighten. They arrive in groups, the brides and their entourages, book into a guesthouse, change into outlandish costumes and go out on the town. This is a mixed blessing for Whitley Bay: the tourist money is nice but the drunken behaviour that comes with it is a blight. Our information fellow suggests that we might find sharing a house with a group of hens less than sleep inducing. He reassures us that Maureen, our landlady, runs a tight ship ... still, it is a risk. A risk we are eager to take. We want a close up of this custom so unlike the bridal showers or stag and doe parties of our countries; we want to meet these hens; sleep can be sacrificed.

Maureen, our hostess at Sunholme Guest House, has large, surprised blue eyes; I don't believe she ever blinks. She takes us in with real affection and deposits us in an attic room declaring she will be back with tea. The room is perfect: crisp sheets, cheerful wallpaper, a huge window overlooking the city, a small but efficient bathroom and even a teeny sitting area where we take our tea and plan our evening.

We are ready to set out in search of supper just as our resident hens are off for their night on the town. They have been rustling and giggling and banging doors on the floor below and here they are in all their splendour. The bride-to-be is Bo Peep and her friends are lambs. She has a bonnet, and a crook and a panniered crinoline, the bodice lacy and low-cut — revealing a vast and creamy décolletage. Her lambs, clad in faux sheepskin, have perky pink ears and cheeky black noses. Given the raw weather outside, the sheepskin seems brilliant except for the fact that they still manage to display acres of mottled blue, goose-bumpy flesh. This is, we soon learn, *de rigueur*: the more skin the better. Out on the street we see scantily clad sailors, fortune-tellers, belly dancers, and ladies of the night. As we watch our lambs teeter toward the town in a cloud of shrieks and giggles, Maureen tells us she sat them all down for a meeting in her front parlour to warn them against becoming a casualty. Her entryway displays a grim poster featuring a drunken girl being hauled off to jail. "I told them, 'Have fun, but be careful.' I'm their mother while they're here. My girls don't get into trouble."

Waving her girls off with the satisfaction of having set them on a path of virtuous amusement, Maureen fixes her unwavering gaze on us, ready to arrange our evening. With a shudder of distaste, she steers us away from an establishment that harbours rats but highly recommends an Italian place further down the street where we are treated royally when we mention her name.

Full of good Italian nosh, we stroll the strand in the long British evening. The rain has stopped and we pause on the beach, imagining those young men, in 1943, shouting, running, rolling in the sand, laughing and happy to be alive. Then we wander back to Sunholme and a computer search for Prudhoe Hall.

Nothing. It does not exist. The name is ubiquitous; Prudhoes everywhere but no Hall in this area that could have made a welcoming Mess for our father and his friends. Yet we have seen its photo. We would like to revisit the library but the next day is Sunday and it is closed. We both believe we have seen a Prudhoe Street but cannot find it on the map. Maureen winkles out an elderly lodger from upstairs but he knows of no Prudhoe either. For years I will, on a whim, Google Prudhoe Hall hoping for enlightenment. It never comes.

Breakfast is sumptuous and we are well-rested, having been only slightly disturbed by the whispers and muffled giggles of the well-schooled returning hens. We say a grateful goodbye to Maureen and her startled blue eyes. We have one other place to visit before we leave Whitley Bay: Holywell Dene. It is one of our father's precise references and we must find it.

In his low-key record, this entry positively bubbles with enthusiasm. *Had a pleasant hike to a very pretty spot by a brook called Holywell Dene — most enjoyable. Bayonet drill in the afternoon.* A Dene is, it turns out, not a brook but a valley. The river, Seaton Burns, flows down Holleywell Dene and into the sea at Seaton Sluice. Our map seems to suggest that we could walk along the Dene from the beach. We park by a hotel and make our way back to the bridge where a kindly local cautions against trudging along the muddy banks. He points out an old walking path on our map. "Likely your dad and his mates took that. It's built up now but if you go in behind you'll find the Dene where he might have seen it." We walk a little way from the bridge finding hundreds of the most beautiful snail shells, but it is unpleasantly soggy and we have the wrong shoes. Back into the car we put ourselves into Fred's hands. He proves fairly useless; poor fellow, his information has not been upgraded for years.

Giggling and cursing by turn, we zigzag into a fifties subdivision of semi-detached homes made unexpectedly sweet by little side gates leading into walled gardens. We park and head through a field toward a distant and hopeful looking wooded area. Robbie stops to pee in some handy bushes along the way. We are, after all, ladies of a certain age, and bathrooms/washrooms/toilets/lavs/WC's (pick your preferred euphemism) are not thick on the ground, so needs must. There will be many such moments. This one is unpleasantly enlivened when she backs her bottom into a nettle and emerges scratching and disgruntled.

At the end of the field we plunge into the valley and it is glorious. Bluebells coat the hillside among newly green trees. Paths wind through the woods. Here and there we see joggers, dog walkers, couples hand in hand. At the bottom of the Dene the river gurgles and splashes. We walk along its banks, following it to a point where it disappears into a hill, bubbling through a mossy tunnel. Leaning over we can see a grate in the distance, the water rushing through, the stone ceiling dripping. Ducks play in the shallows. The sun flickers through the trees. We are dappled and blessed. This is the first time we are able to stand in a spot sure that this is his experience. *Most enjoyable indeed*, my gentle, laconic father.

Hut 17

From Whitley Bay they are moved back to Brighton to wait about for a few more days, then they are posted to Dumfries in Scotland to finally begin real training. All this chugging about on British Rail from north to south and back again seems crazy. But it is accepted with fairly good grace, if some weariness: *Went through usual procedure prior to posting.* They are old hands at this by now. Kitted up, they are marched to the Brighton station and sent to London, where they wait for a connection. It's raining but they find shelter and coffee at St. Pancras after storing their kits on the tender. Once aboard their train, they *secure a carriage among we four.* They hunker down, smoking, chatting, snoozing, as the fields of southern England slide behind them. Huddled in their now soggy greatcoats, they stir occasionally, shift position and stare out the window of the darkened carriages at the sleeping towns, more scattered as they head north, cross the Pennines and, in the early morning, are in Scotland. Do they have food, we fret, do they manage enough sleep? In the early morning they *pass through very pretty autumn scenery* and then they are at the station, loading kit bags on a tender, and heading for the base, a few miles beyond the town.

Seventeen hours. My trip from Canada, including the waiting about in Schiphol airport was, at most, twelve hours. Even Robbie's marathon from Australia was not much longer. No whining on Arthur's part though. He is happy to be posted with his buddies, Dutchy and Baldy, Elger and Pearson. *Place stiff with planes, mainly Wellingtons (Wimpys) and Ansons.* After breakfast (hurrah, they are eating) they get blankets (no sheets, we note sadly) and settle into a hut, which already has some fellow Aussies.

From Whitley Bay Robbie and I, in turn, make our way to Dumfries, pronounced "Dumfris" we have learned and diligently practise saying. As we cannot check in at our B&B until four in the afternoon, we decide to try and find the base first. We'd imagined a nice historic plaque at the entrance, a booth with tours perhaps, some celebration of its history. But no. We find ourselves in the Heathhall Industrial Estate. At the entrance there is a large map of this huddle of low brick buildings and Nissen huts. The street names — *Spitfire*, *Hurricane, Halifax, Lancaster* — tell us something to do with the war and the RAF has gone on here.

We wander about, dropping in on a couple of the rather desperate looking businesses. A pathetic antique store with a skimpy inventory and no discernible proprietor is no help. The workers at a repair shop look blank when we ask about a World War II airfield, but one of them has a brainwave: "There's an air museum, over there." He waves vaguely and gives us garbled instructions, telling us cheerfully that we just have to look out for the planes, we can't miss it.

For some time we manage to miss it quite successfully and when we finally pull up at a chain-link fenced area the gate is firmly shut. It looks unimpressive. A compound next to the sadly dilapidated museum houses a bunch of decaying planes. The website makes a desperate attempt to turn a collection of ratty unkempt aircraft into a virtue: visitors can joyfully clamber all over and sit inside these machines — they are already falling apart so why not? I squeeze through the gate, walk up to the museum and peer in the window at a mishmash of tired bits and pieces. The original tower has been refurbished and is home to some more relevant stuff including reconstructions, using slightly creepy shop window dummies, of life in the control tower and in the huts. This is where our father's war really began and, after our months of research and our long journey, it is depressingly anticlimactic. We want bunting and marching bands; instead it reeks of disinterest.

We are tired, both still a little jet-lagged, but we go back to Heathhall Industrial Estates, and drive the streets with their evocative names. We have photos of our father with Dutchy and Baldy lolling in the weak autumn sun outside a Hut 17, which he shares with nineteen other men for the bulk of his time here. Before us is a hut. We imagine we might be looking at his very hut. We decide we are. It is enough for now.

***

We have a group photo of the men who occupy Hut 17. Shoved together by random chance, they are all Australian, and often that is all they have in common. They get along because they have to. Some friendships are strong and lasting, others fleeting and soon forgotten. In our photo, twenty men in uniform are arranged in three rows. The front row is seated, arms folded across chests. The left side of the row begins with men in a more relaxed mode, their arms loosely crossed or resting in their laps. As the row of eight progresses to the right the arms are more and more tightly folded across increasingly constricted chests. The eight men in the second row stand, arms behind backs. The final row of four, on a bench to raise them up, is also standing. In this short back row, at the far right side, is our father. I search for him first every time I examine this group, checking to see if he is still there. Some believe that the dead disappear from photos. Of course, if that were the case, then there would be many holes in this picture. Of the twenty men, seven will die in action. And, of course, now sixty-six years later, even those who survived the war are now most likely gone. But there are no ghostly absences.

I also always check for Dutchy. Our father compares him at one point to a Polled Angus, a hornless breed of cattle. When he has one of these animals pointed out to him by a chuckling Arthur he is understandably unimpressed by the comparison, but there *is* something sweetly bovine about his round, wide-eyed face. I note that he, more than any of his mates in the front row, is totally relaxed: his arms are unfolded, his legs akimbo, not neatly crossed at the ankles as they have most likely been instructed to do. He seems worry-free. That's a relief, because in the listing under the photo he is marked, quite inaccurately, as having been killed in action.

Next to Dutchy is Ern Baldwin, who is recorded as a survivor. Also not true. Arthur, Ern/Baldy and Dutchy were each other's best friends. Of the three, two will not come home. The errors in this record are doubly galling because, by the time we have finished scouring this diary and peering into the aging black and white photos, we have some knowledge of these men and we are proprietary. Robbie and I both contact the RAF website pointing out the mistakes. The reply is official but dismissive: it is a long time ago and errors are inevitable. Robbie is relentless in this crusade for accuracy and eventually one correction is made; Dutchy is no longer a casualty. He is allowed to go home, marry, have a life. Then the second error is put right and Ernie Baldwin's death is acknowledged. He does not go home but we have set the record straight. See, we are taking care of your mates, we tell our dead father. You couldn't do it, so we are.

In this task of finding truths many decades down the road, we are always aware that any information we might be gathering is suspect. A smaller error, but still annoying, is that our father is listed as having been on 203 Squadron. We have become very attached to 207, his actual squadron. I'm sure 203 is also a fine squadron. But it isn't his.

We cannot know everything — often we know nothing — of the men in this photo, but we want to. I try to discern personalities in the angle each man has set his hat. Daddy's is firmly and sensibly on his head. The chap next to him seems in danger of losing his. Others are either pushed back or tugged low over the forehead. They don't look easy things to wear.

I remember the toe on the bronze statue of St. Peter in his basilica in Rome, shiny and worn wafer thin by the millions of reverent kisses bestowed by the faithful. It's as well that gazing at photos does not have the same effect; this image of those men in the hut in Dumfries would be erased by the intensity of our interest.

***

Cowan Farm Guest House sits atop a small hill. Our little car chugs valiantly up the track from the road. Sheep, many with tiny angel-wing-white lambs tugging at their teats or leaping about as only lambs can, fill the fields, gazing at us as we pass. We pull through the gates and onto the gravel of the fenced courtyard. A couple of farm dogs in cages go mad with joy at our arrival. The air is perfumed with strong hints of cow, sharp undertones of pig, hay accents. We breathe deeply.

We began as country girls. Robbie now farms once again and her cows are her joy. I love my garden but have become more attached to city life. These few nights in the country acknowledge our roots; they also pay homage to our father and to our mother. Perhaps they hoped we would also make a life on the land, but farm kids long to escape; I couldn't wait to leave Orange. Now when I go back, I cannot believe its charm. How did I not notice it when I lived there?

Like most of the farmhouses we have passed, this is whitewashed, low to the ground, solid. By the front door is a large window featuring two huge stuffed hares, posed on their hind legs and seemingly about to tear each other to shreds. Inside there is a common room and a large dining room, both decorated with the loving efforts of the local taxidermist: a fox, a badger, a pheasant, many mounted fish. It is all very *Field & Stream*. Behind these two principal rooms our host and hostess have an apartment. We will not be sleeping in the main house and are shown to an attached long, low building. Inside is a narrow corridor with a row of doors to eight or nine rooms. Ours is tiny, with two trim single beds, a shared bedside table, a minute wardrobe and a bathroom that does not encourage much turning around. It is clean and comfortable and its large window looks onto an apple tree in bloom, a happy coincidence as we remember our mother's dream. Two bird feeders attract a flock of customers. Beyond the tree is a pond. In the winter, we are delighted to learn, it freezes solid and the cows sleep on it.

After unpacking, we explore the property, making friends with some scruffy looking pigs. As we lean on a whitewashed stone wall and take in the view from our little hill, green fields stretching in all directions and clusters of white farm buildings filling the hollows, Robbie, inspired by the pigs, launches into a story about one of her neighbours. "Honestly, he's hopeless. His animals are always attacking him."

"Good grief."

"Yes, his pig bit him right here." She points to her upper leg alarmingly proximate to the groin area. "He went for stitches. They slapped a bandage on. Told him it was waterproof so he, the absolute duffer, marched home and waded into his dam to find out if they were lying. His dam is a nightmare, full of dead animals. Of course he got a horrible infection." She is hooting with laughter. "The hospital had little sympathy."

"And no wonder. You do know the maddest people."

"Yes. I seem to."

Back at the farm office, we tell our bubbly young Londoner why we are in this area. She finds our quest sweet and quaint but is too young to be much interested. We know there must be local people with memories that go back to that time. A ten-year-old then would be seventy-eight now and might recall the men in blue wandering the streets of Dumfries, or sitting in the cafés. He would certainly remember the planes overhead. We know we should be trying to locate such people but we are timid at this stage of our search; we hope our courage will grow.

It is late and we need to eat. Our hostess has a suggestion: we can drive into Dalbeattie. Really, we cry, Dalbeattie? Arthur played rugby there not long after coming to the camp. We can find supper and perhaps get a glimpse of the playing field. We are directed to the King's Arms where we have a bowl of soup followed by a rhubarb crumble. It seems the ideal thing, weary as we are from our travels. Our simple meal in this English pub is in sync with our father's first night in Dumfries. Granted we aren't, as he and his mates were, dining on powdered eggs, but we are being a tad austere in solidarity with his world.

The moon is very new, a silver flick above the dark trees. The crunch of gravel in the Cowan Farm yard is a welcome sound and our simple room is a comforting haven. The hamster in my brain calms and I am instantly asleep.

Robbie is an early riser. By the time I drag open reluctant eyes she has been awake for a good hour and is propped up in bed drinking tea and reading. Over steaming cups we lay out our campaign. After breakfast, among the stuffed critters, we pack up our little car for a day of exploration. A few minutes had been spent debating going back to the remains of the base and the airfield. This is where most of his three months here are spent. But yesterday's visit was discouraging. Those buildings may or may not be the originals; nobody knows or cares. The museum is not particularly devoted to that airbase, and its dispiriting collection of moth-eaten planes seems to have little to do with our father's life. We could go back, we mutter, but would it be helpful or simply depressing? Would we know more of him?

The first month of the diary at Dumfries is all about the camp. It is a world he enjoys. In fact, when granted a forty-eight hour leave just over two weeks into his posting, he declines. Some higher up decides to put him on duty, which he accepts, but then he *goes to see* (code for complains to) the squadron leader and is back on leave. Still he does not want to go away: *Much too comfortable here.* The weather is balmy; he has time to write his stack of letters. So comfortable does he appear to be that it is two weeks before he and another fellow make it into the town. We guess there is a bus although they could have walked — it is about four miles. His first impressions don't shout out for a second visit: *A dull hole forsooth and the people both broad of speech and narrow of mind.*

Harsh, we think, from our easygoing chap. Why? We can hazard a guess. In the main the men in blue are seen as saviours: patted on the back, offered free drinks, admiration, and gratitude. But to some, particularly the local young men, they are a threat. The women find them glamorous. How does a chap in civvies compete with those smartly uniformed fliers with their aura of danger and courage? Perhaps they encounter some locals seeking to even the odds. And then there is that Colonial thing. Australians are particularly galled to be looked down upon as inferior dependents on Mother Britain, a country to which they have travelled far and for which they are prepared to die. Are they sneered at, patronized, by some broad speaking Scot in a dingy local pub? Something happens on that first visit and it is a while before he goes back.

When he tackles Dumfries next it is with Ern. They buy bikes. Fully equipped, his sets him back nine pounds ten pence, a very expensive purchase, but he is pleased. This bike stays with him throughout his war, opening up all sorts of adventures. Most of the men have bikes, some have motorbikes, a very few have cars.

We wonder what happens to his bike after he dies. Robbie reads somewhere that items that cannot be shipped home are often auctioned off by hut-mates and the money sent back to the family. So, we think, that may have happened to this highly satisfactory purchase. Then, months after we return from this trip, Robbie goes to Canberra and gets her hands on a cache of documents concerning his death and its aftermath. Several quite complex letters, to do with the bike, arrive eight or nine months after his death. First there is a wordy request to my mother to consider the fate of the bike. In a kindly tone it explains that shipping it home is out of the question. She may will it to some person of her choice in the British Isles; failing that she may give permission for it to be sold and the money will be sent to her. Believe me, the original letter is not nearly this succinct. It meanders on for a page. Her reply, seemingly involving the assistance of a solicitor, is fairly terse: sell it ... thank you. A third, equally verbose letter, acknowledges receipt of this response. What a lot of paper over a ten-pound bike. And multiply those by the hundreds, or even thousands of such bikes warehoused somewhere until the war staggers to its end. It may be bureaucracy gone mad, but it also may be bureaucracy at its finest. Such care. Such love, really.

***

"Was he a bit lazy, do you think?" We are zipping through the Scottish countryside headed for the city of Dumfries when Robbie asks this.

"I don't know. Maybe. He certainly goes on about his love of a good bludge."

Robbie is beaming, happy to find a real fellow behind this virtuous paragon we are in danger of creating. There is little nobility in being labelled a "bludger," a word with its origins in Aussie slang. It can be harsh: flung in disgust at the man (and it seems to mostly refer to men, having its roots in pimpdom) who ducks work, lets others do it for him, shirks it.

"Now," says Robbie, smacking the steering wheel with the flat of her hand, a signal that a story is on its way, "did you know, and I've forgotten who told me this, one of the aunts I think, that Daddy was a great reader. When he was a kid he always had his nose in a book. Often not to be found. He'd be curled up somewhere, at the back of a shed or off in the dunny. Can't you just see him, sitting on the pan on that wooden bench, pants around his ankles, not caring about the flies or the spider webs, nose in a book, dodging work..." She is chuckling in delight. "What a rascal. I suppose that was a sort of bludging."

We consider this boy, the youngest of seven, perched on the throne — an outhouse, all that would be available in the days of his youth. Outside his six siblings and two elderly parents grumble that he has disappeared — again.

Childhood bludging is easily forgiven. But bludging in uniform? A bludger in a world at war is not so charming. The diary, it seems, is peppered with this word. "Bludge" — it sits squat and gelid on the page, a lump of something nasty in the mouth.

Meanings shift and soften. Think of kids' use of "wicked" and "sick" to mean "awesome" and "amazing." A bludger is to be sneered at, a fool who "couldn't get a root in a whorehouse." But the act of bludging can be almost benign. "Can I bludge a cigarette?" we'd ask in the days of our smoking, in our late teens and early twenties before life became accountable. It is a small thing, more honest than "borrow," but there is the understanding that the bludger will later become the bludgee; the habitual bludger who does not reverse roles is not regarded with favour. This is a jokey sort of transgression. Not serious. The word has lost its edge.

I think that he used it that way most of the time. On the troop ship across the Pacific there is not one bludge reference. Everyone on that ship is at work simply by being transported. The fool who smokes on deck is not bludging — he is simply a fool putting them all at risk. When they all opt to read and relax or write letters home instead of attending the well-meant hymn sing (organized by the unfortunate padre with the "nice solo voice") it is not bludging, it is simply choosing to use time in a saner fashion.

Finally in England, warehoused in the rather upscale Grand in Brighton, they are in for a period of waiting. Much of life in the air force, and I am sure all of the services, is a matter of sitting about wondering what will happen next. So they mooch about, taking in the sights, looking for a way to fill the time. "Bludge" becomes doing nothing where there is nothing to do. He *bludged around the hotel.* Church parade is neither popular nor mandatory; twice in Brighton he *bludges* rather than attending.

There is no mention of bludging of any sort when he first arrives at Dumfries. They are promised a month of ground training: learning base routine, going on flight duty, getting to know the ropes. Then they will go "on course" taking their skills into the air, emerging ready to be crewed up, one step closer to doing what they came for. He is, they all are, anxious to get going, eager to learn.

His group arrives at the beginning of November. By the start of December they should be into the real meat of this experience. *Beautiful weather*, he declares, and *much interesting work*. He gets useful gen on Marconi gear, does *some Morse on Tom's oscillator*. He is busy and happy. *Am getting the hang of things and I think I am a little help to Tom now instead of a hindrance.* We will never know who Tom is; somebody he works with in something called Minor Inspections. In the second week Arthur is transferred from there to Flying Control, requiring him to be on duty at the aerodrome when flights take off for training. At first he finds it confusing but then cheerfully reports that he is getting it sorted.

Then we begin to count the reports of flying scrubbed. They are frequent. *Flying scrubbed again. I seem to be always writing that down in my diary but that's the way it is.* And it is. Training in Britain is hampered by its persistently nasty weather. Bad enough to be in training in often dodgy aircraft without trying to take off into zero visibility as fog and rain blanket the runway and cloak the Pennines. So, night after night flying is scrubbed and, if there is no flying, ground duties are not needed. He gears up, waits around only to be sent back to the base, over and over. The "bludge" word begins to creep in. He is not avoiding work: there is just no work to do. Hanging about, doing nothing, filling time: bludging.

November 11, 1943

Around mid-month, when Armistice Day rolls around, he shrugs it off, *made no difference to us.* It is, after all, a day honouring the close of the Great War. They are anxious to get on with their training and do what they came all this way to do: fight in this one. In the meantime: *Mail coming regularly which is giving things a rosy glow.*

Getting very cunning at 500 and draughts from constant practice.
Spare time on the bludge allows honing of these skills. On this relaxed
day reading his mail and playing games with his mates, shrugging off
the significance of this Armistice Day, he does not know that, in
exactly one year, he will be dead.

As their first month ends, to their general disappointment, they
are told there is little likelihood of their starting the course for many
weeks. They want to start flying. They want to sharpen their skills in
the air under the tutelage of instructors. Time to stop buggering about
and get on with it. November and December of 1943 mark the
beginning of the great slaughter that flowers into the hideous Battle
of Berlin. Crews are dying at a high rate and the young men on the
base know this. Certainly trained crew are needed and the sooner the
better. It is just one more puzzle in the conduct of this war. Robbie
frequently wonders out loud how the British Empire managed to
stumble across victory.

Knowing what men like them, in Bomber Command, are facing
each night in Europe while they sit about, their training inexplicably
stalled, makes this delay even harder to bear. The Government, to
preserve morale, may try to play up the victories and gloss over the
defeats but everyone knows the danger. Newspapers and newsreels
trumpet the losses; letters arrive telling of friends now dead. They
know what is coming.

In late November Dutchy receives word of a cousin's death on
Ops. He is, our father writes, *very cut up*, adding, *and I don't feel too
happy myself*. Daddy helps Dutchy get away for the funeral. We
wonder how that is — Dutchy pushing back tears, Daddy in
sympathetic misery, perhaps polishing his shoes, helping him gather
up socks, a shirt, reminding him to pack pyjamas, a toothbrush.
Maybe they rustle up an iron and press his uniform. They cope by
getting busy.

The next day, with Dutchy off burying his cousin, our father's
frustration is on the boil. People are dying and the course is on hold.

Day off to-day. Slept in late and did S.F.A. My father does not swear. Neither did my mother. Her most explosive expletive, and when it came you knew she was seriously riled up, was "Bum!" Charmingly innocent and adolescent compared to the truck driver mouth I have rather deliberately cultivated. Even if he only expresses it in shorthand, Arthur is really disgusted with his own phoney war. Time to be doing!

Over by Christmas. That is the rumour round the camp. A long shot but they know the tide is turning. *Nooney would be pleased. I don't think I'll see action.* His few explicit musings about mortality are always about her. In early January he hears of the death of another friend, Migner, and he marks the news with a fatalistic, *And so they go.*

In contrast to our increasingly dark view of the British war machine, many others are filled with admiration for the training the crews receive. "Imaginative, thorough, efficient," croons one analyst. The men mooching about the base looking for ways to occupy themselves in a cluster of Nissen huts and brick sheds might argue with that last adjective. As much as many love a good bludge — our father is not alone — this is a bleak time. Their sense of purpose dwindles. They have signed up to be part of something big, not to spend their days being given busy work assignments or trying to fill the time with endless card games, darts tournaments, or visits to the pictures in town. They begin to sleep in more. Beds go unmade. Bludge starts to mean time wasted. It begins to have a bitter taste.

There is a lacklustre attempt to keep these young fellows fit. Games days are planned but often don't happen. Arthur Plowman is a keen Rugby player and his skills are in demand. He and Dutchy play for the Aussies against the Station team. He plays rake, a sort of enforcer, perhaps explaining the numerous scars recorded in his enlistment medical. He does well, getting the ball all the time. This he puts down to the weakness of the English rake rather than his own superior skill, but he is appreciated. *Got quite a few pats on the back — very nice,* he says before cheerfully recording that they were beaten 15-0. We glimpsed a field in Dalbeattie that may be the very one he played on.

For another game his team travels to Carlisle where he plays in spite of coughing and feeling lousy. At still another his overcoat goes missing. This causes his motherly daughters some grief; November and December in the damp chill of Scotland demand that he at least have the comfort of a sturdy coat. It pains us that there is no record of its replacement.

These infrequent football matches are the only organized physical activity. In early December, after several days featuring not much more than sleeping in, playing draughts, eating bad food, and avoiding bed-making, he has *a kick around with some of the 34 course boys. Puffed like a steam engine*, he notes in disgust. *No condition at all.* He starts each day with a vigorous session of Jumping Jacks. My heart is squeezed by this image of him earnestly trying to keep in shape in this time of corrosive waiting.

There are the ENSA nights, the well-meaning Entertainment National Service Association, which valiantly attempts to provide amusement for the troops. There are certainly, on occasion, good shows, but with so many troops and so many stations, and a limited supply of Vera Lynns, George Formbys, and Gracie Fields, many are rather painful affairs. ENSA begins to stand for "Every Night Something Awful." But, even when these nights are less than stellar, some entertainment results, and the men are grateful for the effort made.

In early December, a week away from the long delayed start of the official course, there is another day of hanging around after reporting for duty, finding that flying is scrubbed — again — returning to the hut, waiting to see if he will be needed. It is taking its toll. *Tempers are getting short — too little to do and too much time to do it in. The sooner we get on course the better for all of us.*

So, as we sift through the diary for signs of sloth, what's the verdict? Is he lazy? When the date for the course to start is finally announced he says with relief: *We start flying on Tuesday next — glad of it.* He knows what hard work is and doesn't believe anything since he embarked from Australia fits its definition. They will be promoted anyway. They will become Flight Sergeants but he takes little pleasure in this: *Six months bludge and we get a 'crown' for it. Ridiculous really but I don't mind taking it even though we certainly haven't earned it.* No, not lazy, just a realist. Not a bludger who shirks work and passes it off to others, just, as they all are, wanting to get on with it while filling unspent time they had not asked for in the best way they can.

***

Dumfries is not a huge town — its population now is around 30,000. This, we are pleased to note, is about the same size as Orange, the little country town of his, and our, birth. We reach its centre with startling ease and rapidity, our GPS coming in for heady praise. We park by the River Nith, tamed, as it passes through the town, by concrete walkways, stone walls and iron railings, spanned by an ancient stone bridge whose curved supports divide the water. Apart from a patch of frisky turbulence, it flows with broad dignity, a solid-citizen type of river. It is, however, prone to wild flooding, though not when our father and his mates ride their bikes to the pictures in early December 1943, peddling joyously through the open countryside and the crisp winter air, bathed in the light of an almost full moon. After the show they go searching for fish and chips, ending up by the river in the older part of town and walking along its banks in the moonlight. They find chips but no fish. Later we must walk there in honour of the night. But first we go hunting for the much mentioned picture palace, the Lyceum.

Whatever we discover it won't be the building he actually sat in. It was torn down and rebuilt in the same spot, but even that was a while ago. Local cinemas are a dying breed. We are not bubbling with hope as we lock up the car, feed the meter, and trot up the hill past the old stone buildings lining White Sands, the street that runs by the river.

I am sure that Dumfries has a venerable and rich history. We are vaguely aware of a Robbie Burns connection and somewhere there is a wedding cake of a camera obscura, but our mission has granted us tunnel vision; all we can see or want to see is what his eyes may have lighted on. The High Street, at the centre of town, has a venerable old town hall. He would have seen that; it has been around for three hundred years. Even when he was there it no longer functioned as an actual town hall. It is a wonder to me that it ever did as it is, in spite of its three storeys, quite small and sits uncomfortably in the middle of the street.

There is little to go on, in this search for his time here. Although we find the residents intrigued by our story and eager to help, all the shop girls we speak to are young, born long after the events in which we are interested. They wrinkle their adolescent brows and tell us in their lilting brogues, "Nooo, I'm sorry. Nevah heerred of a Lyceum." So we accost the elderly, our contemporaries, until finally a lady behind a counter recalls a cinema. "Down the street near the arcade." Buoyed with hope we find a fairly new arcade but no sign of a cinema.

On a bench in the domed concourse sits a gentleman who is likely in his eighties: worth a try. I pounce. Is he a local? Aye. Does he recall a cinema, the Lyceum? He does. It was once where at least part of this arcade now stands. He can't be more specific than that. I recount my findings to Robbie and we agree: it's good enough. We are here; we have seen the High Street. We are very close to the Lyceum. All is well.

In a period of six weeks from late November until early January Arthur records going in to town to the pictures a startling eleven times. And there may have been more, as his diary keeping is a little erratic. The biggest concentration of picture going, almost every second night, falls in the period of waiting about for the course to begin. With not much to do, this diversion is welcome. The beautiful weather of their arrival has gone and Nissen huts are drafty things. The only way to keep warm is to sit right on top of the fire. Cinemas are cosy places to hunker down. Airmen all over England escape their cold billets and the austere life of their bases for a night at the pictures. Once they are on Operations it is also a way of keeping fear at bay.

Trips to the pictures continue up until Christmas and into the New Year. After that, the diary is all about training. He may have nicked off on his bike over the frost-hard ground for a meal in the local tea room and a warm seat in the Lyceum as a break from the grind that training becomes. If so, he doesn't tell us. He does however, and this seems odd, go to the pictures on Christmas Day.

We have to accept that our father does not pour his heart into these pages. That, we believe, is reserved for the letters home: the letters our mother destroys, the letters we covet. At times we wonder about his reason for keeping the diary; for whom is it written? I think, in the end it is just for him, a record to look back on when the war is over, a reminder of names, dates, places. But at times, not very often, and precious to us, it becomes a confidante and he lets his feelings slip.

In early December he hopes that something will come of the Big Three Conferences. Maybe this war will all be over soon. With his first Christmas away from home approaching, and six months of UK training under his belt, feelings are a little closer to the surface, tersely acknowledged. In early December, as they all wait irritably for the course to start he admits, *Home pulling me more now than at any time since leaving.* Good, we think, get in touch with those emotions. But then he does the man thing: *Once again, it's probably because of having too little to do.* On Christmas Eve his musings are almost enough to drive us mad. *Feeling very downhearted for some reason.* Really? You want a reason? I believe I can give you one or two.

Twelve thousand miles away the woman you love is pulling together Christmas for your two small children. You are not with them. Instead you are about to celebrate the Yuletide with a bunch of men with whom you've spent the last two months, crammed into a cold Nissen hut, breathing in, mixed with the smoke from the belching coke stove, the perfume of their farts, their beery returns from nights on the town, their infrequently washed bodies, and their even less frequently washed clothes. You like most of them, but some get on your nerves. There is no privacy. Much of the time you are cold. The food is grim.

The beer is watery. You have only just started to do work that seems to be leading anywhere or have bearing on why you set off on this journey in the first place. People have died. You know that your death is a real possibility. You are afraid. You do not know that this is your last Christmas on earth, but you know it could be.

You try to cheer yourself up with a few drinks of *foul whisky* in the Mess before being temporarily diverted by a very Scottish dinner party on Christmas Eve: *the men crowded into the W.V.S., a seven-piece band, plentiful food, the pudding piped in with much ceremony, soaked in brandy and set on fire in the darkened room.* In spite of general agreement that it is a great evening, later in the Mess you *lack the spirit to drink enough dishwater posing under the name of beer to get drunk*, and mooch back to the hut to play 500. Christmas Day brings a lunch of Spam sandwiches and flat beer. The afternoon is spent, still feeling depressed, playing cards in the hut. You cheer up a little when a fairly sumptuous (well at least plentiful) Christmas dinner is provided. You note dolefully that there is no snow. That at least would have been a lift for an Australian longing to experience a White Christmas. While all the single fellows head off for a dance at the W.V.S. you *write a very groan-filled letter to Nooney* before heading out to the pictures with Ernie Baldwin. And, after all this, you still seem slightly clueless about the source of your gloom.

He does not record the name of the picture he and Baldy see that Christmas night. There is a limit to what one can Google successfully in a search of the past but this is a particular fact I would like to know. I hope for a well-made, well-cast, brilliantly plotted, and absorbing flick to take their minds off their homesickness. Ern is engaged, a good and loyal man, and, like our father, not about to go off to a dance. They will pedal home after the show and fall into their bunks to try and sleep through the merry return of the revellers.

Next day they hear the details. Daddy, the old married man, listens indulgently. *Mistletoe*, he notes, *was much to the fore.* These are more innocent times and stolen kisses are a source of much excitement. Not everyone is chaste, of course, and those leading a rich sex life are regarded with some awe. *The boys are very intrigued by the Canadian in the N.C.O.'s room at the end of the hut who had a sergeant WAAF in his room the last two nights. She seems hot stuff so I guess he enjoyed himself.* Then — is this envy? Appreciation? Or just amusement? — he adds *Whacko!* His good mood is back. Or at least his practical nature has overcome the blues. There is not much point in being miserable. This is the lot he has chosen.

He confides his gentle, almost fatherly, exasperation with the antics of some of his hut-mates. Dutchy and Ernie announce that they are going off on a tear, bound for a night of unrestrained drinking. He is dubious about the extent of this boasted Bacchanal: *I hae me doots.* He has chosen friends who are not, however much they may think they want to be, given to excess.

There is one young friend whose foolishness sorely tries Arthur and Baldy's patience: Phil Elger, one of the trainees from Parkes and a fellow traveller on the *Denbyshire*. He gets a mention for being sozzled the last night aboard. To be fair, our father notes that most are pretty merry. They've made it across the Atlantic without being torpedoed; a few too many beers are understandable. Beer, it turns out, is not Phil's only weakness; he constantly and stubbornly falls in love. There is mention of a woman in Whitley Bay and once they are in Dumfries he falls hard for a WAAF. As November drifts into December and early January the diary is sprinkled with the concerns of the more mature for Phil's foolishness. It is never clear what the problem is. They do not appear to disapprove of Jeannette. Somehow Phil is being a goof and they feel called upon to set it right. In early December Ern Baldwin, a staidly engaged, and experienced fellow, *tries to put Phil wise to the folly of his ways in very plain language.* Phil is unimpressed. Daddy shrugs and declares that *he'll just have to learn the hard way.*

What foolishness is Phil committing that his friends feel the need to sort him out? As December and this blighted romance proceed our father carts Phil off to the pictures and during this excursion tries to convince him that *there is no such thing as a Platonic relationship between a man and a woman.* Robbie and I are torn between amusement and amazement as we both believe that such relationships can and do exist. But what is Phil up to? Young and innocent as many of these lads are, there is, for many, the aching possibility of dying a virgin. To leave this earth with that rite of passage unexplored seems a cruel trick. On the other hand they are also young and idealistic, and, we can see now, shaped by the beliefs of their time. Any woman good enough to love is elevated to near untouchability. What a conundrum. If our father is as persuasive as he seems to believe, exactly in what direction does he steer this frustrated and conflicted lad? Is his advice to just get on with it? Or to worship her from a safe distance?

Christmas, depressing and gloom-ridden for our dad, comes and goes. While the unattached guys in the hut enjoy the mistletoe opportunities at the post Christmas party, Phil, Daddy notes, *has the time of his young innocent life.* A week later, as 1944 rolls in, Jeanette dumps poor Phil. There is a bit of "I told you so" in that diary entry. *So ends a beautiful Platonic friendship. Ah me!*

But amorous Phil is not easily deterred. Five days later he *has taken up with a hard-faced little WAAF and is making fool of himself as usual.* Our father is clearly exasperated. *Thank God,* he writes, *I got calf love out of my system when I was still in the calf love stage.*

We wish we knew the story of each and every one of the twenty men in Hut 17, the seven who died and the thirteen who survived. Of some we know a little; thumbnail sketches at best. In one entry our father tries to catch the atmosphere in the hut where two of the livelier guys keep them roaring with laughter. They are both, he says, *hard cases.* Are they delinquents? Are they criminals? No, "hard cases" are simply very funny fellows. One, Cowell, who will die, reminds our father of a pirate with his curly black hair and black gleaming eyes. He is the teller of tall tales, an amiable rogue. But he has Blackbeard's ruthless side and would, our father thinks, *stop at nothing, for he grew up among a tough element and knows how to look after himself.* On one visit to the Lyceum this wrong-side-of-the-tracks-and-proud-of-it-Cowell *scandalizes the lady in the seat behind us with his comments, in good Aussie, on the show and the girls around.* It isn't hard to imagine our father's delighted shock. In small towns you mind your manners: everyone knows everyone else and memories are long. You sit quietly in the pictures, sucking the chocolate off your caramel-centred Fantails, keeping your thoughts to yourself.

Cowell's comedic partner is Eric Henry: *a benevolent Dutch uncle with his big bland face, his spectacles, and his huge cherry-wood pipe. He stands six feet and has a deceptive air of clumsy staidness about him.* This benign façade hides a fellow our father describes as *about as staid and respectable as a randy tom cat and just as active.* He'd run an off-course betting joint and was involved in his father's estate agent business. Daddy imagines him *giving out his bland smile and raking in the coin.*

In a land where class distinction is accepted as a given, the RAF becomes a great leveller. It is pretty clear that being born to the purple will still get you a commission faster than the working class chap but, in the training huts and later in the Bomber crews, it is what you can do, not your bloodline, that matters. Ordinary men like our father are judged on character. The rough and ready Cowells and Henrys are the same. They take care of each other, this disparate group, sharing their care parcels from home. Daddy loans his bike to *some joker who rips the spokes out.* The joker has no name and he brushes it off cheerfully with a *reminder to self not to lend bikes.* A laissez faire attitude helps in those crowded and comfortless quarters.

One night he stays in the Mess reading between arguments with a WAG about land taxes and birth control. He describes it as a *lively evening* but fails to tell us what exactly his opinions are. The latter topic is of particular interest to us. Robbie and I are eighteen months apart; how much birth control was exercised there? Can we leap to the conclusion that he would happily have kept our mother barefoot and pregnant. That, had he come home, we would have grown among an ever increasing brood? And as for land taxes ... well, we'll never know where he stood on that.

Not long after the discussion with the WAG, he chats, while on duty, with the Flying Control chaps, all British, getting their take on the Royal Family. They are lukewarm, *leaning toward a Socialist state*. His impression is that this is a predominant attitude. And how does that feel to this fellow who has packed up and left his family to protect King and County? Does he wonder what the Hell he is doing here when the Brits themselves show no such loyalty?

We are guessing where he stood on matters like birth control and the Royal family, just as we are guessing that he preferred friends who were not drunken sots. Obsessive need to know everything; growing resignation that this will not happen.

***

Well content with our wander along High Street and our discovery of the vague location of the Lyceum we start back to the car. He mentions a tearoom where once he had second helpings causing the waitress' eyes to pop. But it is sixty-eight years ago and the chances of that tea room being in the same place, wherever that might be, are slim.

We return to the river to walk along its banks, imagining the young men in their uniforms, late at night, the moon reflected in the water, fresh from a picture at the Lyceum, munching their chips (*sans* fish) from newspaper wrappings. They are young and happy to be together. Later they will ride home, which is what that camp out in the countryside has become, home, for a little time at least.

Briefly we contemplate the possibility of driving back that night and seeing the river as they saw it. Practical considerations get in the way. We really don't fancy a nighttime negotiation of the narrow roads around Dumfries. I have a pang of sadness at this. Where did the two daring sisters we once were disappear to? Long ago Robbie sailed around the world in a small boat with her husband and two kids. I have travelled, hitchhiked across Europe, and done some ocean sailing of my own. Now I am a quivering mess in traffic and my sister flinches at the thought of night driving on skinny Scottish country roads. But we are what we are. No point in scaring ourselves in order to walk by the Nith at night. I clinch the matter by pointing out that we would not, as they did then, experience a full moon. "It wouldn't be the same anyway." Robbie is pleased with this way out. "Good point," she says, "so where to next?"

Sweetheart Abbey

Scouring the diary for places we can visit yields little. Almost everything that happens to him in his three months in Scotland happens on the base, and when it is elsewhere it is often vaguely *in the country*. So we pounce on the smallest things.

Here is one: *Country around here is undulating with one very high hill into which a Jerry plane once crashed while shooting up the 'drome — Kiffir mountain.* In our Google searches, "Kiffir" takes us to South Africa's appalling racial history and after that to a dead end. We had both given up until this morning at Cowan Farm when we mention it in passing. "Oh, you must mean Criffel Mountain." It turns out we do. Our hostess knows nothing of a German aircraft. We are beginning to think she is in denial of the entire war. Given our single-mindedness, perhaps hers is the healthier path.

We have a sketchy idea of the direction we need to take to locate this place. The Information Centre on White Sands provides us with a map. In vain the young girl behind the counter suggests other thrilling things we might do. All we want, to her bewilderment, is Criffel.

It is supposed to dominate the district but we have chosen a day when the hills are flattened by a blanket of mist. But away we go through leafy forests, past impossibly picturesque villages. Wild garlic and bluebells bloom by the roadside and all is touched with the tender green of spring. My youngest daughter is expecting her second child in a couple of months and has requested a baby blanket in spring green. Perhaps I will find the yarn to match this ethereal landscape while I am here. It would be a delightful connection for this coming grandchild.

For a moment, in my mind, I am mothering my thirty-seven-year-old daughter rather than my twenty-seven-year-old father.

At the foot of Criffel sits Sweetheart Abbey. There is a walking path to the summit somewhere nearby. We have no ambition to climb a damp and fog draped mountain to pay homage to a German pilot; we just want to cross this reference off the list. The abbey is roofless and in ruins. In spite of the rapturous description in the petite gift store housed in a rustic cottage, I cannot warm to it. Perhaps it's the impossibly smooth green sward where stone floors and wooden pews once stood. Perhaps it's the meaty look of its red stone that I find a little creepy. We have washed up here almost by accident. It seems, at first, to have little to do with what we are in search of, so we spend our time patting some inquisitive cows who amble over to say hello. Then the gift shop serves up the poignant history of this collection of cloisters and transepts.

It is seven hundred years old, built by a grieving widow, Lady Dervogilla of Galway. It would be hard to make up a name like that, let alone her story. After her husband's death she has his heart embalmed and places it in an ivory and silver box. When she dies she is buried in the Abbey still clutching the box containing his long-still heart. What else could the monks call this place but Sweetheart Abbey?

It is impossible for us to hear this story and not think of our parents. Practical and unsentimental as they are, neither of them given to desperately romantic gestures, they might find this saga a tad over the top. But there are connections. They are, we know, completely devoted to each other. His metaphorically embalmed heart in its silver and ivory box is her constant companion until she dies. "Sweethearts" is such a gentle and lasting way to describe their love and I think for her it never stops. She and Lady Dervogilla, separated by centuries, have much in common.

Months later, at the funeral of an uncle, also an RAAF man, Robbie spots a fellow in his eighties who has what she describes as "an Orange face," referring to its origins not its hue. Those round-cheeked, rugged faces populated our lives in that long ago hometown. She goes to talk to him. And she is right: not only is he from Orange, he is distantly related to us, and he had known our parents. He speaks so fondly of them, telling her they were very much in love: "Sweethearts, that's what they were."

Among the postcards Paddy mails to his Nooney during the war, there is one from Sweetheart Abbey. He never mentions going there, and this postcard, like many he sends home, is blank on the back. He often buys them to show where he has been, or simply as a typical scene, as he has no camera. He is never too keen on visiting churches, but this one is an arresting pile. Perhaps he did stop here. I imagine him, having heard its story, standing in the ruins, suspicious of sentiment, cant, and religion, but thinking of Nooney, wondering how she will, like Lady Dervogilla, find a way to stand it if he doesn't come home.

As we drive away from the Abbey we peer into the fog creeping down the side of Criffel Mountain and take a moment to remember the German pilot, Oberleutnant Martin Piscke, who on March twenty-fifth 1943 flies over the Scottish countryside to shoot up the airfield beacon at RAF Dumfries before ploughing into the top of this mountain. He is interred, we learn, in the Troqueer Cemetery in Dumfries having been afforded full military honours.

So the enemy is treated here at that time. Things are often different across the Channel. Noting this contrast helps us remember why our father left his young family to go and fight a war far away. In all the frustration, inefficiency and lack of focus that those first six months hold there is a purpose. The world is at war and the foe is evil.

Even as I write this, I know that human decency is in no way completely absent in wartime Germany. RAF crews, shot down over Germany, are also accorded funerals with full military honours, at least at the beginning of the war — although that will change. And, while German civilians, standing in the ruins of their homes, their dead about them, are often moved to murderous rage when they come upon the men responsible ("It is," I once read on a T-shirt, "inadvisable to bail out over an area you have just bombed"), German Military Police mostly step in to protect these terrified young men from being torn to pieces. War is a place where barbarity and humanity often walk hand in hand.

The very fact that a Jerry aircraft can penetrate the western edge of Scotland and shoot up a 'drome, something Daddy finds arresting enough to record, brings the reality of this war they are in training for a little closer. There are, even in this relatively benign base, close calls, often brushed off in the excitement of finally flying. Just after Christmas they set off *taking along a pigeon for good measure.* It is a productive trip with a good staff wireless operator to coach him. Then his navigator *takes us all by surprise when he cuts the engines while winding up the under carriage.* "Surprise" seems an inadequate response.

The mention of the pigeon sets us on a flurry of research. They were indeed taken along but why? Some kind of canary in the coalmine thing, I suggest. If the cockpit starts to fill up with noxious gas, a toes-up pigeon might be a timely warning. But reading descriptions of what happens when a bomber is hit makes us realize quite quickly that only the dimmest crew would need a dead pigeon to alert them to danger. No, they are taken as a way to communicate the crew's whereabouts if the plane ditches in the North Sea. The navigator hastily jots co-ordinates and attaches them to the bird's leg, tosses it into the air, and it flaps home allowing for a speedy rescue. That is the theory anyway. And it does, remarkably often, work. Pigeons are true heroes, saving lives of men who would otherwise have frozen or drowned, or winging their way across the Channel bringing messages to and from the Resistance. The most valiant are even awarded medals. These are the astonishing facts we discover. However, just why the pigeon is on board the day of the navigator's surprising lapse in judgement we will never know.

On another training detail, a message telling them to divert fails to transmit and they come into the base with a visibility of thirty feet, abort, and end up landing successfully in West Freugh. My sister and I briefly consider driving to West Freugh to honour this moment, but we are aware of time constraints: we cannot see everything he saw. He flies down England's spine, above the Pennines, icy cold in the dead of winter; he dips over Leeds, he glimpses Ireland, a patchwork of greens, its rivers swollen and muddy. We won't be visiting those places either.

One night he has a double detail. The first, down the centre of England, is warm enough as the heater is working. It is three and a half hours followed by another three and a half with no heater and horrible conditions. Dead tired, he neglects to change his roll neck sweater before going to the Mess and is *ticked off unpleasantly by a b. of a W.O.* The men are expected to be in their full uniform in the Mess. Rules can be, and often are, broken — but you don't always get away with it.

This is a time of hard work for all of them and, most of the time, it seems sane and useful. There is some skipping of lectures but he also writes of waiting about for instructors who arrive late or not at all. It goes both ways. They sleep in a lot. Butch Harris, their ultimate commander, loves his airmen, his "old lags," even as he hurls them night after night into death-dealing peril. He wants them focused and on task in the air, but when they have spare time it is theirs. This is part of the culture of the Air Force. However, when the lads take to this laxity with excess enthusiasm they have to be reined in.

From the beginning of their stay in Dumfries they are, as any group of young men away from home would be, less than keen on housekeeping. Many have left homes where mothers swept and polished, cooked, and did the laundry — skills not passed on to the sons of the house. No wonder most of the huts are a sty. They are reluctant to attack the gathering grunge and clutter that piles up as they sit around the coke stoves at night, chatting, playing cards, eating anything they can scrounge, passing around their care packages. Food is a constant topic. *Sugar*, he writes, *is as rare as sovereigns here.* Doubly sad for this man who has a sweet tooth.

One of Robbie's small gems of memory involves her sharing a can of condensed milk with our father. They are sitting together on the platform that holds the small water tank supplying the packing shed. The tin has two holes punched in the top and they pass it back and forth sipping blissfully. This gooey, sticky delight is an Australian staple and adored by our family. Robbie, who cheerfully admits to a greedy streak, once asked for a tin all to herself for her birthday. I watched with a mixture of envy and admiration as she, a bundle of single-minded intensity, devoured it in the garden. What a genius to ask for such a thing, I thought. The lid had been fully removed, none of those triangular pokings that, although they allow delicious sipping, leave too much trapped inside. No, take a teaspoon, tuck in, and finally wipe the sides of the tin clean with a slippery finger being careful not to slice that finger on the jagged edge. Her memory of the moment when she and Daddy share a tin, both eager and greedy, fuels this childhood birthday request.

She has a twin memory to this one, less vivid, just a scrap, but it also involves food. She has refused her dinner and is sent to the bathroom as punishment. This room is not particularly scary; the shame lies in being cast out of the family circle. Our generation grew up with the guilt of not cleaning our plates when "small children are starving in China." I'm sure that the war and rationing were on both parents' minds if not spoken of. Food was not to be wasted.

In sugar-starved Britain, the food parcels sent by family are treasured. Dutchy and Arthur often share their cakes from home, but sometimes the gluttony is solitary: *Joy of joys — a parcel from Nooney. Everything in perfect order and beautiful. What I did to the fruits and nuts is nobody's business.* Later he gets condensed milk from his brother and gives it *a lacing.* We have a good idea what that involves. All of them, many still growing lads, can never get enough to eat, and much of their eating goes on in the hut. They are always on the scrounge. When all else fails, they grab bread and margarine from the Mess and enjoy a good feed. The sticky mugs, crumb-flecked plates, wrapping paper and general detritus accumulate. At one point Arthur compares the state of their hut to a brothel. We doubt he has much to do with brothels. Neither do we, but we are pretty sure they don't feature stacks of unwashed dishes or mounds of dirty clothing.

Every so often the C.O. descends, demanding that beds be vacated by nine a.m. (these fellows are notorious over-sleepers, not surprising as they are often out very late on flying detail), then made, and that the hut be cleaned. One visit finds him in a particularly picky mood, vigorously laying down the law and scolding our feckless Dad for not being on duty even though flying was scrubbed. The C.O.'s irritability might, Arthur thinks, *be attributed to the fact that one of the boys nearly brained him with a poker during inspection.* After another inspection we learn: *Hut looked unreal after its clean-up this morning. R.O.R. today said, "No grass in Australian hut today. Soil must be poor."* I find this pretty funny. Our father's comment is *English humour??* The initials "R.O.R." are a puzzle. An ex-air force friend comes up with an explanation: a successful inspection results in a Release on one's Own Recognizance. If the corollary is some form of "confined to barracks" then the verve with which they get stuck into cleaning up is explained.

The group in this occasionally tidy hut, all Australian, all of independent mind, take those in the higher ranks with a healthy grain of salt. From the beginning they find their British accents comical (and you may be sure that the compliment is returned). There is always a faint bristling when power is exercised in a way that they feel to be petty or unreasonable. They are fairly low on the totem pole of RAF Dumfries but that doesn't mean they tolerate having their noses rubbed in it.

Arthur writes with some amusement that the permanent Staff Sergeants have screened off a section of the dining room. Inside this exclusive and rarefied space they are waited on instead of serving themselves as the lower orders do. This arrangement is christened the "hen coop" and the hens therein are subjected to some good natured, but pointed, ribbing. A day or so later the hen coop has been removed and its occupants are back to waiting on themselves. *Some of them*, he observes, *must have a sense of humour.*

He seems to be a fair man, our father, taking each of these authority figures as individuals, not pre-judging. One is *a dry stick* whose humour he appreciates, another is *a good egg* who chats pleasantly with the Aussies and seems *genuinely interested.* And, tellingly, he sums up their W.O. this way: *doesn't seem a bad chap but like all Air force chaps, scared of the men above.* Intimidation by those who out-rank them does not seem to be something the men of this particular hut, including our father, suffer from.

With the course underway, life changes. There is an urgency to get skills in place and to demonstrate them as they fly above the winter countryside. There is much emphasis on Morse, the wireless operator's language. Morse practice takes place in Harwell Boxes, which loom large in his life as the course unfolds and December seeps into January.

"Boxes" is a fitting name for these contraptions: a sort of freestanding broom cupboard containing an aircraft seat that faces a daunting bank of dials and knobs. This is the w/op's equivalent of the dreaded Link Trainer, into whose cramped interior pilots in training are stuffed, sweating in the dark in front of a panel of instruments as sadistic instructors call for impossible manoeuvres while it bucks and jerks like a plane under fire. Harwell boxes present similar challenges to the w/ops: dark, hot, stuffy, and claustrophobic, session after session, in full flying gear, doors closed while they receive and send, listen to crackling messages, decode and reply. The drone of engines is fed in to add realism. It is what they will face alone in their cramped cubicles aboard aircraft headed for enemy targets and they know they must get it right if they want to keep their crew safe.

A cartoon from this time sums it up: an octopus stands on a wooden crate, two tentacles acting as legs are stuffed into a pair of army boots. It has earphones on its head, and is facing a couple of consoles covered with dials and bristling with antennae. His remaining six arms are frantically busy, turning knobs, adjusting dials, writing notes. "The Perfect WAG" he is labelled. It is an in-joke even a civilian can get.

In mid-December Arthur spends an hour and a half stuffed into the airless cupboard making a mess of it, before stomping back to his hut *fed up.* From then on Harwells appear regularly in the diary. One night he finishes a session but *mad with zeal* heads back for a second one. On another occasion he gets to bed very late, explaining simply: *Harwells.* He is however, never again as frustrated as the first time. He chides himself for being slow, worries that he is still having trouble with the Receiver. Finally he labels a session *fun* causing us to sigh with relief and swell with motherly pride. "Nailed it," we cry. "Good for you."

Fellow Traveller

The last man in the front row of the photo of the men in Hut 17 is also an orchardist: Ernest Hugo Traeger, known to everyone as Snow or Snowie and he and Arthur are, for a time at least, friends.

December 19, 1943: *Sat up 'til late talking fruit with Snow Traeger — a nice chap.*

"It's not a big place," our father, the younger man, leans forward, cigarette glowing in the dimness of the hut, "we just have thirty acres. Twenty-three are planted."

"But it's working," says his companion, encouragingly, "you're doing alright."

The first man smiles and nods, "Yes," he says, "it's an old orchard but bears well. Yes, we're doing alright."

They are talking fruit, these two RAF w/op trainees in a drafty hut at the camp in Dumfries, a week before Christmas in 1943. By sitting very close to the fire it is just possible to keep the cold at bay. The wind finds every crevice in the walls of the hut, stirring the flames coaxed from the stove by means of the poker. The hut is quiet. Some of the men are flying tonight. Others have stayed in the Mess playing cards, keeping warm. Others have ridden into Dumfries for the pictures or a night at the pub. The few men left are reading or sleeping, ignoring the two chatting by the fire.

Arthur is always eager to learn. He explains the difficulties posed by his small orchard in Orange, New South Wales. His companion, Snow Traeger, is five or so years older and a fruit grower from South Australia. They exchange stories: black spot, brown rot, coddling moth, pruning, harvesting, packing, storing, and marketing ... all absorbing topics to these men of the land. They know the humility of watching a season go bad, wiping out a year's labour; they know the quiet pride when trees are laden and the harvest goes well. Each year is a new challenge; they dwell always in hope.

Both have wives who are struggling to keep their distant orchards going. Snowie and Ivy, Paddy and Nooney: two couples torn apart by the war, keeping in touch through aerograms, the women being strong, the men waiting for their care packages, aware of the sacrifice they demand.

We do not know if Snow and Ivy have children. And of course we cannot know if this topic comes up in their talk. Our impression is that such things are not widely shared. Close friends know of wives, fiancées, children, but generally the package called "home" is held tight to the chest.

A week before these two talk fruit, as our father and the other men in the hut huddle together by the stove, he is invited to show pictures of his family. He doesn't say who asks, but it is clear that he will produce such a private thing only on request — maybe it is Snow, although I have no idea if he is even there that night. Our little family is *passed around to enthusiastic admiration*, he records with a touch of pride. Perhaps one of the photos is of us on the back of that truck. So if Snow is in this group admiring photos of two small girls or a pretty wife, perhaps it is part of the conversation a week later.

We squint at the blurred image of the airman at the end of the first row, trying hard to make out the features of the man who sat by the fire with our dad. He has a square face and, of course, he is blond: "Snow" is the traditional Australian tag for the tow-headed. Physically, he's the Aryan ideal fuelling this war. His family came to South Australia from Silesia in the mid-1800s, fleeing the oppression of the Prussian state. I wonder if that fact comes up as they ponder the state of their crops or latest chemical sprays being touted by the Board of Agriculture. If it does, the irony might have struck them as rich: having fled German tyranny this family has, close to a century later, shipped back one of its own to fight a new incarnation of the same brutality.

They might have explored our father's family as well. The Plowmans had come in the 1850s, fleeing the raw uplands of Caithness, to settle and prosper in New South Wales. And now, here is one of their sons back in Scotland, at the end of a busy day of training to defend the land they'd left a century before.

What richness we have found in Snowie Traeger considering he has only two mentions in our father's diary. The first is that night when these two slightly older, married men sit poignantly talking fruit. At the end of the entry Daddy notes with satisfaction on an evening well spent, *he's a nice chap*. The second, written as they finish their time in Dumfries, tells us that Snow and two others, also German speaking, are off to Doncaster. Our father does not explain why; he doesn't know. Nobody in their group, including Snow himself, does. After that we hear no more of Snow from him.

Robbie and I become so enamoured of this twice-referenced fellow that we dig deeper. I find a picture of his parents' gravestone, elaborately carved with an inscription on the base to honour their lost son. It fools the cemetery into declaring that he is buried there. Like all the other bereaved parents of sons and daughters dead far from home, August Henry and Anna Pauline, Snow's mum and dad, do not have the finality of a funeral or the comfort of a nearby grave to visit. This little inscription manages to circumvent that loss. Perhaps by leaving instructions to slide his name in at the base of their tombstone, they manage not only to persuade the cemetery that he has come home, but also themselves.

When he dies, these parents do not know his entire story and nor does Ivy. Actually, I doubt they ever know it. Our father certainly has no clue why the three German fellows from his course are being sent off together. But we know the story now. We know why the three German-speaking graduates from Hut 17 are spirited away and something of what happens to them. Hardacre and Marks are the others and, ironically, we know less about these two because they survive. The dead are documented; those who make it through and go home are harder to pin down. As is right, they slip back into the world they've left. Many of them will not, or cannot, speak about what has happened. How can such an intense and terrifying time be understood by those who weren't there? So, home they go and get on with life.

Of Hardacre we find almost no trace, though in an uncharacteristic burst of impatience, Daddy once describes him as *a pain in the neck* before cheerfully admonishing himself to *remember to suffer fools gladly*. Marks pops up in a photo in one of the many books we read, posed with his crew and looking very pleased with himself. Blond and handsome, he is, like many men diverted into this special and secret program, Jewish.

As a group, these young Jewish airmen know better than most the evil of the regime they are fighting. Many speak Yiddish and German; they can, they are pleased to discover, turn this talent into a weapon. But this choice has a dark side: should they be shot down, captured, and identified as Jews, horror awaits. They certainly know this; suicide is chosen over capture by at least one such recruit.

As far as we know, Hardacre is not Jewish and we know that Snow is Catholic. All three are plucked from the wireless operator course in Dumfries simply because they have listed the ability to speak German on a survey put out in anticipation of the value of such a skill. A secret plan to confound the enemy is in the works. They are hooked out of the base, popped into a covered truck, dropped off at a train station, directed to a carriage and sent on their way. More mystified men join them at various stations. Nobody knows where they are going or why. Before they can be deployed they have to get ten hours of flight time on Lancasters. They are ultimately headed for Ludford Magda, a base in north Lincolnshire, home to 101 Squadron.

Two months before Snow Traeger and Arthur Plowman chat by the fire in Hut 17, 101 Squadron has been chosen to be home for a new top-secret weapon against the Germans. Each Lancaster there is re-fitted to carry a very special 640 pound wireless set, bolted to the floor aft of the spar, right over the bomb bay and hooked up to three seven-foot antennae that sprout, two on the fuselage and one on the nose, from the aircraft. German speakers, both wireless operators and others, are recruited, speedily trained, and assigned to these planes that now carry a crew of eight instead of the usual seven. These men need to know how to operate the special sets, they need their German to intercept ground transmission and recognize codes; they need to think fast, to be imaginative and cunning. They do not need the other array of skills required of the regular w/ops who are melded into a working crew.

Focused training and a crying need for their skills means these special wireless operators are fast-tracked into combat. Snow, Marks and Hardacre arrive at 101 on February 18, 1944, just eleven days after leaving Dumfries. The training for this new and secret role is not more than a couple of weeks. In a short six weeks Snow, our "nice chap," will be dead. By contrast our father, and the other w/ops from Dumfries, will be shipped off to a series of training bases and will not see combat for another four months.

While these more conventional airmen are hopping from training base to training base, flying in rackety aircraft and learning to work with their new crews, Snow and his companions are engaged in sorties over Europe. Their work is shrouded in secrecy. The special equipment and extra antennae can scarcely have gone unnoticed by the crew but this is not discussed. The Special Operators are ordered not to explain what they are doing and the crew is told not to ask. Discipline requires that there be no questioning, however oblique, of this eighth airman labouring at his intrusive equipment, alone in the dark. Nobody is to speak of it, even when home with families on leave. To the world they are just regular Bomber Command. When photos of these crews are taken they are shipped to nearby bases and posed in front of conventional, unmodified Lancasters. I suppose there is an element of glamour and dash in all of this but it must have felt very lonely.

In any crew there are jobs that are isolating. The wireless operator, the gunners, and the navigator are in their separate little worlds. But they are, at least, joined by the intercom; they can speak to each other. They are in this together; their job is to have the other fellow's back. Not so for these Special Operators. They work away from the crew, their closest companion being the nearby feet of the mid-upper gunner. Hunched over the specially installed desk with its three transmitters and cathode ray screen, they are further walled off from the rest of the crew by a curtain. The intercom threading human contact among the crew is, for them, switched off. The pilots can use a red call light to alert them in case of an emergency but otherwise they are alone. This part of the aircraft is unheated. Temperatures in winter, high above the night clouds, can plummet to minus fifty degrees Celsius. So they fly encased in the same electrically heated suits worn by the gunners. Ice builds up on their oxygen masks. Their clumsy gloves make manipulating the set difficult but bare skin would stick to metal and rip off. I have one record of a Special Operator using the intercom to warn his crew that they are coming into an area thick with night fighters, but this is an unusual contact. They have to get used to the isolation and the discomfort. They have a job to do.

The original code name for this cloak-and-dagger enterprise is "Jostle," evoking something that might happen when trying to get through a department store door carrying too many parcels. And the Special Ops are jokingly called Jonahs by their crewmates who may be unclear about what they are doing but know damn well it puts everyone in greater danger. Scattered through the Bomber stream, these Lancasters from 101, with their Special Operator on board, are giving serious grief to the Germans. As they judder their way across Europe, Snow and the other SOs listen in to the enemy ground controllers who are gathering radar information about the direction of the stream of allied bombers before coordinating and relaying it to the night fighters.

In their isolated "offices" the SOs concentrate on jamming these German transmissions by pouring a stream of loud and jagged notes into their irritated ears. To keep ahead of the enemy, they have to know their codes, recognize if and when they are being fed misleading information, switch frequencies in tandem, and occasionally throw out their own inventions to confuse or subvert. The Germans respond with martial music or sounds of screaming women. Often these lonely men doing this bizarre task hear orders given to shoot down a plane, or a *nachtjager* announcing going in for a kill. They grit their teeth and hope their plane isn't the target, then suffer combined relief and guilt when they realize some other poor sod has copped it.

The Germans quickly realize what is going on and it is not a great leap to intuit that the planes with the huge antennae are the culprits. Add to this the fact that these planes are constantly breaking radio silence, making them easier to locate and attack, and they become prime targets. Because their skills are in high demand, the crews of 101 fly more sorties, further reducing their chances of survival. No surprise that 101 claims the unenviable statistic of having the highest casualty rate of any squadron during the war. It doesn't help that they are often required to carry a full bomb load, no allowance being made for a 640 pound wireless set and an extra crew member. As those magnificent Lancasters charge the runways, Merlins screaming, dragging an impossible burden into the air, every man aboard fears that an annihilating fire is seconds away. Jostle? Poor Snow. The ability to speak German has placed him there and painted a bull's eye on his back.

The night Snowie dies the dice are even more lethally loaded. It is March 31, 1944. Most men on the base of Ludford Magda think this will be a stand down night; there is a gleaming half-moon. They look forward to a quiet evening in this bucolic village, which sits in the middle of the base — barracks to one side, aerodrome to the other. It is a comfortable pairing, the town and the base. Time in a local pub, perhaps a dance, or the pictures; that is the plan for the night ahead. Then the Ops Board lists twenty-six crews. They dutifully assemble in the briefing room where the target is revealed to groans and derisive whistles. Not only will they fly out under a moon, their course is a long unbroken leg to their target. The usual turns and evasions designed to confuse the enemy are missing, allowing an easy radar fix by the Germans on the ground and easy pickings for the Messerschmitts in the air. Hoping for cloud cover, hoping for a break, they trail out to gear up and head for their planes waiting, fuelled and bombed up, in Dispersal. By nine p.m. they are trundling toward the runway, engines growling. And then they are in the air. Our fruit growing, "nice chap" Snow sets off into the bloodbath that is the infamous Nuremberg raid.

The sixty-eight mile long, seven hundred and ninety-five strong bomber stream forms over Reading, west of London, and heads for the coast. They are carelessly sent out, moonlight glinting on their wings, into the eager arms of the German fighters waiting for them at the Belgium border. The hoped for cloud cover does not appear. The wind predictions are wildly out of whack. The bomber stream drifts north, breaking apart and losing the protection of the mob. The German ground controllers see through dummy raids and direct their fighters to do their worst. The Luftwaffe has twenty-eight night fighters in the air before the bombers have even entered enemy air space. The *nachtjagers* slip into the now scattered Bomber stream. Flower bursts of exploding bombers light the sky; the ground below sprouts piles of burning wreckage. Eleven point nine percent of the total planes dispatched are lost — Bomber Command's worst night of the war. The massacre continues all the way to Nuremberg where the higher-ups have ignored the warnings of cloud cover over the target. For all this paralysing loss of life, little damage is done to the enemy, a sinful waste. Out of twenty-six aircraft dispatched from 101 Squadron, seven aircraft and crew are lost that night. Do the math and howl: 39 percent loss. Snow and all his crew form part of this statistic.

They are not however, like the other six aircraft from 101, lost in the raid itself. They escape being shot down over Europe; they survive the German fighters long enough to head for the coast. Rather than making straight for their home bases, the Bomber stream has been ordered, for its own safety, to return by a circuitous route. The Americans are setting out on a raid in the early morning and will be forming up over central England. To avoid collisions the survivors of this disastrous raid are diverted to cross the south coast at Selsey Bill, head for Reading, east of London, and then split off for their home bases. This Snow's plane obediently does, although they are in serious trouble. All engines are still working but the tail gunner is badly shot up, his body riddled with bullets, suggesting that the plane is attacked from the rear as it returns. They are perilously low on petrol and they have lost their radio. And then ahead of them, just north of Reading — how joyful the sight must have been — is a brightly lit airfield, a haven for a wounded aircraft and medical help for a wounded crewmember. This is Welford, an American base. Even if it occurs to Snow's crew that their Lancaster, with its alien antennae, will be difficult to identify, without a radio they can send no distress signal or colour of the day to clear their way. They line up for a landing.

What they do not know, could not have known, is that just a week before, this base had been attacked by a lone German raider who, attracted by its lights, had rather ineffectually attempted to shoot up the field. As a result, standing orders have been given that should an unidentified plane approach the base at night the lights are to be turned off. As Snow and his crew drop toward the base, shot up, low on fuel, carrying a wounded crewmate, but heartened by the sight of the welcoming glowing runway, wheels down, safety beckoning, the lights go out.

***

At debriefing tables in RAF bases all over the country, exhausted, shattered young men face up to what this night has done. One of their jobs during a raid is to log every plane they see go down: every collision, every explosion, every disintegration. On this night the tally becomes unbearable. Pilots tell their crew to stop counting; it isn't helping, this ghastly score keeping. In the Mess they watch as the tally of missing crew is chalked up. Some weep. In Snow's squadron, 101 — the hardest hit of all — there is shocked bewilderment. The next day in the Mess they are told to sit together to minimize the horror of all those empty chairs. Snow's possessions are, as is customary, gathered up to be sent home to Ivy, who will carry on alone. He will never be able to tell her about this extraordinary job he has been called to do and for which he dies a mere six weeks from his graduation as a wireless operator.

Snow is buried in Botley Cemetery in Oxford, but where he crashed, in Welford, a special plaque has been placed in the memorial gardens of the RAF base. There is also a plaque honouring our father in a rural park in the district of his birth. They share more than they know, Arthur and Snow, hunched over a smelly coal fire, joined by a passion for the land, just before the Christmas of 1944.

My father does not know of Snow's death, although the horror of that Nuremberg raid is certainly known. The day after the raid the Daily Express placards scream "96 down," and the tannoys at the bases blare the news of this disaster. At a time of plummeting Bomber Command morale, the hideously wasteful string of operations over Berlin has its climax in this Nuremberg massacre. Daddy must wonder, as they all do, just how many of the dead in this gut-clutching night are men who have passed through his life. And of course he must also wonder how long it will be before his turn comes.

Poor Snow, I think, before flying into a protective rage on discovering an error in a report of his crash. The actual wireless operator, not Snow, is credited with being the "Special Equipment Operator." One day I may write to somebody to put this right. We have accumulated a tidy stack of errors. Perhaps madness is setting in; two dotty old women on a mission, firing off polite letters full of barely suppressed indignation, calling record keepers to account. We are aware of the comic potential, but somehow truth must be honoured.

Our search for Snowie, long and time-consuming, raises a vexing question. What are we doing? Every person mentioned in the diary, every connection, calls out to be explored. The threads lead us on, then tangle or disappear. Sometimes we despair, question our sanity, but still we do it. In the end it feels right; each of these tiny stories, each fact, each detail, is part of the whole we are trying to reconstruct. I think of those patient archaeologists with their tiny whisks gently brushing dust from splinters and shards, building whole urns from scraps, imagining entire scenes from a toe, an elbow, the drape of a toga. This, it seems, is our task. Or perhaps it is more like those cunning composite portraits built from thousands of miniature pictures arranged so that, when the viewer steps back, suddenly there is a recognizable face. If we collect enough, understand enough and arrange it well, will we one day step back and find our father there, looking back at us?

The Pact

As we drive away from Sweetheart Abbey through the countryside our father came to know, as we meander through picturesque villages, their old houses fronting the road's edge, it is clear that not much has changed in hundreds of years. Did he see these precise houses? Did he pass this way? When he writes of riding along the country roads and lanes, we want to know precisely which roads and which lanes. But he gives no hint of the direction or distance of his explorations. He and Ern and Dutchy leave their bikes at the foot of a steep hill, clamber to the top and admire the vales of Scotland, a patchwork of crops and neat green squares dotted with sheep or cows. On the way down they encounter a hedgehog. *My first.* Daddy's initial delight gives way to concern. It is sick, curled up and sad. He contemplates taking it home but decides against it. His two animal-besotted daughters are enchanted by his concern. He admires the albatross, the flying fish and the porpoises on the Pacific crossing. He loves to watch the sea. The sight of farmed fields quickens his pulse. To all of this we can relate.

Having decided, probably wisely, that a Nissen hut full of airmen is an unsuitable place to bring a sick hedgehog (we feel his regret), he and his two best mates leave it curled up on the hillside, climb onto their bikes and pedal back toward the base, exuberantly and dangerously, leaning down and picking up stones without dismounting as they fly along the country roads. This diversion lands our silly dad on his head in a ditch. He seems unscathed but it does remind us that there are lots of ways to die in a war — some less heroic than others.

The young, of course, consider themselves invincible. That explains how they can do the things asked of them. Youth also explains some of the antics on the base. A favourite diversion is jumping a fellow hut mate and ripping his clothes off. Plympton, a fellow we have discovered little about, is, before they go for a run around the aerodrome, *forcibly stripped to the detriment of his buttons. He spent a quarter of an hour after the run dolefully sewing them on again.* Poor Plympton, we think, but it is not a rare event, this communal debagging. Our father loses his trousers on at least one occasion. *We are all kids at heart, I guess, and it's a good way to be.*

Toward the end of their three months in Dumfries the training becomes more intense and Hut 17 gets a possibly well-deserved kick in the behind. After all of them *accidentally* sleep in until 9:30, the hammer falls. In what, we are to learn, is a fairly common method of grabbing the attention of a group of young men who have developed some slovenly habits, one of the bigwigs gathers them together and reads the riot act. They are, he announces, the worst Australian crew ever to pass through. He wonders aloud if they actually want to fly, adding ominously that if they do not they should come and tell him. I spent thirty years teaching adolescents in three different countries and this is pretty standard shaming procedure.

They have their forty-eight hour leaves cancelled, returned, cancelled again. Somebody wants their attention. Somebody gets it. Sam, the hut spokesperson, whose other mention is stepping in to tell the sexually athletic Canadian and his alluring WAAF to lower the noise level, volunteers to march off and inquire what exactly is meant by the suggestion that they do not want to fly; is their courage in question? Up to this point the course itself has been pretty sloppy, seeming to encourage a casual approach. They are accustomed to rolling into lectures an hour late or missing them altogether and nothing said. On several occasions even the lecturer fails to materialize. Sleeping in and missing a lecture or two in a course that seems to be pretty lax itself, has nothing to do with courage. But the hoped for tightening up is achieved.

The bigwig who has set this in motion has another chat with them. I would like to have been a fly on the wall at that meeting. Some of the men in that hut are not shy; perhaps they point out the sins on both sides. Whatever is said, my father reports that *all the misunderstandings are cleared up, and they are now all right on the mark*. Mission accomplished. From now on everything is *fair dinkum*.

An Air Vice Marshall is about to visit: Panic is at its peak. The tongue-lashing administered to Hut 17 and this august event cannot have been unrelated. All this is reported in the most matter-of-fact manner by our dad. There is the slightest whiff of cynicism, but generally he seemed to let most nonsense run happily off his back.

And so the course rushes to its end with all of them anxious to know: what next? He is about to say goodbye to many of his fellow hut-mates who are soon to be scattered. Some he will not see again and some will go with him to the next stage of training.

When the course ends there is a graduation, a course pass-out dinner, in Edinburgh, where they go for a forty-eight hour leave. We have a photo of Daddy with his two best friends, Baldy and Dutchy, on a ferry with the Firth of Forth Bridge behind them. They are all wearing their greatcoats making us happy. Knowing that our father lost his at a November rugby game, we have fretted that he will be cold as the winter sets in. Many of the men use their coats as bed coverings in the chill of those porous Nissen huts. We know he doesn't care for the cold — he is the only one wearing gloves on that chilly February ferry ride. They look content, these three fast friends. The sun is shining; they are squinting into its weak Scottish rays.

They are going together to Silverstone so they will not be separated just yet. But, once they are crewed up and moved into different huts, they will see less of each other. In a crowded Edinburgh pub, after a day exploring the castle, they escape from the raw cold, steam rising from their greatcoats as they shrug them off onto chair backs. They carry frothy mugs to their table, cigarettes are lit. They talk and laugh and tease as they remember the days and the months behind them. But then they are serious for a moment. With the end of this course, they are that much closer to combat, and even training has its perils. This new adventure is a beginning that could also be an end, so they make a pact, promising to look after each other's families should the worst happen. All three have living parents. Baldy has a fiancée. Arthur has the burden of knowing he may leave a widow and two small fatherless daughters. Those left behind will be visited and comforted and cared for, they promise each other. "We'll be OK, of course, but just in case. It would help to know somebody was looking out for them. Somebody who knew what it was like over here."

Some months before this Edinburgh leave, in early January, they receive official photos from the camp photographer — a record showing them wearing those new, and possibly undeserved, crowns. They autograph each other's for sending home. We have Baldy's and Dutchy's, neatly mounted in little cardboard folders with messages to our mother. They wish her the best and Ern adds, "Don't worry about Old Man Canobolas as I am looking after him for you." Dutchy promises something he knows he cannot be sure of delivering: a speedy return of the "Canobolas Kid." They are younger than Arthur and they look up to him, perhaps a little in awe of his mature marital status and his fatherhood. They mean those words. We look at those young faces, such babies really, and wonder all over again how they stood it — the stupidity, terror, ugliness, and waste.

***

On our way back to our second night at Cowan's farm, we stop at the fish and chip shop in Dalbeattie to pick up a supper to be eaten in memory of those young airmen wandering at night along the Nith. In our room, perched on our beds, we enjoy this crunchy, greasy treat, topping it off with tea before turning in.

The next morning, in the dining room, with its grimacing band of stuffed critters, we tuck into yet another sumptuous full English

Breakfast. Secreted away are two eggs. As our trip progresses so does our cunning. We order a brace of boiled eggs each for breakfast: two hard-boiled for Robbie, two soft for me. We have a soft boiled each and pocket the hard-boiled for lunch. With a worrying lack of shame, we settle up with our hostess. She comes to the door, stands on the steps by the duelling hares, and waves us goodbye as we pull out of the yard and point our car south.

Band of Brothers

In early February of 1944 the twenty young Australians who had shared a hut, a Scottish winter and, for seven of them, their last Christmas, are scattered. Bundled into their greatcoats, kit bags slung over their shoulders, they gather in groups on the Dumfries railway platforms stamping their feet to keep warm, dragging on their cigarettes, waiting for the train that will take them to the next stage: deployment to an Operational Training Unit. There they will be trained to fly into danger and they will be trained to destroy and kill.

I have no proof that anyone in the upper echelons cares enough to make sure that Arthur and his two best friends continue to train together so that, even after being crewed up and separated, they are able to see each other, but it would be nice to think that's how it happened. Here they are, among the six setting off to Silverstone, Old Man Canobolas, Dutchy, and Baldy: three mates off on a new adventure and sharing the same hut at least for the first part of the course.

They leave Scotland in the bitter cold of early February. It is not such a great distance, but manages to take them a full day, twenty-four hours, of stops and starts. At Carlisle they are off-loaded to hang about while their luggage speeds merrily south without them. Hoping to catch up with it, they pile out of the train at Bletchley, but the luggage has now been spirited even further south to Euston station in London. It will be days before they are reunited with their meagre but important possessions. After hanging about the station for a while they board a train for Blisworth. A sympathetic guard drives them to Towcester where they meet up with an RAF group of similarly bleary-eyed fellows, all awaiting the tender to take them to their camp five miles outside of the town.

"Honestly," Robbie fumes, back to a favourite gripe, "how did Britain manage to win the war? They couldn't even transport a bunch of Airmen about efficiently." She goes on to tell me about the first civilian casualty of the war, a hapless warden who, upon spotting a third storey window not sufficiently blacked-out, clambered up a drain-pipe to tap on the offending window. Unhappily, the drain-pipe parted company with the wall. Not the most noble way to die but a wartime death nevertheless. "I shouldn't laugh, but really. Hardly a well-oiled machine." She is giggling now. "And poor Daddy and his mates spending their first night freezing in those miserable huts with no sheets and no pyjamas."

We tut-tut, mother hens, never wanting to think of him cold, or fretting over missing bags. Arriving at dusk they dive into hut number 13 *and scrounge to such good purpose that within two hours, besides having tea we have one table, three chairs, one light and a poker.* We of the papery skin and aging bones are glad to hear they also have a fire going. Old hands at this, they are good at surviving the ineptitude of those running the show. And they are eager to get on with the next chapter. At the end of Operational Training, they are told, there will be a leaflet-dropping exercise over France — *what fun.* There is also some apprehension: *Seems we have to keep our wits about us now as the game is getting a bit fair dinkum.*

A day or so after settling in, the new arrivals are assembled in an empty hangar, are supplied with tepid, watery beer, wished good luck, and let loose to choose their crews. Each one of these men milling about is intent on one thing: find five other men who look like a good bet. Pilots, navigators, wireless operators, gunners, and bomb aimers wander about sizing each other up. In these early days, when they will be flying twin engine bombers, they do not need an engineer; he is added later when they convert to four-engine heavies. For now they are looking to assemble a total of six men who, in some way, seem a fit; men you feel you might trust with your life. It doesn't always work, but for the great majority this freedom to choose is brilliant. Men from different worlds, separated by class or country or education, manage to form solid, loyal teams ready to have each other's backs in ways that continue to astonish.

And so our father's crew is formed. Sadly we, his fact-starved daughters, for a long time have very little idea who they are. In those aerograms that he wrote so faithfully to our mother he would have listed their names, their role, their stories. She certainly knew all about them. We would kill for those letters now for nowhere in his diary is a neat list of their names and crew positions. "These are the men I will fly with. They will hold my life in their hands; I will hold theirs. These men will be closer to me than any before or likely since. Here they are." Such clarity is missing.

This seems to us uncharacteristic. In a neatly ruled chart at the back of his diary he documents the number of aerograms he writes to his Nooney, often six at a time, and, with great joy, the number he receives in return. He writes regularly to friends and relatives — all carefully recorded. He likes people, cares about them, keeps track. But he fails to record for us the full names and backgrounds of these vital men in his life.

All we know is that they are all Aussies but one. Thanks for nothing, we grumble. Then he begins to mention these men — Bruce and Alf, Mike and Cliff, Bill, Stan — in the way people do who assume back stories are known. We feel like the unfortunate outsiders at a dinner party, smiling gamely as people of whom we have no inkling are animatedly discussed.

Perhaps they are all dead, unable to shed the light we long for. But perhaps not. Most are younger than our father who would be well into his nineties had he survived. They could be mid-eighties, spry and hearty, tempered by the fires of war. We have seen Remembrance Day ceremonies attended by lovely old veterans with their canes, their wheelchairs, their medals and their pained pride. Perhaps one of our six treasured crew-mates is still out there for the finding?

Yes, We Did It! The Finding of Mike

INTERLUDE and ENLIGHTENMENT

November 11, 2011

Remembrance Day, six months after our Daddy Project trip, bristles with significance. The CBC had chosen the day before to highlight Armistice Day, 1944, the day my father died. Then on the day itself comes an interview with a wireless operator, shot down and interned in Buchenwald. He survives only because, even though he is very ill, his companions move him each day to a new bunk. Had the Gestapo observed a sick man lying in the same bed day after day he would have been lethally injected. I spend the day gulping back tears on this special date, not only for its poppies, guns, and haunting piper, but because this anniversary is personal. We know now so much more vividly, what we have lost.

As well as crying, I am also packing. I am bound for England, the second time in six months, this time with my husband, Tony, instead of Robbie. As we take off into the thickening dark of this Friday evening I know that sixty-seven years ago to the day, my father flew out of Spilsby on his last journey. Although Robbie cannot join me on this trip, it is thanks to her that I am doing this again. She does not conjure up visions of Miss Marple for nothing.

Since our return we had continued to read and research but there remained the vexed question of the first crew, not the men he died with but those he trained and flew with for six of his fifteen months in Britain. The puzzle itches in our brains. We cannot leave it be.

From the diary we know their names: Mike, Alf, Cliff, Bruce, Stan, Bill and, of course, our Arthur, but we know no surnames, and we are not even sure of their positions on the crew. For a long time our only resource is a photo of 207 Squadron, crews and commanders, posed in front of a Lancaster. One hundred and ninety-two people, each face not much bigger than a caraway seed, but still we find Daddy in the back row standing in front of the inner starboard engine. On the following pages the picture is broken up into ten expanded sections. Not every person is named but many are. We find Daddy's section and the sleuthing begins. A Cliff Morton and a Stan Fletcher are next to Daddy. Stan, we think, is the engineer who joins later. By the time this photo is taken the crew is no longer flying together, but their powerful connection remains; they still share a hut, go drinking together, and worry about each other.

Robbie notices that a Michael Madigan is one of the identifiers — the men who after the war volunteered to attach names to the faces in these photos. Could he be our Mike? Of the one hundred and ninety-two men in the photo, only ninety are identified. Among that ninety are Daddy, Cliff, and Stan. There is also a Bruce and an Alf. If Michael Madigan, the identifier, is the Mike we seek, then we have six of the seven. We feel we are getting closer to the truth.

In mid-October, five months after we have returned from our trip, Robbie is sifting through the various photos we have inherited. Many have been pulled from albums — Mummy divided them up, a package for me and another for Robbie. They were originally pasted into the black paper albums of the day. When torn out, they carry that paper with them obscuring anything that might have been written on the back. Robbie sets to work. "By wiping gently on the back of one photo I found that Bill, the pilot, is Bill Watson and Alf's name is Copsey, he is mid-upper gunner. Mike Madigan, as I suspected, is the navigator, and Bruce Hill the rear gunner. I think Daddy said Stan Fletcher was a gunner so now there seem to be too many gunners, I thought Cliff Morton was a bomb aimer but can't remember why, he also went up with Bill and seemed to fly, perhaps he was second pilot, but who was flight engineer? This first crew seems so important to me. They billeted together, went about together."

I begin poking about in the relics that I have on my side of the world. There is a letter Robbie had given to me in England: "You should have this. I have so much. I have the Diary!" Written by the mother of one of the crew to our mother very soon after Daddy's death, it is a short but gracious note and, although the handwriting is beautiful, it is hard to read as the ink is blurred and bleeding through the pages. It was at some time soaked, perhaps with tears. I know I cannot read it without weeping.

Dear Mrs. Plowman,

I have just received a letter from my son, Pilot Officer M. R. Madigan, telling me the tragic news of your husband's death. In his own words he says, "Without question, he was the most honest man I have ever known, and for whom I held the greatest respect." He goes on to say how much they all liked your husband and how sorry they are.

There is so little one can say at times like this — you will know how deeply I feel for you, for my boy is facing the same dangers day by day — it could so easily have been he, instead of yours. And so we bear one another's sorrows.

Please accept my sympathy — I wanted you to know how much your dear one was esteemed & liked by his comrades, & how much they feel his loss....

The signature is a puzzle. The name is Madigan, Mike's mother, but what is her given name? It begins with "W" but is not decipherable. Having no expectations, I Google the address, which is just a house name and a town. Then, there on the screen is a Rosemary Wynnis Madigan; Wynnis, surely unique and must be the mother's name from the bottom of the letter. This Rosemary must be the daughter of the kind and compassionate Wynnis, meaning she is our Mike's sister. We have a connection to one of the crew who, in his misery after our father's death, writes to his mother. She in turn, touched by this grief, writes to our mother. And now we have found his sister. She is a sculptress with a detailed website. She is eighty-five. She is alive; at least she was a few months ago because she held an exhibition. Quivering with excitement I phone Robbie. "You must find her. But do it fast. She's not getting any younger."

The next day Robbie calls triumphant. "I've spoken to her! She's lovely. But there is good news and bad news. I think you should sit down." I do. Robbie continues, "Mike is alive and well. He's eighty-eight. Oh, and they don't call him Mike — he is Michael to his family, or Rowie. BUT, and you won't believe this, he lives in England. In Bishop Stortford, east of London. We were probably no more than five miles from his house when we were driving south. If only we'd known then."

I take this in. The answer seems obvious. "I think I have to go."

"I think you do."

Will he want to see me? Many who return from the war cannot or will not speak of it. Our uncle, Mummy's younger brother, the same age as Michael, and also in the RAF, will not talk of his war. He dabbles in Tibetan spirituality, owns a prayer wheel, and cultivates a lushly beautiful garden. He pursues peace. We have to wonder, had our dad survived, would we be any wiser about his war? Would he have turned his hand to growing fruit, raising his girls and loving his Nooney, refusing to visit the past? Perhaps our magically discovered Michael will politely decline to unearth his.

I gather my courage and write to him. I begin to look for flights to England. Tony says he will come with me, partly I think because he fears I will mow down half of south London if put behind the wheel of a car on an unfamiliar side of the road, but also because he wants to be part of this. Rosemary — she and Robbie are becoming quite thick — gives the go-ahead to phone. She and Michael, products of their generation, do not email and are not in frequent contact, but they remain close. She thinks he will be open to a visit. Nervous as any school girl hoping for a date, I make the call.

Apart from the expected quaver of age, his voice is strong and he sounds genuinely delighted at the prospect of a visit. He frets that he cannot have us to stay as his wife is in hospital having broken a leg. "Oh really, that is very kind, but we do not expect you to put us up." We set a date. "I don't go out much," he tells me. "I'll be here."

A month after Rosemary popped up on my computer screen, we are pouring off London's ring roads into the November countryside of Hertfordshire. Crossroad cenotaphs are laden with poppy decorated wreaths. My eyes sting with tears as we speed by. Remembrance Day, sixty-seven years since Daddy's death, and we are about to meet somebody who knew him well.

The country byways get narrower and narrower until Tony is driving in the hedges to avoid local traffic that whizzes by heedless of the fate of side mirrors. At one point we pull into a car-width lane convinced we have found the Mill where we are staying. I have to get out and guide him back onto the road.

Once arrived, we call Michael to confirm our appointment for two p.m. the next day. I am awake early, nervous and snappy with anticipation. To fill the time until our appointment, we decide to explore Great St. Mary's, an imposing church dating back to the Doomsday Book. Built of clunch, a mess of local stone folded into mortar, it should not have lasted this long, it seems to me. The walls are enlivened, and possibly strengthened, by knapped flint, chipped to shapes reminiscent of a stealth bomber. The result is, counterintuitively, charming and dignified. In the churchyard, laden with fresh wreaths, is a memorial to the war dead. I admire their poppies: more elegant than those in Canada. Although, of course, John McCrae, who made the poppy an emblem for this day, was a Canadian. As Tony moves from ancient gravestone to even more ancient gravestone, carefully deciphering moss-clogged inscriptions, I murmur to this simple country memorial: "If ye break faith with us who die/ We shall not sleep, though poppies grow/ In Flanders fields." Is this what Robbie and I, and now my patient spouse, are doing, keeping faith?

Bishop Stortford, where Michael lives, is not far. The town is packed; we have arrived as their Sunday Remembrance Day Parade is ending. Many churches are just finishing their services, their front yards alive with the red capes and white cassocks of clergy and choirboys. Parishioners mill about in their Sunday best. Traffic moves at a glacial pace. We pass boy scouts, army cadets, medal-encrusted veterans, and band members carting instruments.

Michael's address, obtained from Rosemary, is "Greenacre." Surely with a name like that it must be a senior's home. We find his street with no problem, tree-lined, hedge-fronted houses, peaceful and established, but with no sign of a large institution. I spot a driver education car, hop out and tap on the instructor's window. He knows of no senior's home in this neighbourhood but begins a search on his cell phone. I lean on his car, waiting and staring idly across the street. "Greenacre" says a small sign at the entrance to a driveway. "Oh, thank you for your help, but I think I've found it."

We park in the courtyard in front of a house, which although impressive is clearly built for one or two seniors, not a gaggle. I ring the doorbell. Gentle shuffling, a little wait, the door opens and there he is: Michael, a.k.a. Mike, a.k.a. Rowie Madigan, a living breathing man who knew my father, trained, flew, and holidayed with him. I feel like Carter opening Tutankhamen's tomb in the Valley of the Kings. When Carnarvon, peering around him, asks if he can see anything, Carter replies, "Yes. Wonderful things."

Michael is tall, very thin, slightly stooped; he walks with a cane. Later he will tell us this is a bum knee, a legacy of his cricket-playing days. His hair is still quite thick, showing very little grey. Tony, much younger but balding and turning silver, is envious. Michael's full beard and moustache are slightly pepper and salt. His eyebrows are wild. His face is long and thin, elegant and expressive; his nose is aquiline. And I adore his ears, which although neatly flat to his head are huge. He is smiling broadly: "Come in, come in. Lovely to see you."

We set up camp around his kitchen table. First we must get permission to tape and film this interview because I want Robbie to feel that she has been here. I did fear he might not be happy with this but he is the most amiable of men. I have my binder and my questions. Tony is in charge of the media side of things. We are ready.

For three precious hours we are led into the world of that crew from early February to mid-November of 1944. Michael kept a detailed and thoughtful diary mature beyond his twenty years. He has read it through and marked each place our father is mentioned. Wonders await. But first we ask Michael for his own story:

After volunteering in Australia, signing up, and going though initial training he reports for his interview to see which branch he will be assigned to. "So I went up before this board. Of course everyone wanted to be a pilot... I walked in and they said, name? Madigan, right, oh well you're a navigator. Well, thank you very much. I had nothing to say..." His fate decided with no input on his part, as it is for all of them who have signed their lives over to their King, he goes on leave before his posting. While at home he gets the flu and, by the time he has recovered, his friends in training have been posted to navigation training schools and he is cast adrift. Then the puppeteers who control his fate dance him onto a troop ship headed for Canada where he does six months training in Edmonton. His memories of this time are fond. "I loved Canada... I saw the Northern Lights. They were lovely. That's unusual ... for a South Australian." After the war he and his wife, Claire, visit a much-changed Edmonton; he wants her to see where he trained.

By the end of 1944 he has completed his tour and is sent to a training station in Enstone in Oxfordshire to instruct. When the European war finished all Australians were to be put in Tiger Force to fight the Japanese but the atomic bomb put an end to that. So then there is nothing to do but wait. He will not be shipped home until December 1945. They just hang about, he says. More waste of time and lives.

We spend some time poring over photos, identifying the crew. He has little knowledge of where any of them went after the war and, apart from our father, little curiosity. He and Claire, on a visit to Australia, drove to Orange to try to find our mother but by then she had remarried. Given the plethora of Plowmans in my hometown, I am surprised and disappointed that they were not able to track her down. Surely somebody at City Hall should have twigged. But they don't and Mummy is deprived of meeting this kind man who would have told her stories and said such comforting things. I am grateful that he tried. As we talk, it becomes clearer and clearer that he admired our father and regarded him as his closest friend.

As the afternoon wears on we stop for tea. Michael manages to make and serve it, an heroic effort, which impresses his sister, Rosemary, when she hears. His hands are shaky and his grip is weak but not a drop spilt. I do not want to wear him out and we finally call a halt as the light begins to fail. He turns aside our attempt to take him out for supper but happily accepts our modest gifts of Maple syrup and Ice Wine — very Canadian goodies.

It is hard to say goodbye.

After a night spent mulling over all the questions not asked, all the puzzles not solved, I am anxious to have a second visit and we arrange it for the day after. Not as long this time, but a feeling of tying up loose ends. We leave with the promise that I can call any time.

In those few hours with him we hear things both sad and joyful. Like King Tut's tomb, in the presence of death and loss, there are treasures beyond price for me and my sister. With these our father's story is enriched and so are we.

Death and the Foremost Girl

With the discovery of Michael and all the light he will shed still ahead of us, Robbie and I are, once again, poring over a map showing Bomber Command Stations during the War. The country is thick with them, the density increasing toward the east coast where Operational Bases need the advantage of being close to the North Sea and the continent beyond. In Lincolnshire, which we are told, turned blue with all those airmen, the bases are heavily clustered around the City of Lincoln, whose cathedral spires, looming out of the dark, lifted the hearts of so many crews returning from operations. We do not seek to know all these bases, just those where our father and his friends served. And High Wycombe, Bomber Command Headquarters, east of London, sporting a little flag and distinguished by its bold lettering — we know it. Even though none of the men we read about in Daddy's diary sets a toe in this exalted place, the decisions made there are life or death to them.

South, around Brackley, closer to London, as we scan the airfield names, there are Silverstone and Turweston, where they trained, bouncing between the two. There is Scampton, tucked in behind Lincoln, where planes fill the sky and he feels the real thing getting closer. Just south is Wigsley, the conversion training, uncomfortable and difficult. Swinderby, Group HQ, is close by. Even further south is Syerston, the Lancaster finishing school. And finally, the crew, deemed ready to engage, moves to Spilsby, closer to the coast. For the most part the bases represented by these little black dots, which became, for a time, home, for so many men and women, are now gone, or changed beyond recognition. We often find them tricky to unearth. Many have disappeared completely.

Silverstone, their first stop, has been reincarnated as something far more splendid: Home of British Motorsports. Young men, and women too, now risk their lives zooming about a racetrack at high speeds for the edification of those addicted to benzene fumes, adrenaline, danger, pushing limits, hoping to beat the odds ... not such a far cry from its purpose all those years ago. For many, the arcane differences as well as the engaging similarities of the airfields that dotted Britain are a fodder for endless discussion. To Robbie and me their triangular lay-outs look remarkably alike and rather uninteresting. What we want is the hut where our father slept, the Mess where he ate, the pub where he drank.

The little town of Brackley, close to Silverstone and its sister base, Turweston, is a favourite watering hole, the location of *many of our hilarious nights*. The pub of choice is not mentioned but for us this town is marked for greatness; we believe it to be a good and necessary place to look for lodging.

Turns out it isn't. Silverstone's racetrack is a tourist magnet allowing inns in the area to hike up their prices, and, as we soon discover, lower their level of service. We choose the Crown on the main street. From the outside it looks not too bad. Inside it is a musty, unkempt place of staggered staircases and interminable corridors. Nobody offers help with our bags as we make our tired way to the most unsatisfactory of rooms: cold, dank, and minus towels or soap and none too clean. One night will be more than enough.

After a short stint in Silverstone Arthur and mates are shot off to Turweston. Here he is lodged in a hut with his new crew as well as two other crews, and a couple of fellows not yet crewed up. Immediately after settling in they are granted leave. Daddy and Baldy go off together for a jolly time in London running into mates from Dumfries and Whitley Bay. For some reason, when the leave is over, he and Baldy do not return on the same train. Given what follows we wish they had shared that last trip together.

After a bit of ear bashing by the ground training staff he begins flying with his new crew. Our father at first has some problems with his air operating: a bad patch. He is worried whether he can cut it. A flying officer comes to his aid giving him two hours night tuition, after which he steadily improves. To be smart enough to know you need help and to seek it out ... we are proud of our sensible Dad. He is also making an effort to get to know these new crewmates. A boozy night out with the two gunners, Bruce and Alf, is pronounced a success. The evening spent with Cliff, Bill, and Mike is not. Given that he and Mike will eventually be the best of friends, we wonder what blights this outing? I could, I suppose, have asked Michael when we sat in his kitchen in Bishop Stortford. I considered it. But by then it seemed unimportant. Whatever happens that night, they get over it. Daddy reports an improvement in his mastery followed by a night of hectic fun in Northampton with all but Alf. They are becoming a solid crew and that is all that really matters.

And then a hole is rent in Arthur's world. *On the 17th Ernie Baldwin and all his crew crashed and burnt at the end of the long runway. The entire crew was wiped out except the rear gunner. So died as fine a type of chap as there ever was and Dutchy and I were particularly knocked in a heap. We wrote to Ruth and offered our sympathy but sympathy's a poor thing at best I'm afraid.*

He thinks, as he tries to find the words to comfort Ern's shattered fiancée, of his wife and children and his own mortality. After the war, in honour of the pact, Dutchy goes to visit Ern's parents on their farm: the people who loved this treasured friend and the place where he grew up. Finding it hard to put into words what he feels, he looks for a way to be of help. The windmill is squeaking. He oils it. There is no ready cure for grief but that earnest young man climbing up their windmill, clutching an oil can in honour of his lost mate, must surely have eased a little of their pain.

A letter from Ern's fiancée, Ruth, arrives in June. *Poor kid has taken Ern's death very hard and no wonder.* We have become attached to and protective of Baldy. He and Daddy, both loyal to the women they love, go off together to the pictures rather than to dances. And now poor Ruth has lost her future. Does she keep his photo forever on her night table? Does she become the spinster aunt, a figure touched with tragedy, at the edge of family gatherings? Or does she marry and, like our mother, tuck her first and greatest love away and get on with her life? We hope she finds some measure of happiness.

Michael, rustling through his diary, finds a day in September when he travels to Oxford and, while there, carries out a small mission for our father. In Botley Cemetery, he records, "I laid a card on Ern Baldwin's grave for Arthur Plowman who had been charged with the duty by the foremost girl at home." How sweet that is, "the foremost girl." We know enough about Baldy to know she was more than that; she was the only girl. Why did Daddy not go on this errand himself? Michael says, "Obviously he couldn't go for some reason." Perhaps he could not bear the thought. He does not seem to have confided much to Michael, who does not know that Baldy had been one of Arthur's best friends. Some things are difficult to speak of.

In the binder we have a photo of Ern's grave in Botley Cemetery, one of the many Commonwealth Graves sites scattered about the country. Snowie is also buried here. These graves hold those who died on English soil. Regardless of country of birth, this is where they have their final rest. The fallen are not brought home, rows of flag-draped coffins loaded into huge military aircraft. These overseas cemeteries are meticulously maintained and records are faithfully kept for a steady stream of relatives and friends. We wonder if Ruth ever makes the pilgrimage. I suppose we could have gone, Oxford is not so far west of London. It would have added a mere day to the trip. But, like our father, we did not visit Ern's grave where he lies "in some corner in a foreign field." Still, he is remembered by us and we are about to travel to the place where he died.

Over the period of the war, the eight stations in a fifteen-mile radius of Brackley house ten thousand men and women, either on the bases or billeted locally. A horrifying four hundred aircraft are lost during this time. Not holed with flak, shot down by *nachtjagers* or out of fuel ditching in the North Sea, just victims of accidents. In page after page the names and details of this waste are bloodlessly recorded. I find Ernie's name in 17 OTU and make much of the connection with Hut 17 in Dumfries. They are flying a Wellington. Of the forty-one crashes recorded on this page alone, all but two, a Hurricane and a Lysander, are Wellingtons. Six men on Ernie's plane are listed as dead, but Daddy has written that the tail gunner survived. There would have been no engineer at this point; just a crew of six. At first I am puzzled by this. If the tail gunner survived, then how can six be dead? But, it turns out, the explanation is simple: this is OTU, Operational Training; a flight instructor is on board. He would have lived through a gruelling thirty sorties over Europe, thanked his luck and gone on the instruct, only to die in a training accident where all but one are killed. There is often terrible guilt in being the one that got away. How does the rear gunner cope?

They were flying circuits at the time, a fixed route taken by all aircraft when taking off, landing, or flying around waiting to land. Training for this means an approach to landing, a "bump and go," then climbing away and back into circuit. If they are a little too far down the runway, the bump is aborted and an overshoot procedure followed: opening up the throttles, climbing away and getting back into circuit. The Accident Record Card, written up after the "incident" reports that the aircraft, poor BK352, "was seen to turn sharply to the right at 600 ft. after a practice overshoot, lose height, crash and burn." And why does this happen? Why is poor Ruth to spend a life without her fine chap? Accident Record Cards, written in haste with little information, are notoriously unreliable. But this one is clear on the choices. When the burnt aircraft is examined, it is noted that the flaps are down. Two possible causes: "flaps lowered inadvertently or creeping down." Either somebody makes a mistake or there is something mechanically wrong, options that could cover almost any training accident. The instructor, P/O Dennis, has a distinguished flying medal but anybody can have a lapse. Or else the less experienced men in training: the pilot, the engineer, even the bomb aimer, perhaps, make an error. Daddy writes that Cliff, *while acting as standby to the pilot during training, cut the throttle six feet above the deck and we did a Hell of a bounce.* These things happen. Failing human error, suspicion falls on the aircraft. Aging, overused, and tired, many of these training planes are in less than perfect nick.

Non-combat crashes account for fifteen percent of all losses. In both operations and training, the planes, although religiously and diligently serviced, often let the crews down. One day I find myself scrolling down a catalogue of horrors in a website devoted to Bomber Command casualties. "Casualties," a bloodless word for what happens to these young men: bodies ripped, shredded, smashed, and burned. Their planes succumb to flak, night fighters, bombs dropped from above by their own planes, petrol tanks sputtering on empty. So many of the deaths are random and stupid. "Door fell off," "wing came off," "came down over the coast," "crashed on take-off," "crashed on landing," "collided," "engine failure," "wireless failure." One bomber crashes into the North Sea when a pilot uses a gadget called a "reflector sight," requiring him to close one eye and depriving him of depth perception. To compensate he relies on his altimeter, which, unknown to him, has a built-in lag time. Nobody survives. Another report comes from a chap fishing close to the English coast who hears a plane approaching and then a "dull thud." He carefully packs up his gear and traipses through the mist, collecting a couple of shepherds along the way. They find no survivors. Over and over the reports tell us "Nothing heard after take-off. Failed to return to base." Burial sites are mentioned but there are countless not buried anywhere. How do their families live with that? One of the saddest: "a rifle with a length of string attached to the trigger was on the floor of the billet." Another records a life lost to peritonitis. Was that any better or worse? He volunteered and he is just as dead as the fellow "Last seen bailing out." And of course, not everything is known. They can only print what they have been told: whatever is seen, recorded, remembered when every night dozens of planes do not come back. One plane that crashes on take-off in a training exercise has two cadets on board, aged fourteen and fifteen. All perish. As I wade through this waste I want to know how the man who is my father copes with this. We also want to know the details of his death. We begin knowing little of what happened to him. We will, eventually, know much more. But, for now, we can be present at the place where Ernie Baldwin, his good friend, crashed and burned at the end of the long runway.

***

On a dewy morning we reach Turweston, still in use as an airfield for small recreational planes. The array of startlingly outdated websites that we have consulted has filled us with anticipation of semi-intact buildings dating from the time our father trained there. Doubtful, but ever hopeful, we arrive at the gates of the Turweston Aerodrome, home of the Turweston Flying Club, nestled on the border of Northamptonshire and Buckinghamshire. Nobody stops us from driving through the gate and up the dirt road. Ahead we can see a fairly impressive jumble of grey corrugated iron buildings: hangers, a business park, a conference centre. A modest control tower pokes out, overlooking a series of runways. Small brightly coloured planes buzz about.

This is a far cry from its life as a training base packed with huts, a Mess building, control tower, the classic triangular runway, bubbling with the activity of hundreds of uniformed men and women, the roar of the two-engine planes they trained in, taking off, circling, touching down, soaring up again.

We drive up to the buildings at the end of the narrow track, and park. There are a few small planes to admire, red and white, blue and white, polished to a high shine, nothing like the long ago tired Wellingtons grumbling along the runways. What once happened here is wiped away. We have heard of haunted fields: tales of hangars occupied by ghostly airmen, the unmistakable sound of combat aircraft rumbling across the English countryside in the eerie dusk but here is bright prosaic sunshine. There is no hint of what once went on.

A little loony perhaps, we feel our hearts lift when we spy a pile of bricks next to a rusting Nissen hut. Something has been dismantled. So far we have seen not a sign of the crumbling buildings promised by those outdated websites but this looks encouraging. We clamber over the large mound of bricks. They look hopefully old — many have maker's brands inscribed on their sides. In a moment we have convinced ourselves that they are part of a building he has entered, these are bricks he may have laid a hand on. We are in his presence. We make a small cairn and Robbie wanders into a field to pick a bunch of wild flowers including a glorious and serendipitous scarlet poppy. We lay this bouquet on our memorial pile. As we leave I pick up one of the bricks. It will go home with me; I have something real.

Still, as we get back into the car and turn toward the entrance, it seems sad that this is all we have found and that we have most likely invented most of it. At that moment a car enters the gate and drives toward us. "Stop," I order Robbie, as I leap out of the car to flag him down. He rolls down his window and I, Ancient Mariner-like, tell him our story. Can he fill in any gaps for us? Well, no he can't, but Peter, on duty in the Control Tower, certainly can. We are invited to follow and he will introduce us.

In between calmly guiding in various one and two-seater planes, Peter and the others manning the tower treat us like royal visitors. They find our story intriguing and have some information for us. The runways are part of those on the original base although the longest leg is no longer used. For many years local kids raced their bikes along it but now it is just a shadow. We can see its ghostly outline, this runway where Baldy died. The original Control Tower can just be spotted peeking through the forest encroaching on the edge of the 'drome. Gypsies camp there, we are told. It isn't a place they would suggest we try to visit. Our saner suspicions about the brick pile are confirmed: no, it did not date back to the war. All those original buildings are gone. There are the remnants of bomb shelters along the fence line of the road leading away from the aerodrome. We pledge to try to find them.

Ready for a snack, we drop in to the little café at the base of the tower where we find a sponge cream cake just like the ones our mother used to make. With a pot of tea it is a deliciously sentimental feast. This now quite satisfactory search ends as we park along the road and go looking for the bomb shelters. We haven't, up till then, considered the possibility of such structures though we know the Germans frequently venture across the Channel to shoot up bases. Of course they would need bomb shelters. Sadly our desire to see them is thwarted. We climb fences, we brave irritated cows, we plunge through underbrush, we find nothing. Not a real problem we convince ourselves as we examine the nasty scratches on our legs. Just knowing the shelters are in there will suffice.

Well on the Right Side

By the time the course at Turweston finishes there is a change in the tone of the diary. Satisfaction shines from the pages, the entries are detailed and personal. We are proud of our smart dad for, in spite of his fears of failure, he has come *well out on the right side.* He, Mike, and Cliff *leave Turweston on a warm and drowsy morning, heading back to the base at Silverstone, riding our bikes, lazily taking our time and enjoying the exquisite luxury of a sunny day.* They are comfortable together. *Mike is delivering some very wise remarks on the modern young girl. Good old Mike. He certainly is a comic strip when he likes but he is also a smart lad.*

When I read this out loud to Michael in his kitchen at Greenacres we are both a little shy. "Now I can blush," he says. Urbane and self-confident, he is suddenly a twenty-year-old, worried about how he is seen by this man he admires: his senior, more mature, less inclined to youthful folly.

"Not at all," I reassure him. I have already decided to skip the awkward first outing but this, I think, is sweet. He is uncomfortable about the reference to his assessment of the modern girl but glows gently at being described as a "smart lad."

It is clear that Daddy enjoyed his smartness. He continues: *Mike waxed very wrath about one patronizing Englishman who was talking down to him in a very "Lord of the manor" style, telling him if he evah wanted any digging, he would be pleased to supply him with a cup of tea. "Of course I can't do it myself. My lumbago you know!"* Mike is typical of these men in the RAF: they volunteered;

they are independent fellows, proud of their choices, proud of what they are doing. They do not enjoy condescension, whether civilian or military. They might cheerfully call themselves Colonials but the hackles rise if the British dare to. And as for indulging some hoity-toity old fart by digging up his garden ... I don't think so.

Michael has no memory of this self-important fellow who treats him like a labourer and seems puzzled now by his own reaction. Perhaps I should not be bringing these long ago moments up. There is later a cryptic reference to his infatuation with somebody nicknamed by Arthur *the Horrible Splendide*. I decide not to explore this. What if she was the love of his young life only to discover that his best friend had such a name for her? We don't know this dignified and hospitable fellow well enough to cast doubt on his youthful taste in women.

In these happier times our father's diary blossoms, becoming almost lyrical. On this idyllic spring day as they head to Silverstone from Turweston on their bikes, we feel he is content. A bonus, on their arrival at camp, is finding that Bill, their efficient skipper, has reserved beds for them in a hut full of *good chaps*.

Daddy confides one worry. *Cliff*, he writes, is *coming in for some censure*. And then the dreaded judgement: *turning out to be rather a bludger*, the word used here in its worst sense. He isn't just enjoying time off; he is ducking responsibility and letting his crewmates down. Alf and Bruce are not with them because they are behind schedule with their gunnery and have stayed at Turweston to catch up. But this is not seen as shirking; Daddy knows that there are challenges. All is well as long as you are meeting them; Cliff, it seems, is not. Daddy hopes this will pass. *All the rest of the crew*, he remarks with great satisfaction, *are bonzer chaps.*

We become fond of Cliff. He is very young and this is his first time away from home. He loves his parents, Alf and Elsie, who live in nearby Northampton, and he nips home a lot. *Cliff is all of an itch to get away to home but Bill is sternly holding him in.* For the rest of the crew, Australians twelve thousand miles from the comforts of home and valiantly sucking it up, Cliff's whizzing off must be galling. Still, to be fair to homesick and twitchy Cliff, until the two gunners turn up, the crew cannot fly. Nobody is doing much. Our father has a satisfying stack of the elusive aerograms and is contentedly filling them with news for Nooney. Why should Cliff be grounded? A little later, Daddy and Bill go in to Northampton for a night of drinking. They have tea at Cliff's home and spend the night there. In the morning they return to Silverstone by bus. After this there is little comment about Cliff's behaviour.

Michael does not know of this visit to Cliff's home. "I wasn't invited," he laughs, hastening to add that there was no harm in that, that they all got on. But he tells us that Cliff is "a bit bristly." One day Michael calls him a Limey, as an Australian would do. He "got quite cross," calling Michael a Colonial. "And I didn't react. I said well yes we are Colonials, what's the problem and you are Limeys. But he didn't see it. So he always called me Colone, And I always called him Lime." Perhaps the invitation to stay at Elsie and Alf's is issued while this little contretemps is still raw, leaving Michael out. But perhaps not. They seem, to us, to be above such pettiness.

Cliff, Michael tells us, is "a pretty ordinary sort English lad ... he was a clicker in the shoe trade, he did something to the shoe, something to the soles." My trusty computer spits out this definition: "A person who cuts out the uppers of shoes from pieces of leather using a flexible knife that clicks as it changes direction." He has moved from this modest role, in a world where class is king, to the vital position of bomb aimer, the man who finishes the job they have been sent to do. There are interesting tensions. We find Michael the most egalitarian of men but he *is* a surgeon, and our later research reveals that he comes from a family of great distinction. Is there a hint of class-consciousness here? We don't want to think so. It never surfaces in his relationship with our father, a simple orchardist whose education did not go beyond high school.

***

Our next stop is Towcester, properly pronounced "toaster," which we take great pleasure in saying. A temperate morning rain mists the windshield and smudges the countryside as we drive into this sweet English village. Watling street unfolds, winding gently down the hill and there, right in front of us, is the Saracens Head and, with it, the voice of our father. *After tea, the evening being so inviting, Bill, Mike and I mount our bikes and ride off eventually reaching Towcester in the quiet of the evening. We dawdle around the town having an occasional drink but, as darkness deepens, we settle down in one place for a pint or two and a quiet talk.* For our father and Mike this is a place worth seeing; they share a love of Charles Dickens and the great man ate here and brought it to life in his writing.

Pickwick, of *Pickwick Papers*, on his perambulations, spends a night in the Saracens Head. He and his entourage arrive, as do we, in the rain. Theirs is not a sweet spring rain but a steady downpour. They are reluctant guests, at first declaring that this place will not do. Sam Weller, practical to the bone, points out that they are soaking wet, that their horses are exhausted, and that the Inn can warm them, dry them, feed them, and put them happily to bed. It does all of these things in good time; what's more it provides a setting for a vigorous contretemps between Mr. Slurk and Mr. Pott, champions of the INDEPENDENT and the GAZETTE respectively. Insults are traded, leading to a taking up of arms: a carpet bag for Slurk and a fire shovel for Pott. Blows are exchanged, and Mr. Pickwick, having placed himself between them as a noble intervener, comes in for the lion's share of the damage. Of course Sam Weller, who must surely wonder why he bothers, calms the waters and sends everyone to bed.

I have owned the two volumes of Pickwick's travels since my mother's death nearly twenty years ago. They are proudly displayed in our living room on the mantle over the fireplace, along with *A Tale of Two Cities* with its heartbreaking inscription. I've read that one, but had never tackled Mr. Pickwick. Somehow it seemed dry. As part of the commitment to this missing parent, I dive in, feeling virtuous and ready for sacrifice. I love Dickens. I know he is not dull, but this had seemed a plotless ramble that I could do without. Of course I am wrong; it is a delicious romp.

We have been told that our father was very funny. Dutchy certainly thought so. Along with everything else, we never asked our mother about his sense of humour. Michael says he doesn't talk much, but he loves Dickens. For us to stay at a place he longs to see, to know that he loves a writer we love too, to imagine him, and our mother, chuckling as they read to each other by the light of the kerosene lamp at the kitchen table — more strands in the tapestry we weave.

It seems an idyllic night for these young airmen. Do they actually drink at the Saracens Head? Have a meal there? We know they see it. Surely they go inside. But perhaps not; with such an exalted pedigree it may be that the dining room is beyond their means.

We also fear that the price of a room for the night might stretch our frugal tolerance. But we must stay here. It is our heathen equivalent of a holy place. We park in the cobbled courtyard behind the mellow red brick building and head for reception. Unlike the Crown, the Saracens Head is clean, sweet smelling, welcoming, and remarkably cheap. In a flash we have a room. Our bags are carried up. Lamps, soap, shampoo, fluffy blankets, a functioning kettle and packets of bikkies complete our bliss. After a brief settling in and a reviving cup of tea, we set out to explore.

Never a man to gush, Daddy tells us that Towcester with its aging brick buildings and its quaint old Public Houses is *almost picturesque*. The curving main street is lined with ancient shops. There is a house built in 1457, for goodness sake. With its paved courtyards, wrought iron gates, and crème caramel stone, it could not have been more picturesque had it been vying for a prize.

Happily, it also offers twenty-first century conveniences; a nearby supermarket can supply us with lunch possibilities and a few sundries. Robbie, keen to get her hands on some food, strides ahead. I rush to catch up.

"My you do walk fast," I puff.

"I do," she responds complacently. "I'm famous for it."

Shopping accomplished, we drive out into the country. We park at the ornate and firmly closed gate of an estate, its noble pile visible across sweeping green fields, a bubbling brook, and picture-perfect stands of trees. The lunch of olive bread and bananas is oddly delicious. Sheep munch sedately and a pheasant struts by. Our world is serene and satisfying at this moment, just as Daddy's is, on his visit to Towcester.

We decide to explore Bletchley, which is mentioned in the diary as a destination, nothing more. Daddy and his mates, waiting on the platform of Bletchley Station, after an uncomfortable night travelling from Dumfries, have no idea that, close by, another kind of crew is working to end this conflict in a very different way than Bomber Command.

During the war, Bletchley Manor, an eccentric architectural hodgepodge, houses the clandestine Government Code and Cipher School. Every person working there keeps its secrets. The young girls who labour to unravel ciphers and codes hop on their bicycles each morning and pedal away through Bletchley village, away from the houses in which they are billeted. The families whose tables they share think them dull little secretaries. Others roar on motorbikes along the narrow back roads speeding decoded messages to war offices. Nobody can know what they are working on. They are sworn to secrecy, can tell no one: not family, not friends, nobody. And they keep that vow. Even into the 1970s, when the public finally hears what has gone on in this place, secrets are kept. Many husbands, wives, mothers, fathers, sisters, brothers die without knowing what vital work their loved ones did in the war. Churchill rumbles in admiration, "They were my geese who laid the golden egg and they never cackled." We admire and thank them too. They are doing their level best to protect our father and men and women like him. They save so many lives; because of them the war is shortened by as much as two years.

Back in the comforting arms of the Saracens Head we organize our belongings, spend a little time poking through our binders and then go for supper. What British restraint we find in this pub so connected to Dickens. Transport this to the USA and it would be a Disneyland of references to Pickwick. Busts of Dickens for sale at the bar, T-shirts screaming: "I slept with Pickwick at the Saracen Arms," "Wot the Dickens!" Perhaps a life size, animated, Sam Weller in the lobby, staff in period costume, Dickensian-themed meals, souvenir carpet bags and fire shovels. No, not a hint of any of this. We do find, on the walls of a back staircase leading to the dining room, a collection of charming silhouette portraits of some of the characters who spent their fictional night here, but that's it.

We have a splendid supper of sausages and mash and, a first for this trip, a bottle of wine. Tony and I are unrestrained wine drinkers and usually chug a bottle at a meal. Not so my sister who, less accustomed, gets pleasantly tipsy. And, as always, we talk and talk. I am telling her about the Museum in London — the British War Experience — that has succumbed to an unfortunate attack of political correctness. Over its entrance, clearly visible from the street, is a giant photo of Winston Churchill, in full uniform, making the V for Victory sign and chomping on a cigar. At least he was, until some jelly-spined revisionist, fearful of corrupting the youth, or offending the anti-smoking lobby, or making a wave of any kind, has his cigar airbrushed out.

"That is so stupid," Robbie sputters, waving her wine glass erratically. "What is the point?"

What indeed. Churchill smoked — constantly. Everyone did, it seems, during the war. Do we think less of the man who led Britain through this terrible time because he was fond of his Havanas? This is revisionism of the pettiest kind. The museum pretends to be astonished, unable to name who did it or why. More spineless behaviour. "And really," I groan, voice rising, wine glass in danger of slopping, "of all the things that might make Britons think less of their war-time leader! Kids can know he smoked. It won't make them take it up. It won't make them think less of him. Other things might. Do they know he turned his back on his friends? Do they realize that he did a bit of air-brushing of his own?"

We sip our wine, silently contemplating our mixed feelings about Mr. Churchill, both saviour and false friend. Luckily this excursion into the dark side does not dampen us for long. We can set it aside for now. Wine is handy that way. We sleep well.

A Heroine of the Highest Order

When Michael opens up his wartime self and his diary, the first thing he reads is, for me, the Hope Diamond of the visit. I have said we set out on this journey prepared for frailties, but, of course, we want to find a good man. What Michael has written, long before he even dreamed of a meeting with his friend's seventy-year-old daughter, is an unsolicited homage: "To me Arthur was always a true gentleman. He never swore, drank or behaved to excess like many of the younger ones. But he was not censorious of us or showed disapproval of our antics. He was always smiling and ready to help if there was anything he could do." A cheerful, willing fellow who did not judge others. How lovely.

Michael's statement that our father does not drink must be parsed. Clearly he does: pubs appear often in his accounts and he is mildly critical of weak beer. That miserable Christmas in Dumfries he sets out deliberately, if unsuccessfully, to get drunk. He was certainly not a wowser — the Australian term for a self-righteous abstainer. When people say, "He drinks, you know," voices dropping a register, eyebrows elevated, they are not referring to the odd pre-dinner sherry; the fellow under discussion is a lush. Daddy did not "drink" in that sense; that is Michael's point.

In April of 1944, life at the Silverstone base develops its own rhythm. The serious business of training is intertwined with the developing friendship of the crewmembers. More nights out drinking in Brackley come in for some mention. *Once more I got talked into going into Brackley with the crew.* The "once more" is revealing; arm-twisting seems not to be needed. On this night his plans are interrupted *by our benevolent Signals Officer having provided all w/ops on with an hour of night Morse.* But, as it turns out there is rain and the excursion is cancelled. The only crewmember deeply disappointed is Bill who is dead set on going as he has *some woman he is keen to meet.*

We know so little of Bill, the skipper of our father's first and much loved crew. He is older, thirty-two, and seems, on what can be gleaned from the diary, to mix less. Michael can tell us nothing of his life after the war but thinks, from something he hears, that Bill returns to Queensland. And, yes, he is single. We are glad to know he is not being unfaithful to some poor woman keeping his home fires burning. He has our motherly blessing to be keen on any woman who takes his fancy.

When this night out falls victim to English weather, it turns into a night of tomfoolery. By the time Daddy gets back from Morse, *Bruce and Alf have been set upon and portions of their mos cut away.* Daddy does not have a moustache so is spared that humiliation, but not other indignities. *We all got stuck into a wrestle during which I was "done over."* Just exactly what those quotation marks imply we can only guess. Some hysterical mortification, likely debagging. Trousers surely back in place, they head off *for a hilarious supper during which some rather revolting remarks were applied to the food.*

Making adolescent fun of what the Mess has to offer is one way of dealing with wartime fare in the UK. Our parents, both raised on farms, ate well. Even during the Depression, when others were making do, there was fresh milk, thick cream, their own butter, newly laid eggs, homemade bread, home grown vegetables, and of course, an abundance of fruit. Daddy, although his complaints are muted, must have been horrified at the food served up by the RAF: powdered eggs, sausages so devoid of meat that they were dubbed "breadcrumbs in battle dress," cartloads of brussel sprouts. This last so ubiquitous that one returning airman writes a book about his wartime experiences entitled *Boys, Bombs and Brussel Sprouts,* elevating these vegetables to equal the drama of the Blitz and the Battle of Britain. They are a staple of the Victory Gardens, which are often attempted in unsuitable soil and unlikely places: bombed out building sites, rubble-strewn parking lots, even the moat of the Tower of London. These little green knobs will grow anywhere. They might be boiled to mush, stringy, bitter, and the object of ribald remarks, but by God they are good for you.

***

One night, Arthur and the two gunners, Bruce and Alf, bike in to the pictures and a late supper before riding home. They see *about 300 Dakotas flying over at low level with all their lights on — one of the most impressive sights I have ever seen.* About sixty land at their base, taking off the next afternoon: *a grand sight.* They love their planes, these men. They are "fly boys," after all, comfortable with the exotica of this world. They *fly their first solo,* Daddy reports proudly, and their *longest trip, four and a quarter hours.* He feels he is operating fairly well now. He records an 80% and an 85%. Even though we don't know what is being measured, we swell with pride.

And it gets better. In the last month of the course they get in *bags of flying hours.* He adds gleefully: *95% yesterday — bang on as they say in the classics.* We are often at sea about exactly what he is doing in these courses, so pounce on a list of what is left to cover at Silverstone: *two cross-countries to do and two fighter affiliation trips and about five exams — not much when you say it quickly.* Mention of flying with fighters brings the peril they will soon face a little closer. And he reports having escape photos taken. These will be sewn into his uniform. Should he have to bail out over enemy territory, survive the jump, and not be instantly scooped up and imprisoned, perhaps he will stumble onto members of the Resistance who will fashion travelling papers that may or may not get him home.

In the photo he looks quite severe. It is a passport type photo after all and he is told not to smile. He is wearing a version of civvies: a striped shirt and a tie. *I look about 21,* he complains of this picture that may save his life, *very callow indeed. Guess I act very callow too as I was all over the camp tonight to avoid having my face blackened — everybody in the hut was done except Mike who very cunningly "laid low and said nuffin."*

More hijinks. Michael is confounded when I read him this section. He seems to have forgotten (repressed?) this particular foolishness, and there were others. Walking on the ceiling, leaving boot-blacked footprints, was a favourite. For a long time we wonder just how this is accomplished. Then comes an explanation: the walker is held upside down by a bunch of his mates and marched across the ceiling to make his mark.

We don't share our father's contention that he looks twenty-one in his escape photo. In the time since he left home his youth has fled. On one of the chaste single beds in our B&B we lay out in chronological order the photos we have of him. These are formal portraits, some taken by camp photographers, others taken elsewhere to send to Nooney. The first, when he gets the flash on his cap back in New South Wales, shows a man who could well have been a teenager: a gleaming smile displays his coveted white and even teeth and he glows with health. The corners of his eyes sport no wrinkles although he does have the endearing little bags that he has bequeathed to his daughters. By the time we reach the end of this row of portraits, the last one taken months before his death, those little bags have become pouches; lines radiate from the corners of his eyes and his cheeks are deeply furrowed. His smile is as charming as ever but this is not the face of a young man. He could easily be forty. And he is not alone in this premature aging. These young men are marked by their experiences. Chasing each other about the camp, having food fights, climbing over furniture, walking on the ceiling, playing the most juvenile of pranks, they wear the incongruous faces of old men.

After a short leave they spend seventeen days at the Scampton base — more lectures, no flying. They are a little north of Lincoln now: *planes overhead as we are surrounded by ops stations. The real thing is getting very nearer — hope nothing happens to me as Nooney is going to take it very hard.* As always he expresses his concern not for himself, but for her. Joyfully, he reports the arrival of *bags of mail, my Nooney is much too good to me but how I love it.* At home, alone, raising two kids struggling to pay the bills, milking cows, running an orchard, missing him — he knows what she is going through. *Poor kid she has had a Hell of a time but never complains — just a heroine of the highest order.*

***

As we zip along the road toward Wigsley in search of their next base, we contemplate how much our mother was loved by our father and how little by her own mother. Robbie tells me of an evening many years ago spent with Mummy sorting through old photos. In one, Mummy, aged about ten, stands by her mother, arms loosely hugging her ample waist. It seems run-of-the-mill, the sort of photo you'd find in any family album, but instead of finding it a delight, fond memories cascading, our mother seemed bewildered. "I never remember hugging Mother," she said. There was no bitterness. It was simply stated as a fact but it explained a lot.

We know families who hug and kiss and pinch and squeeze and say "I love you" with ease. We have never been like this. In a world where the social kiss is mandated, I have a nanosecond of discomfort before surrendering to these intimacies. Hugging my sister or brother is always preceded by a stutter of reticence. We are getting better but old habits die hard. I have few memories of hugging or kissing my mother. She was kind, thoughtful, and a wonderful listener; we never felt unloved, or neglected in any way. We just didn't go in for cuddling. I have, to my delight and amazement, managed to raise three daughters who are free with their affection. I am grateful that the family reserve has not claimed another generation. But it is interesting to trace its origin to the matriarch of Mt. Pleasant.

We called her "Jimmy" — her husband's pet name for her. To us she was an amiable but distant grandmother. We loved to visit her and our even more distant grandfather at Mount Pleasant, their large, badly designed house. I remember her baking in the ridiculously small, cramped kitchen. On an open and cluttered shelf sat a fat jar of boiled lollies, slightly fluff-covered but enchantingly decadent. She had a kerosene fridge — the first in the district. It smelled funny but beat our icebox hands down. The dining room, also rather cramped, included a chaise longue under the window where she lolled of an afternoon, sipping sherry, smoking one or two wicked cigarettes and reading romance novels. During this period of rest we made ourselves scarce, running through the garden, chasing the barn cats, wandering in her two greenhouses among the stag-horn ferns. On special occasions we were permitted to play with a collection of tea cosies kept in the bottom drawer of a chest in the hall. Celluloid kewpie dolls had been sliced off at the waist and supplied with voluminous crocheted skirts, slit to accommodate a teapot. I found them captivating, even more so because the treat of enjoying them was strictly rationed.

We loved our grandmother and it was years before we realized her shortcomings. Jimmy's house — not ever a home — was thick with gewgaws: decorations for their own sake. I fear I have inherited her love of the fussy and frilly. I don't recall Robbie being as taken with those rather creepy tea cosies as I was. The shotgun hall that ran from the rarely used front door to the never opened back door was dotted with tables holding large, hectically painted plaster statues of country folk frolicking among lambs, eating grapes, or staring pensively at a sylvan scene. Although never forbidden, the large and rarely used lounge room felt out of bounds. I tiptoed in to contemplate the brocade-covered couches, the urns full of dried palm leaves and peacock feathers, the elaborate lamps. A high plate rail ran around the room displaying a dizzying collection of objets d'art. One wall held a line of ebony elephants ranging from impressively large to adorably tiny.

There were vases, ceramic animals of all sorts, plaster busts, and bronze figures. On the mantel above the marble fireplace, within touching distance (although I never did) was my favourite: a little ceramic bathtub containing a dainty ceramic lady, her hands modestly crossing her naked chest. It was, I found out by eavesdropping, a gift from a male friend who accidentally barged into the bathroom to find my grandmother in the tub. A risqué scenario for a seven-year-old to contemplate.

All the bedrooms opening on to that long hallway were themed. There was the blue room, the pink room, the green room, the yellow room. They were museum-like and impersonal. Apart from the cluttered kitchen, it seemed a house for show rather than living. As a child and young woman growing up in this house, our mother's job, one of many, was to dust these rooms and every fussy, decorative, and, to her mind, useless item they contained. Having fled her childhood home to the small cottage where she and our father set out to make a life, she avoided accumulating any such stuff. On her death we marvelled at how little she left. When her own mother died, she packed up boxes of all these bits and pieces, memorable to her only as a pointless chore, and gave them away. Our grandmother's jewellery, an impressive collection, showered on her by an adoring husband, was similarly stuffed into a couple of shoeboxes. For a week she drove about the district calling on friends and family inviting them to choose something. She got rid of all of it. She wanted nothing as a keepsake or a memory.

"'The children of lovers are orphans,'" Robbie murmurs. Jimmy and Pop, our maternal grandparents were, indeed, lovers. He worshipped and spoilt her. Every morning he brought her breakfast in bed, she had all the latest labour-saving devices, she wore fur and modish outfits, diamonds hung from her ears and sparkled on her fingers. And, although he clearly loved our mother — his only daughter — and she adored him, he was apparently content for her to be an unpaid skivvy who kept the house running and raised his two much younger sons, freeing his precious jewel for her afternoons on the chaise. Our mother and her two brothers, outside this circle of love, like The Little Match Girl peering, from the cold street into a warm bright world they could not enter, were, indeed, orphaned.

Mummy's ambition, as a young girl, was to become a teacher — Home Economics. When the second brother arrived, a preemie, sent home in a shoebox lined with cotton wool, his fifteen-year-old sister's hopes were smothered. She was taken out of school to care for the baby. Jimmy lay abed in the large master suite, awaiting the wicker trays of tempting dainties carried by a doting Pop. Our two uncles, one seven years younger than his sister, the other fifteen, both declared their sister to be more of a mother to them than the woman who gave them life.

We know of our mother's stifled hopes because she told us over the years. I don't remember hearing bitterness, but surely there must have been some. She was determined that her two daughters be educated; she wanted us to have choices. "You need to go to University," she declared. "You need to have an education in case your husband dies." This, said many times, sank in. Off to University we went and, somewhere in the back of my mind, after I married, I waited stoically for the inevitable death of my husband.

Robbie wonders, "If Daddy had lived, would we have been orphans, too?" Good question. Somebody told me of coming across them once, before they were married, in the days of courtship, walking along a country road, laughing and playing a game of stepping in each other's shadows. "They were so in love. It was wonderful to see." They were certainly lovers absorbed in each other, but to the exclusion of us?

In another of Robbie's cache of memories she and Daddy have been shopping in town. He has bought her a small gift: a little hinged metal case containing six square cakes of watercolour paint, a small brush tucked into its groove. It comes with a colouring book. They are both quivering with anticipation, Daddy even more than his daughter. In the cab of the ute he removes the packaging, eager to begin, but there is a snag: they have no water and these tantalizing blocks of colour cannot be released without it. Robbie recalls what happens next with amusement and love; her ingenious, enthusiastic Dad spits onto the lid of the small case and they are in business. No sign of orphaning behaviour in this cherished moment.

After her Paddy died, our mother didn't speak for a week, not because she didn't want to but because she couldn't. Words would make it real. She stopped lighting the oven and cooked for us on a little Primus stove. One day Robbie asked politely, "Why are you starving us Mummy?" Jolted back to the reality of two small kids to raise, in spite of the evisceration of grief, she returned to us. But if he had come home, walking up the drive as he'd done in that long-ago dream, into her arms, would their love have been like Jimmy and Pop's, so all-consuming that the children are incidental?

The Heavies

Not all airfields, whether training or operational, are created equal. Some, Woodhall Spa for example, are situated on the commandeered estates of the aristocracy. Airmen find themselves sleeping in high-ceilinged suites with snowy plaster walls and long windows looking out onto velvet lawns. They dine in panelled halls, and lounge in former smoking rooms. While their lives are no less under threat, the luxury is appreciated.

Then there is Wigsley. This is where our father and his crew are sent after their training at Silverstone and its satellite drome, Turweston. It lives up to its foul reputation. Daddy's assessment of its muddy and scabrous bathing block, *Ablution facilities are shocking*, is likely understated; the men shower up to their ankles in mud. He also comments on its biggest drawback: *it is very dispersed and we are away on one side of it at the edge of the wood.* The village is in the middle of the base creating very long treks to the Flights, the hub of the airfield. This means *walking a Hell of a distance.* To add to the discomfort, his bike has not arrived. It will be nearly a month before it turns up. With or without bikes, Wigsley is a place dreaded by many. Our dear Arthur Leslie tries to look on the bright side: *I think that on the whole it will be pleasant enough when and if the sun shines.* Then he adds with some gloom, *We had a long and tedious series of Bullo talks this morning which didn't enhance our opinion of the station.*

***

There is little left of this inadequate muddle that housed him so long ago, but we visit what we can. The huts are gone but the village still exists and so does the control tower. There are few of these left so it is a must-see. But first we must find it. To no avail, we stop frequently to quiz various and sundry farmers, dog-walkers and loiterers. There are no helpful signposts; nobody seems aware of its existence. When we do stumble upon it we feel we've pulled off a minor miracle.

It is a three-storey brick building, just off the road, next to an aromatic pig farm and, although battered and scarred, it has a certain dignity. Like an elderly veteran, creaky, wrinkled, covered in age-spots, eyebrows sprouting, valiantly pulling himself to attention, it stands tall in an overgrown field, bearing witness. We park on the nearside verge, negotiate the fence and stumble through the high grass. It isn't an easy building to approach. Certainly not for two old ducks like us, but teenagers, it seems, have found it with ease. Its red brick walls are richly festooned with graffiti. Once inside, which requires climbing over piles of rubble and through broken windows, every interior wall is decorated: protestations of love, complaints against the world, a huge nude with bull's eye breasts. Candle stubs and broken beer bottles litter the floors. It could be worse; there are actually, on the top floor, a few windows still intact, and the place does not reek of urine and feces. It has been treated with a little respect. Kids come here to defeat the boredom of living in the sticks, nine miles from Lincoln. One wall sports a large, black "RAF" so some of these visitors know what it used to be. I wonder: do they ever think of the men and women on this base and the life they led there?

Wigsley, for our father and his crew, is their home for a little over six weeks: 1654 Conversion Unit. Here, after flying the two engine Wellingtons, they will convert to four engines. They are now a crew of seven; Stan has joined them.

Our knowledge of Stan Fletcher is skimpy: he is English, he survives the war. Michael says he was an "ordinary sort of chap" and seems unsure of his role in Civvy Street, before he became their engineer. Something to do with cars? Michael's diary suggests that Stan is a little on the sidelines at first. He is not mentioned at all when they go off drinking. Then there is the matter of repayment of car debts. Michael buys a car but needs to borrow in order to pay for it. Later, he records meticulously his settlement of money owed. It is quite a list. Bill, his skipper, owes a whopping twenty pounds one shilling, Alf forks out four pounds, other men part with various sums: seven, nine, six, four, one pound. Arthur, we are told, owes two. Of course it is in the interest of all these fellows to float the loan for a car in which they will ride. It is this car that takes Daddy, Alf, and Michael to the Lake District, their best leave. Stan is not part of this elaborate car-financing scheme, but he does get to ride in it later. And then he begins to feature in pub nights as he becomes part of this tight group.

The Stirling is a giant among the World War II bombers. Our dad, when they first arrive, entertains the worrying prospect of their operating on Stirlings, adding hopefully: *I don't think there is any possibility of that, thank goodness.* For the men who fly them into combat there is unwavering loyalty, but these planes do not have, if you will pardon an awful pun, a sterling reputation. Arthur and his crew, to their relief, will not fly them in operations but do their conversion, moving from two to four engines, on this behemoth. Michael says they are "enormous aircraft, I've never seen such big planes. And every now and then an engine would catch fire." More stupid ways for men to die. "We didn't do much about it," he adds nonchalantly.

References to training mishaps stud the diary. Once, they are *diverted to Carlisle to pick up a crew that had pranged while trying to do a three engine landing when another motor cut out causing them to crash in a field, tearing through overhead wires and ripping off the rear turret.* Happily the injuries are slight. A less fortuitous ending awaits a Winchester kite, which *went in a couple of miles from here — caught on fire at 3,000 feet but for some reason no one bailed out and it ended up wrapping itself around a tree killing four of the crew and injuring four others.* On at least two occasions a tire in their Stirling bursts.

Another time the undercarriage won't retract, aborting their flight. They make two three-engine landings in the space of two days. All this is recorded quite unemotionally. The prevalence of *rotten* teas (the evening meal so longed for after a tough day's flying) is invested with more disappointment than the inadequate aircraft they deal with. A wag posts a notice board in the crew room "*in regard to Ben Bowering: dying through overeating at Wigsley — no flowers by request.*"

With May easing into June, the weather is better although it still rains quite regularly, interrupting planned flying. Even so, spirits are better. A warm hut, even when leaking asbestos fibres from its decaying roof, is more hospitable than a damp and chilly one. The early lecture stage ends with Arthur topping the course — the first time he has done such a thing. We are puffed with pride.

And then comes news of the long awaited D-Day — the Second Front has opened. *The first official news I got was over the R1154 when I was doing a D.I. and I felt delighted — 4,000 ships and several thousand smaller boats were engaged in the landing.* Soon he will be an operational flier in Bomber Command whose squadrons play such a vital role in making Operation Overlord the beginning of the end of the war. One thousand, two hundred sorties on the night before the landing, the greatest effort of the war, the largest tonnage of bombs dropped in one night. To the brave men scrambling toward the beaches air cover is vital. Over a thousand planes are sent out on the night of June 6th to make the Normandy invasion possible. The war must have felt so much closer to its end, our father closer to going home. Present happiness is just fine, even if the future is unsure.

***

Robbie and I are not, in any real sense, children of war. We lost our father, but in a world far away. Australia remained, apart from poor bombed Darwin, largely unscathed. When I first arrived in Europe in my early twenties, goggle-eyed at the antiquities of Italy, I was startled to see bullet holes in buildings, souvenirs of the war we had, in so many ways, ducked. The combination of quotidian domesticity and bullets is a shock. People lived through (or not) this kind of peril. In those days, working in London and hitchhiking through Europe in my 1960s version of the grand tour, it was all new and wonderful. Now huge chunks of it are forgotten, but I retain a vivid mental photograph of that house, made of dusty caramel-coloured clay, scarred by lethal pockmarks. After the war our uncle, our mother's brother, returned to the Italy he had flown above in the war unleashing bombs. He stood in the cratered buildings, saw what he had done, and wept.

By the time I arrived in London in the sixties, there was little to mark the Blitz. London picked herself up and slowly rebuilt, but with something so devastating, all traces will never be removed. In Bethnal Green, where I taught Cockney kids, I remember, again with amazing immediacy, the Roman Road. It runs through the town, an original Roman road down which Centurions once marched. It was also the route of soldiers tramping south to gather on the coast for D-Day. They trekked day and night through Bethnal Green. Women made urns of tea and stood on the road to fill the soldiers' extended helmets as they marched by. With them came the tanks, churning along the Roman cobbles and often crushing the concrete curbs. When I was there this damage was still to be seen. I stood on the smashed street corners and wondered: how did people live through these things? I cannot believe I did not think of my father when I saw these signs of war. While those tanks rumbled south and those men marched, gulping welcome steaming tea from their helmets, he was in Wigsley. This was his world and yet I gazed with amazement at those tread marks in the concrete, pleased to be so close to history, and gave him no thought at all.

Now, drowning as we are in so many details of the war and his life, we are very aware of how sheltered we have been. We are children of the fifties who grew up in a world prosperous, peaceful, and a little smug. The cold war gave us a jolt. We came through the Cuban crisis with bated breath, there was Korea and then Vietnam but it was all far away, this killing and potential mayhem. We are part of a favoured generation; we are white, middle class, educated, cosseted. Since the war, which we do not remember, there has been no global conflict. We are now, too little and maybe too late, trying to understand just what it was like for these parents we long to know.

There is also a connection between the place where I taught in London's East End with Bomber Harris, head of Bomber Command. Butch (short for Butcher) Harris was, after the war, scorned and vilified, along with his beloved "old lags," those young men with their old faces. It was a long time before his contribution to defeating Hitler was acknowledged. Fifty years from the anniversary of the first thousand bomber raids, the Queen Mother unveiled his statue near Trafalgar Square. As she valiantly, and I am sure sincerely — she was, after all, in London during the Blitz — spoke of his contribution to the winning of the war, she was interrupted by shouts from those who saw him as a war criminal. "Mass murderer," they screamed, safe in victorious Britain, too young to remember any of it, full of righteous fury. Later red paint was thrown on the statue. But not everyone was convinced of his calumny. A wreath appeared thanking him and his Bomber Command for what they had done. It came from the East Enders. For a year, I worked among those grateful for my father's sacrifice, and I never knew.

On June 6, 2014, the seventieth anniversary of D-Day, Robbie has her ear tuned to her kitchen radio as she works. In Normandy, the town of Caen, a group of men from Bomber Command is being honoured. There are six of these elderly veterans from Australia; two dozen more from other allied countries. They are in their nineties. The powers that be have decided it would be unwise to wait for a seventy-fifth anniversary; the men who have travelled here will likely not make such a journey again.

The Australian Broadcasting Corporation is focused on its own: six Australians. The pilots among them are given France's most coveted award, the Legion of Honour. The other heroes are dubbed Chevaliers. It is a moving ceremony. As Robbie weeps into the lunch she is preparing, she is shaken from her sorrow for the long-dead, and her admiration of those who endure, by the name of one of these celebrated chaps: Phil Elger. Galvanized, she kicks into research mode. Can he be the romantic young Phil whose love life caused such discussion and intervention in Dumfries? He is a wireless operator, he is the right age, it is an unusual name.

She calls Dutchy's widow. Lynn is quite clear: yes this is the very Phil. He and Dutchy kept in touch; he is godfather to their daughter. We had not imagined such a connection. He is an Air Force celebrity, his story written up by Veteran's Affairs. After the war, he returned and got on with life, became involved with greyhound racing and was good at it. He is modestly pleased to have this recognition; to be honoured at his age is a wonderful thing. "I'm ninety-three," he says, "I didn't expect more." In this time to remember the fallen, those who didn't come home, he must surely think of our dad? He speaks of his own crew's "enduring devotion to each other, regardless of country, rank or role." It was far, far more than just mateship. "I had seven men on my crew, three Australians, four Englishmen, and I'm the last one. Only the good die young." Terrible theology, but there does seem to be something, if not exactly criminal, then at least feisty, in those who survive into old age. All of the lovely old dears, as Robbie calls them, who knew our father and still walk the earth, are men of mischief, rare good humour, and gentle determination.

On D-Day, Phil's task, with his now-dead and admired crew, is to divert German planes from the landing sites for the one hundred and fifty thousand allied troops heading for the beaches of Normandy. He is part of the complex planning and cunning that went into pulling off Operation Overlord. To be connected with one of the players, no matter how distantly, is our own Legion of Honour.

Daddy, still several weeks away from active duty, would have been proud that his Dumfries hut-mate is involved. He might have felt some frustration over the timing. Here he is, still in training, while Phil, who graduated from Dumfries at the same time, is already on active duty.

Robbie manages to contact Phil. It takes a while for him to respond; he is tired and frail, he tells her. Finally a letter arrives. "We use to look after each other," he says, adding, "Arthur was the one to control us." Interesting choice of words and, on reflection, perhaps not inaccurate. Daddy is often in mother hen mode to his boys: he comments when Dutchy goes off with a young woman and notes with relief his arrival at camp shortly after, he tries to buy fish and chips for the chaps back in the hut, and he attempts to moderate Phil's romantic urges. I'm not sure he controlled them, but I think he would like to have done.

Wigsley's shortcomings as a base are offset by the power of the work they are doing. Arthur and his crew are concentrated on finishing their training and logging the hours required to move to the next, and final, stage.

The role of the wireless operator is, though perhaps not as isolated as the rear gunner in his vulnerable turret, one of the loneliest. Daddy records one day spent flying circuits and landings. This is important stuff but for Daddy not so engaging. He is on strict radio silence so just sits there feeling the plane dip, bump, rise, circle, and then do it all again. Curtained off from the crew, it is only by standing up that he can get a glimpse of the outside world. *In twenty-two hours of flying, spread over five days, all over England and hardly a thing did I see.* When his pilot has to corkscrew, boredom rapidly evaporates. The plane is flung sideways into a deep rolling dive, a manoeuvre to take them away from whatever is menacing: fighter attacks, trapping cones of light, bombs falling from above, imminent collisions. Inside the aircraft, chaos reigns; pens, pencils, protractors fly up to the ceiling, rapidly followed by crew members, none of whom are strapped in. Glued to the walls or the roof by G-force, they hang on while their pilot fights the controls. In any real world those planes should have simply ripped apart. But they don't. They struggle back into the bomber stream, men peeling themselves off, clambering back into seats, reassembling the tools of their trade, going on.

In his offhand way, our father remarks that, during a series of corkscrews, he *manages to see quite a bit of the country*. A comic strip visual reels through my mind: Daddy jammed by G-force to the Perspex window over his seat, eyes plastered open but gratefully taking in the scenery from his now upside down aircraft. Such comic moments of revelation aside, he is mostly, with his ears glued to his set, listening to its whispers and crackles, in a world removed from his crew.

One of the questions I ask Michael is whether their training for survival in the event of bailing out or ditching prepares them for the real thing. Do they actually experience deploying a parachute, for example? "Well, no," he says, adding with composed certainty, "but we knew what to do." Daddy's description of their training does not support this optimism. He and Mike spend one morning trying to fly a dinghy kite but *not enough wind so we had to clamber over a Manchester fuselage*. Later they travel to Clifton to watch ditching films and then to Rampton where there is a pool in a mental home. Splashing about in a pool getting a dinghy inflated and climbing aboard seems a far cry from ditching at night in the North Atlantic's turbulent and icy waters, but better than nothing, I suppose.

As the course winds down each crew is intent on finishing the required flight hours but uncertain weather means there is quite a lot of waiting about. Time is filled in various ways. Michael tells us a tale about his attempts to reserve a place for lunch for him and the boys. "I rang up to book. The lady answering the phone said she couldn't book us so I said, 'This is Mr. Madigan speaking.' At once she said 'Wait' and coming back said it would be quite alright." The young Mike is clearly chuffed by the success of this approach. Much older Michael is more bemused than amused. "Now why on earth I said that or why it had any effect I have no idea. Nobody could possibly have heard of me or Madigans."

What a funny, bold fellow he is, and how he must have enjoyed that lunch. He has told us this story because Daddy is mentioned, but in this case it is because he doesn't come. He stays at home to write letters and deal with the swag of aerograms that have just arrived. *Alf, Bruce, Cliff and Mike,* he notes, *are out on a tear again tonight.* As Michael says, "He didn't say 'you drunken lot,' he just went his own wonderful way." And as for chasing women: "I can tell you he never went out with a woman. Absolutely never. He was as faithful as anyone could be."

Without knowing if we were prey to wishful thinking, we've always believed in his fidelity. When my playful sister-in-law, hearing that my father served overseas, wonders if we might have some unmet siblings in the UK, my hackles rise. I have always, somehow, known that he is, as Michael tells us, "a most honourable man." He sits in his hut writing his letters, sporadically filling in his diary and, if not sharing the drinking and womanizing of his mates, happy that they are having fun, never "censorious." Alone in the hut after an afternoon spent writing to Nooney, he is content. *The evening is soft, mild and overcast and the cries of the birds come clearly in through the open window. Hope tomorrow brings fine weather again.*

Comfort, for him, comes from these tastes of the country life he has left. *One night after night flying and supper over at Clifton we walked back to bed. It was lovely at that time of night with the dawn breaking and a cool breeze blowing. Made me think of the times I had landed home from Sydney at that time of the morning.* Home. It is always there, tugging.

With the gift of a stretch of fine weather, the course rushes to an end. In a jubilant diary entry Daddy writes that he has topped the course. *Very lucky I think.* ("Again!" cry his proud parent children.) And then, in the early morning, he sees a large formation of Lancs heading for France. The future creeps closer.

"Lancaster Finishing School," where they go next, has a debutante ring to it. In two weeks at Syerston, southwest of Lincoln, they move from flying the giant, slow, four-flammable-engined Stirling to that quintessential symbol of Bomber Command, the Lancaster. The men who flew in bombers grow to love their aircraft; whether flying Halifax, Manchester, Wellington, or Stirling, they loyally and passionately defend their plane. But all acknowledge that the Lancaster, with its giant bomb bays, its long range, its grace in the air, and its mighty Merlin engines, is nobility. The idea of a Lancaster Finishing School seems apt enough.

Daddy finds the base compact, tidy, and attractive. More Finishing School vibes. The billets are comfortable, if crowded: thirty men to a room. The ablutions facilities are splendid, making a nice change after the horror that was Wigsley. He is not so sanguine about the course. The lectures, he tells us, are tiresome and contradictory. He sums the whole thing up as being *duff*. After wading through definitions of this word that include some startling anatomical and sexual content, I find that he uses it in the sense of "worthless, poor quality, undesirable."

In the next entry he lists the names of friends who are missing in operations. How, we wonder, do young men in this war, or any war, cope with this constant loss? And it will get worse. They are about to enter a world where, every night, names of men who have shared their lives, are listed as missing or dead; a world where every night they go out knowing that their names may be destined for those lists.

This two-week course is covered in his diary in a single rapid-fire paragraph, again all clipped phrases and dashes. He sounds impatient to have it done. After all this training it is time to get into the real job. They are slated to be posted to Waddington, an Australian Squadron. This, for five members of the crew at least, is the best possible place to be. But poor Cliff comes down with tonsillitis. It is a week before he recovers and by then Waddington is no longer a choice for them; they are told they will be going to 207 Squadron in Spilsby. This is a bitter disappointment; it means saying goodbye to long-time friends. We imagine Michael pondering the role of illness in his Air Force career: first he gets the flu in Australia and is set on an entirely different journey than his mates, ending up in Edmonton. And now this thing with Cliff and his wonky tonsils. Random, but, I think, not unwelcome for him in the end. Canada is a great adventure, and he survives the war. Perhaps another path would not have been so lucky for him.

For Daddy and Dutchy, such firm mates, this parting of ways is particularly sad. Dutchy is off to Waddington. They will never see each other again.

A Name in a Book

A cameraman from *Central Western Daily*, our local paper, met me at the cenotaph in Robertson Park, a scruffy space with a reputation for shocking teenage trysts. In the resulting photo I am wearing my full school uniform — black wool tunic, black wool blazer, white shirt, black and gold tie-pin — and I am the farthest thing possible from a shocking teenager. My hair is cut short, my famous plaits having been recently hacked off, my fifteen-year-old attempt to dip my toe into a more adult world. It is after my sister has left home for university — had she been available for this moment it would have been she, the older sister, chosen instead.

I don't recall how it was arranged. Was I driven there? Did somebody collect me when it was done? I would have missed the school bus home. But somehow I got there. A small door in the cenotaph was opened, a large metal book retrieved, its pages turned. The photo clearly shows a hand hovering ready to snatch it back the moment the photo is snapped. I am staring at the page, eyes properly lowered, serious expression in place. They must have been delighted with the result. It appeared on the front page of the paper, timed to mark another November 11th. Reverential, tasteful, tugging at the heart strings: "Orphaned by World War II local girl holds back a tear as she reads her father's name in the honour roll..." or something like that. But what I remember most is that I was barely able to make out his name, that there was no time to linger. All they wanted was a photo for the front page.

***

"Curses upon this useless piece of excrement!" I snarl. "What cretin decided it was a suitable Instrument to guide two aging daughters about the English countryside in search of their father?"

We've just had a close call on a roundabout; we're feeling rattled and our patience has been sorely tried.

This time our rage is not so much directed at the wee Scot of the reedy voice and his misplaced certainty. He can only do so much, poor confused lamb. No such tolerance is extended to the hire car agency. It is consigned to the flames.

We are trying to find Leicester Cathedral. In Leicester, mind you. Some years hence they will finally discover the bones of Richard III languishing, for over six hundred years, in a forgotten grave under a parking lot. Perhaps this is a city adept at losing its history. But surely they cannot have mislaid a cathedral; it should be here somewhere. The town seems intent on keeping it from us. Not a signpost do we see. Hadrian's Wall had been at least acknowledged as being in the area; not true for this venerable, ancient and, I do need to add, world famous house of worship. It is getting late in the day. What if it is closed? Desperation dews our brows as we blunder about. We actually have a street name but even that isn't helping. Robbie pulls into a large used car lot in an industrial part of town.

"We need to ask someone," she says.

I agree. Men avoid asking directions. Even after they have metaphorically disappeared up their own bottoms, even when they know there is no way out, they carry on, too proud to pull over and seek guidance. We have no such problem. Besides, I need to pee. For a wonder, Robbie does not. I am in extremis. I can no longer think clearly and don't much care if we find the cathedral or if we don't. No bushes present themselves. I find myself envying Robbie's stinging nettle experience. All that I am offered is rows of cars. I suppose I could stagger into the used car office and throw myself on the mercy of a bunch sniggering Leicesterites; a lot full of used cars seems friendlier.

Out I hop and scurry in a few rows and hunker down behind a van. Relief gushes forth until, alas and fuck, I realize that asphalt is the opposite of porous. The generous stream I have produced is winding its way downhill, under the cars, heading for the spot where I can hear Robbie quizzing an employee.

"The cathedral," she says, speaking slowly as if to a dolt, "in Leicester. Leicester Cathedral. Can you tell us where it is?"

"Naw," he says. "Don't know it."

As I emerge adjusting my clothing and acutely aware of the small river snaking its way from beneath the cars and heading in the general direction of our parked vehicle, another gormless local saunters up, leans against the car and joins in the conversation.

"Didn't know we *had* a cathedral. Lived here all me life. News to me."

I nod at them, climb into the passenger seat and hiss at Robbie to skedaddle. Any minute now, these fellows will notice the incriminating stream and then, however astonishingly dense they may seem for never having heard of the greatest landmark of their city, they will look like pillars of the community compared to a woman who would sully their parking lot with a torrent of urine.

A church appears in the distance. We are still giggling about my perfidy and the opacity of the local lads. With a blessedly empty bladder, I am back in the game. Robbie pulls up beside the ancient churchyard, which sprouts a crop of rakish gravestones. This is, sadly, not our cathedral. It is St. Margaret's, but it *is* a church and there is a, hopefully more knowledgeable, group in the churchyard clustered around one of the headstones. I leave the car and approach them.

They are quintessentially English, possibly a rarity in this city that boasts the highest ethnic minority population in England. They are pale, almost colourless. The women wear sensible shoes for this graveyard excursion, shapeless skirts and wan, flowered blouses. The men are bearded, their trousers a faded grey. Everyone wears owl-like glasses and sloppy cardigans in various shades of beige, hands plunged into their sagging pockets. A donnish looking fellow lectures them on the significance of the lichen on the tilting monument around which they gather. I have fallen into another time. I clear my throat, apologize humbly for interrupting them and ask for the cathedral. There is no problem. In the refined tones I'd expected they twitter out directions and wish me luck before turning back to their contemplation of elderly moss.

Parking at the cathedral is a challenge but in we squeeze. Then we are inside. It was, we learn, once called St Martin's Cathedral but this does not seem to let our ignorant local lads off the hook. It smells of cold stone, antique dust, and wood polish. Tourists wander about peering at guidebooks and staring awestruck at its vast interior. We are more single-minded.

We've been pretty clear on our disappointment in the dearth of recognition for the sacrifices of these men we have come in search of. But, here, in the south aisle, under the standard of 207 Squadron, in a glass-topped case, is a roll of honour. Our father's name is in it.

We ask one of the attendants for help and are promptly assigned a guide. We've already noticed her. Hard not to. She is hectoring a group of cowed looking day-trippers on the arcane pleasures of this building. Her voice would shatter crystal; it reverberates around the cathedral, bouncing off the stone walls, swooping into the rafters, and sliding through the fretted screens. She is hard to miss, and suddenly she is ours.

In a bustle of self-importance, she guides us to the south aisle, trilling stentoriously. Now everyone in the cathedral knows our mission. Good. Some recognition at last. She has a key; she wears white gloves. Reverentially, she opens the case, carefully turns the pages back to November 11, 1944, traces her finger down the page, and stops at Arthur Leslie Plowman.

It is a lovely, solemn book containing the names of those who died in the service of 207 in both wars. It does not include prisoners of war or evaders. It honours this most final of sacrifices. Every morning the case is opened and the page turned to display and honour those who died on that date. Each name is traced in the elegant calligraphy of Mrs. Vivien Holmes. I imagine her: slender, pale, and serious, fingers ink-stained, crouched over the heavy book, carefully spelling out the names of the dead. I bet she wears a cardigan. I bet she knows about headstone lichen.

We look as long as we want. Unlike that awkward moment in Robertson Park when I was fifteen and too intimidated to insist that time be taken, this is our moment, and we may take as much time as we need.

By now quite fond of our silver-tongued docent, we thank her, wish her well and ask to be directed to a washroom (bathroom, ladies' room, W.C., lav, toilet ... pick your euphemism). Yes, AGAIN. We are directed to an inner sanctum, through heavy oak doors, down an echoing corridor, past intricately carved storage cupboards, and into a clean and ancient water closet. This time our iffy waterworks have book-ended the most wonderful adventure.

Battle

Courage does not always roar. Sometimes courage is the little voice at the end of the day that says, "I will try again tomorrow."

—*Mary Anne Radmacher*

With rain pouring down, Mike drives our father from Wigsley to the Spilsby Base in the car he and his mates have helped to fund. In the village of Spilsby they meet up with the rest of the boys who have travelled from their old camp by bus. A fair is in progress but it fails to lift their mood.

The conversation as they drive toward this base, that is not the longed for Waddington with its Australian squadron, is glum. Arriving, they are full of misgivings. *We hated the idea of Spilsby*, our father writes. They are still Colonials, owned by the RAF. But it is not long before the gloom lifts and Daddy's natural optimism asserts itself. He finds the accommodations not too bad, the food a happy surprise: *The Mess is top of the line. Looks like we haven't missed the bus after all.* The most pleasant surprise is that, now that they are no longer students, the level of respect has risen. *Everyone is very decent to us*, he says, apparently surprised by this cordial treatment. How, exactly, were they treated in training? Whatever ... they are now fully trained fighting men with all the gravitas that implies.

His only complaint is that *the kites have no Monica, only Fishpond, which to my way of thinking is a poor substitute*. Both Monica and Fishpond are a form of radar and, with the prospect of operations ahead, he wants the best. The longed for Monica is tail-mounted and points rearward scanning for fighters sneaking up behind. When one is detected, the device emits a series of beeps, audible to the crew, and a helpful warning to shoot back or take evasive action. This sounds like a godsend and certainly that's what Daddy believes, but we have an historical overview beyond his reach. From the early 1940s until mid 1944, when our father mourns its replacement, Monica is estimated by some to be responsible for more bomber losses than any other single device of the war. One problem is that, in a crowded Bomber Stream, enemy fighters can sneak up unnoticed, hiding among the beeps generated by other bombers. Worse, many night fighters are equipped to lock onto these warning beeps. Once they know exactly where the Allied bomber is ... BINGO. At first we sigh with relief — our father is safer in the arms of Fishpond — until we are told that it is equally dangerous. Is it too much to ask that the cushions fashioned for their comfort do not end up smothering them?

It is ten days before they go on their first operation. In the meantime there are practice runs and a couple of Bullseyes. These are night flights set up to simulate, as closely as possible, an Operational sortie. One of Britain's larger cities stands in for a German objective, a target at its centre. The crew in training carries out a bombing run over the dummy target, which, while lacking flak, serves up mock fighter attacks and the dreaded coning. Enemy searchlights probe the sky trying to lock onto a bomber as it approaches the target. Once one is successful, other searchlights clutch the aircraft, lighting it up, making it an easy target for the guns. Being "coned," impaled by light, is terrifying. The only way out is to fling the plane sideways into a desperate corkscrew trying to shake the talons of the cone loose. A pilot needs to do this well and, often with the aid of his engineer, must drag his aircraft out of the corkscrew, avoiding the melee of planes around him, and finding his way back into the stream. As they make their run over the target they take a photo to gauge their accuracy, just as they will for the real thing. Those thirty seconds of steady flight after the bombs are dropped are agony, flying straight and level, an easy mark for the guns below.

While they practise, actual operations are going on at the base and Arthur records, with unusual fidelity to detail, the casualties of each one. Calculating the odds, perhaps. He also ponders which aircraft they will be assigned. Rumour has it that they will get A-Able. This is good news as it is a new kite, but he says, resignedly, *time will tell.*

On July 26, 1944, twenty months since signing up, a week short of a year since he left Australia, and with a little over three months to live, our father, Arthur Leslie Plowman, sets off on his first operation. *The event for which we have been training for so long.* Robbie and I mine obsessively every word in his brief and irritatingly low-key description of this night. The briefing is at 18:15. They head for the kite to *run it up and lie about in the grass waiting until time to take off.* Michael adds the tiniest detail in his one mention of our father as they "run up" the kite. "Alf tested the intercom and oxygen while rotating turrets, Arthur obtained a frequency check from base, Bill dived and climbed etc." What efficient fellows, we think, what marvels they are.

When this is done, they wait for the time to take off, relaxing on the grass under the wings of their Lancaster, which will soon take them into danger. We see them there, this crew with whom we have become a little familiar, and quite fond, each dealing with his own mixture of pride, anticipation, fear, and bravado.

There is a slim quarter moon that night. They are detailed to bomb a small railway junction in Lyons, France where there is a large concentration of German soldiers. With allied boots on the ground, greater care is taken to avoid killing civilians or allies. They are, however, going out with the express aim to kill people: the enemy, but fellow travellers on this planet nonetheless. Of course this is a war and of course they know death will follow their actions but this momentous first time, how does that feel?

They leave on time, in the air at twelve minutes past midnight, and are doing well until they encounter a large concentration of cumulonimbus: *very difficult to get through*. Pushing their way into thick cloud, not sure they are on course, concerned about nearness of others in the stream and very aware that this is their first test, they plug on, arriving on time over the target: 0202. It will be twelve agonizing minutes before they are given the order to bomb. In any average day, twelve minutes zips by unnoticed, but every second when tooling around over a target increases the possibility of fighters arriving to pick them off. Luckily, they are left alone. *We bombed at our leisure*. Oh, I think, I don't like that expression.

Do I long for hand wringing and high tragedy? I know this man well enough now not to expect that; and Michael has been very clear that this is not a crew of hysterics. They are all business, which is the best chance of survival. "The crews I flew with," he tells us, "were disciplined. Some crews, especially Americans, they were chattering and talking all the time. We never did that. We only spoke when it was necessary."

Warming to his theme, he leans forward, his giant ears twitching slightly, his voice gaining strength. "Why people survived ... there were various reasons. One was luck of course. If some anti-aircraft gun happened to fire and hit you, that was luck. A fighter might strafe you, all sorts of things. But the main reason, the biggest reason, for surviving was crew and crew discipline. If you all did your jobs properly and stuck at it you had a far better chance of survival than not. We knew some people that ... you know, didn't take it seriously, and very often they wouldn't last long." He stops, afraid he has oversimplified; my father is, after all, dead. But then he gathers his ideas and finishes firmly: crew discipline is no ultimate guarantee of survival, "of course not. But crews that were useless never survived. Put it that way."

So, having navigated the thick and confusing cloud, they arrive on time, patiently wait until ordered to drop their bombs, send them down accurately and without haste or panic, turn for home. Mike, Daddy reports without comment, *got a little lost and we were still over*

France when daylight came. I had to identify coming over the coast as we were well behind ETA. We eventually made base with just enough petrol to land after ten hours and sixteen minutes in the air.

Exhausted, they debrief and stagger to bed. They are thankful that an expected raid the next night does not come off. All in all a very satisfactory blooding, especially since two experienced crews "boomerang," (return without getting to the target,) no doubt flummoxed by the cumulonimbus. Our lads are complimented; *good show for the first trip was the general verdict*. Arthur is feeling proud of his crew and, waiting in his hut, there is a parcel and two letters from Nooney ... euphoria.

Two nights later comes their second raid. It is reported so laconically that I almost pass over it but later I do a little research. The next day Robbie receives this email from me: *Have to tell you this — maybe you already noticed — but our father was a remarkably unflappable fellow. On the night of July 28/29 — his second op — he went to Stuttgart and declared it "more difficult" than the first. Light flak ... two fighter attacks but no shots fired on either side.* Not a piece of cake but no hysteria either. Then I read *Men of Air*: Losses of 7.9 percent. Combined with a Hamburg raid that night, 65 aircraft lost. The last big cock-up of the war. "Never again would so many bombers be lost in one night or day." The complacent fools at High Wycombe sent a huge bomber stream out with a brilliant half moon glinting on their wings, silhouetting them against the night sky, making them easy targets. And, for the third night in a row that Stuttgart was the objective they followed the identical route. When the men saw this they were stunned. The Germans were ready for them. The Bomber Stream was infiltrated as they crossed the coast and they were picked off at will. Same thing on the way back. It was historic and quite dreadful. But for our placid fellow just "more difficult."

I begin to regard my father's descriptions with deep suspicion. The day after this night of unremarked horror they go on a daylight raid southwest of Caen. Their job is to clear the way for Allied troops retaking France. The target is, again, massed German troops. There is, he says, *a tremendous concentration of Lancs — rather thrilling. Then, three minutes from zero hour we got "abandon mission" — we were all very disappointed and it did seem a Hell of a waste.* But the night's excitement is not over. As they head back the starboard inner engine fails. They feather and carry on. Then, just over the English coast he receives a message that they are to divert. A discussion follows: they are in trouble, have only three engines and a full bomb load, so they opt to return to base. There is evident pride in the successful landing. *Bang on*, he cries, exhibiting some welcome enthusiasm to his passion-starved daughters.

Landing a Lancaster, we are told, is a tricky thing. It requires skill and nerve. Arthur admires his skipper; more than once he comments on how well he handles the plane. For a crew to function well, every member of a crew must inspire confidence, but the one who gets you into the air, knows how to dodge and turn, and sets you down, is the core of the team. They are the leaders. Over and over we hear of pilots staying at the controls of a burning plane, flying straight and level so their men can bail out safely and many times dying as the plane explodes or disintegrates. Bill is a good pilot and a solid leader. Our father does not lie awake worrying if his skipper is up to the job.

In between raids there are nights of freedom. One evening the crew sets out for Boston, a quaint coastal village well supplied with pubs. Bruce has acquired a motorbike, nicknamed "the outfit," Mike has his car. Alf, Cliff, and Stan bundle into the car while our intrepid Dad climbs on behind Bruce. Bill does not come. Possibly he has other fish to fry. There is no comment on this. They live and let live. Living, now, being the foremost aim in their young lives.

There is a second daylight raid two nights later, this time to La Bretagne, targeting a Flying Bomb site. There must be great satisfaction in this. Our father, on a brief London leave, has seen the damage they're doing, these terrifying doodlebugs: miniature unmanned airplanes, launched in their thousands from Pas de Calais, across the Channel. Londoners come to know their sound: an airborne lorry. While you can hear it you are safe; when it goes quiet is the time to worry for, at that moment, the flying bomb has run out of fuel and is ready to crash and explode. By October 1944, Bomber Command has successfully ended this reign of terror.

This first bombsite raid is summed up as *serving up fighters and a small amount of flak*. The second one, two days later, has no details, just the destination: a Flying Bomb site in St. Maxime. No drama, no detail. About as heart stopping as a laundry list.

We have, at times, wondered what it would have been like to grow up with a father. Art, (there are far too many Arthurs in this story) our stepfather, never really got the hang of being a dad. Once, in a foolish attempt to force him into this role, I backed him into a corner asking permission to go to a school dance. He wanted no such responsibility, turned as pale as lard and sputtered, "Ask your mother." But what would Daddy have been like? Would we have sat adoringly at his feet like some Victorian lithograph, or would we have argued, butted heads, found fault? I might have regarded his fondness for understatement somewhat annoying.

I am feeling that exasperation now. For, having met Michael, I know that Daddy's curt cataloguing cries for a more detailed telling. So here, from Mike's rich diary, is a less phlegmatic look at their fifth operation over St. Maxime:

Went as a group today with leader and shepherd. There was about three tenths cumulous over France. But looking out I could see many areas covered with bomb craters. As we approached the target the shepherd collected us in a group. In the rural area the predicted flak was bloody accurate, bursting all around us. We could see all the boys windowing like mad and Lime was chucking it out on time. Our target was as dangerous as Hell being staggered at all heights from about 15 to 18,000 feet. I looked up and saw three Lancs above, they were at 17,000 feet, with bomb doors open, bombs ready to go, I warned Bill and he moved over. Just then Bruce reported a Lanc having been hit by

*a bomb behind us and the starboard outer engine, caught fire, fell out
and the thing went straight in, a mangled wreck. Alf reported seeing
another going in, hit by flak. Coming out of the target which was raided
by the boys yesterday, I could see bursts covering the area. We had some
72 hour delays on board.*

*One kite was spewing petrol from the wing while N Nan had one
engine feathered and another cutting, only able to do 155 mph. The
shepherd ordered us to slow to 155 to keep with him. A Lightning and
some Spitties kept watch. When we landed we found that our starboard
bomb door and fuselage had been holed by flak.*

Well, that's more like it: action, detail, damage. We are now very
familiar with the jargon. For example "Window" is to dump out
bundles of aluminum strips to confuse the radar. Young Cliff is
heaving it out with a will. Good old Lime. We understand the
nightmare of one plane above, let alone three, with those great bomb
doors running the length of the plane, the bays stuffed with death,
open, ready to drop their load on the plane below. The 72-hour
delays, new to us, Michael clears up. They are, he reports cheerfully,
"bombs that had a 72-hour delay. The Germans would be clearing up
and bang, we'd blow them all up." The Shepherd with its gentle
Biblical whiff, directed operations. Our seven precious fellows stay
with a crippled aircraft on his orders, Spitfires buzzing protectively
around them.

Back at base, they spend a few minutes poking their fingers into
the holes made by the flak. Perhaps the hole in the bomb doors causes
a quiet moment. When they go in for their bomb run, doors open,
listening to Cliff's "Right, right, left, steady, steady," waiting
breathlessly for the blessed "bombs gone" they know that their belly
full of explosives, now naked and unprotected from the spewing flak,
needs only the tiniest spark to turn their plane into a fiery ball of
death. But the flak hit when the doors were closed. No harm done.
The ground crew will get to work and patch it up. They thank their
lucky stars, debrief and enjoy the post Ops breakfast. Then, Michael

tells us: "Arthur and I had a quiet game of snooker and billiards, had a shower and went to bed."

There are many accounts of young men, back from a dodgy Op, shaking so badly they decide not to have a cigarette, as they cannot hold the match steady. For some it becomes a permanent state: "the twitch" it is called. But our two cucumbers opt for snooker and billiards, surely requiring a steady hand. Then, more news from Michael. The next night he, with Bruce, Alf, Cliff, and Arthur, trot off to the pictures — Lana Turner and Robert Young in *Slightly Dangerous*, an apt title given what they were up to the night before.

And so it goes. There are more Ops on August 5, 6, 7, 10, 12, and 13. *A long stooge*, Arthur says, *boys done in*. Not "I'm done in," but his boys, barely out of their teens. They are moving toward a well-earned leave. But before this they endure six raids in nine days. These raids are recorded in sparse detail. He admits to neglecting the diary — hardly surprising given the pace. However, Michael does not slack off. He writes eloquently and at length and he fills in some gaps.

Bois Casson, on August 6, is, to placid Arthur Leslie, fairly *uneventful*. They drop a 13,000-pound bomb load on ammo dumps at this site near Paris. Ho-hum. They land at 1400 hours, Michael tells us. Somehow the daylight raids that bring them home at two o'clock on a sunny afternoon are harder to imagine. On examining the plane they find a dent in the spinner and another under the starboard wing. So flak is involved and damage, slight but real, is done. The spinner, by the way, is the cone in front of the propellers. A little too close to the engine for our taste.

The next day, damage neatly patched, one hopes, they set off for a battle area near Caen to provide support for ground troops. This is a night raid with artillery fire. That much is revealed. On the way back they are diverted to Moreton-in-Marsh, not far from Oxford, and it all sounds a bit of a lark and a holiday. After a mix up over the drome they eventually get down. We know enough now to be sure that this economical summary hides something dramatic and possibly perilous. Once on the ground, they are fixed up with good billets. Stan, Alf, and our niggardly diarist bunk down in a hut away from the rest of the crew and distinguish themselves by sleeping in. Bill has mandated that they be airborne by nine a.m.; they aren't conscious until ten. Michael records that they don't roll in until eleven-thirty. Bill, our father notes, is *hostile*. Michael has written of this too, but he describes Bill as having "a set of pups as he always does when we are late." Poor Bill, a mature thirty-two-year-old lumbered with these fellows. My father might have been twenty-seven, and should have been more responsible, but we already know his love of sleep and his ability to do it with purpose.

Leave is granted, revoked, granted again, and then in jeopardy because, we learn from Michael, the army has got itself into a mess near Caen and the RAF is required to bail them out. This description comes from the Wing Co and there is more than a hint of rivalry between the forces. Drunken airmen are hooked out of bars and pried from amorous arms to be sent off in no condition to fly, let alone to drop bombs very accurately. Stan, a wise fellow, refuses to report and goes to bed. Bill announces that he is too drunk to go. Not one crew is complete. Men roll in, half tight, greeting the Group Commander with a cheeky, "Howdy boy." He is not amused. Michael cobbles together a crew that includes our father and Alf. Cliff is briefly considered but dropped after he is quizzed on how much he has consumed. The Squadron Leader is laughing all through the briefing as this debacle unfolds. In the end the Operation is scrubbed.

I believe that, in spite of tension, exhaustion, fear, and danger, this time since they became a crew has been the happiest of their Air Force lives. They are finally trained, they trust and admire each other, and they have done well: eleven raids in nineteen days.

Next day, leave reinstated, they go, turning their backs on the RAF Spilsby, free for two glorious weeks to wander among the meres and fells of Cumbria's Lake District.

The War Far Away

When Robbie and I set out for the Lake District to investigate this leave, we are brimming with optimism but our GPS has other ideas. Round and round he takes us, in and out of the same village whose charms are rapidly evaporating, steadfastly refusing to set us on a sensible road to Ambleside. Finally, we are directed off the main road onto what looks like a cattle track pointing across barren and rocky land toward the Pennines. We give in. "How bad can this be? At least it is in the right direction." And in the end, this detour proves to be the very definition of serendipity.

Standing stone circles pose a puzzle so far unsolved. Sometimes they are associated with burial sites but this is rare. They were not lived in, not even lived near, but somebody built them, not just one or two, not just a dozen, but hundreds scattered across the British Isles. They don't tell the weather, or the date, or the movement of the planets. They just are their enigmatic selves and, to our astonishment, we have found one. From our forced turn-off onto the cow path we have bustled our way down into a valley before labouring up the next rise. At the top of this hill, where the road makes a sharp turn into the next valley, is an unmistakable stone circle. It has no signage; nobody is selling tickets or tempting us with Devonshire teas. All that has passed it by; we don't. Some mysteries cannot be solved. Sometimes it is just enough to marvel without knowing everything. Walking among these primeval blocks, feeling they are ours because we discovered them so unexpectedly, is a bequest from our incompetent Fred. We are inclined to forgive him his trespasses.

Back in the car our road slides down the hill by a line of ancient gnarled trees. Just who would have planted them there, in an otherwise treeless world is another mystery. Stone walls slice across the landscape; grazing sheep dot the bare fields. Once we are trapped in a flock being moved along the road by a farmer with a stick. We are far from the motorways and roundabouts, travelling in a timeless land.

There was a copy of *The Decameron* on the shelf in the lounge room of our childhood home. As we drive on toward the Pennines I ask Robbie if she knows where it is now.

"No, it wasn't around when I cleaned out the house, not that I remember. That must have been the one he read in Whitley Bay. I wonder what happened to it."

"Maybe Mummy destroyed it along with the letters. It was pretty racy."

"Did you read it when you were little?"

"Yes, at least I tried. I knew it was a bit naughty but most of it went well over my head."

I recall clearly what it looked like and where it sat: on the mantel in the seldom-used lounge room. Given that the house was of modest size, having a pleasant, comfortable room that mostly remained empty, used only for special guests, seems foolish. But that was the way with all the farm houses of our childhood. This room contained our few treasures: a vase featuring the Pied Piper and an avalanche of fleeing rats, a Pickwick plate, a painting of a geranium in yellow pot, and four or so special books: two volumes of the *Pickwick Papers*, leather-bound *A Tale of Two Cities*, and *The Decameron*. There may have been others but these I remember. It is telling that the one I chose to poke around in was *The Decameron*. Somehow I knew it might relate to sex, a bucket of mystery to me; any enlightenment would have been welcome.

The list of belongings sent home after the war included "six books." The titles are not given. We know the Dickens arrived much earlier, but what were the others? Surely one was *The Decameron*? What can the fellows, packing up our father's things in the early morning of the night he died, have made of his choice of reading matter? We find it intriguing that he would have, on a visit to London, chosen Giovanni Boccaccio's frisky take on his fourteenth century world. His comment: *Sure is revealing* gives us a chuckle. Months after we return from this trip I check a copy out of the library to refresh my memory and it *is* revealing. The priests and nuns frolic in unseemly ways while maintaining a hypocritically pious façade; the aristocracy is no better.

As kids, in the La Doré world of the 1950s, we were told fantastic stories about the wicked Catholics. They sinned like crazy all week, went to confession on Sunday, wiped the slate and got stuck into it all over again on Monday. We believed there was a tunnel from the convent to the priest's residence; why do you think nuns wore those flowing garments if not to cover up the results of clandestine visits? And so on. Titillating as this was, I had trouble believing it. After insisting I be taken to church, I became disenchanted. Sunday after Sunday the dried up prune of a Presbyterian minister railed against the Catholics. This wasn't what I was seeking. By the time I arrived at university I was a firm atheist. We don't know what Daddy believed. We know that Mummy turned her back firmly on any kind of religion after his death, though I don't know how much stock she put in it even before she lost him. As we drive toward Ambleside, we assemble what evidence we have of his attitude to things other-worldly.

"One of the aunts told me," says Robbie, "that he was very cross with a girl who worked at the house when she went on about the portents of her dreams. He had no patience for such stuff."

"Right. And think about some of the postcards ... not much reverence there." In the stack we have, sent home to record his travels, only two showing churches have comments on their backs. One from Somersby says, *Just another church. The place reeks with them. This one is very old — AND looks it.* And one in Spilsby: *Typical old church — don't ask me what it looks like from the inside.* An in-joke for Mummy; of course he wouldn't bother *entering* a house of worship.

That and his frequent mention of deliberately ducked church parades tell us he does not hold religion dear. How is this viewed by his Presbyterian family? They are church-goers and the Catholic-despising Reverend Torrance is frequently at their house for Sunday afternoons, sitting on the wide verandah speaking in Gaelic to our otherwise silent grandmother.

I wonder what Daddy would have made of my marriage to a Catholic. In the town of my youth each group keeps to itself, the Catholic and public schools corral the kids in their solitudes. Some of the hissings and whisperings that I overhear while admiring the La Doré wedding photos have to do with gleeful outrage when a "mixed" marriage has occurred. Social mingling is rare and frowned upon. Our mother, we notice, has not embraced this particularly; one of her best friends is Catholic and another converts in later life. Mummy sees this as no impediment to their friendship. Still, I feel I have to mention Tony's faith when I call home to tell her I am engaged. "I don't care if he is a Sikh, a Muslim, or whatever, as long as you are happy," she says. I believe she and my father shared this sane tolerance.

So I hope the reading of *The Decameron* is revealing of the ways of unbridled sex rather than any kind of confirmation of the anti-Catholic rumours rife in our little country town. In this dangerous, and ultimately fatal, adventure our father has embarked on he is far from that town and free to explore new worlds. He has met men from all classes and religions. Those differences are never remarked upon. Once he has harsh words for *an unpleasant dwarf*. We cringe a little; Australia, our home and native land, is not a hill of tolerance, even less so in the 1940s. This is, after all, the country that invented dwarf-tossing as a sport so it would be hardly surprising if he had a blind spot or two. Then we discover that this particular vertically challenged chap is labelled "unpleasant" because he struts into the Mess where a card game is in progress and proceeds to be loudly critical of Ern Baldwin's playing. He offers *to take Ern on, teach him a lesson*. When he is later bested by Ern, and creeps out, humiliated,

Daddy is jubilant, not because the man is a dwarf, but because he is high-handed to one of our father's best mates.

We have graduated from the dirt track to a narrow paved road, A592. For most of its length stone walls hug it closely. Every so often we glimpse fast flowing streams next to our road. Meeting a lorry or a camper van coming the other way is momentarily heart stopping. Kirkstone Pass takes us from Patterdale, to Ambleside, winding its way through the high fells of the Cumbrian Mountains, rising steeply on either side, bare, apart from sure-footed black-faced sheep, and a scattering of scree. It is breathtaking in its stark wildness.

Daddy and his fellow travellers drove along here. Among the postcards he sends home is one of the Pass still looking very much as it does today; it was then a dirt track, but the steep slopes and the stone walls on either side look exactly the same. At the end of the pass Brothers Water gleams. The photo was taken on a bright summer's day: the stone walls cast sharp shadows on the road, the grass on the bare hills is green, the sky a pale blue. How often does it actually look like this? On the back of the postcard he writes: *Very typical countryside around the Lake District. It was not always so highly coloured as this while I was there, rain and mist playing a big part in the scenery.*

***

In preparation for their trip Mike goes to the adjutant for a fuel allowance for the communal car. Bruce rides "the outfit." Stan, Alf and Arthur take turns: car, sidecar, pillion. Cliff has scooted off to his family in Nottingham. Bill is away on his own adventures. Their first night is in Harrogate where Stan lives and he arranges accommodation in his small semi-detached and at a neighbour's down the street. The next morning, Mike, Alf and Arthur climb into Mike's car and wave their friends goodbye.

This much anticipated leave, for Daddy, tops all that have gone before. His first, just after arriving in England, was a cringe-making disaster over which he prefers *to draw a veil*. His curious daughters work to pull this veil aside. We uncover four awkward days, before he manages to flee. His hoped-for country posting finds him trapped in the village of Hathersage, with a landlady he nicknames the Dragon, who, in spite of Daddy's marital state, is single-minded in her mission to score an air force fellow for her spinster daughter, "Little Audry." Daddy contacts his mates seeking escape from this minefield; they send a creative telegram calling him back to base for a fictitious emergency. He leaves as graciously as he can, given that they have generously taken him in. As part of a Government organized scheme to provide holidays for men in uniform, the Dragon and her daughter house holidaying servicemen for no remuneration other than their increased ration cards. They may be deluded, but they are big-hearted. Released and relieved, Daddy flees to London to meet up with friends whose leaves have been stellar and who have a good chuckle over his.

Daddy spends more ink on his disastrous Hathersage leave than he does on the highly satisfactory two weeks in the Lake District. Clearly he is having too much fun for detailed diary writing, summing it up in a scant half page. But it is a rich half page; our three days in the Lake District will be barely enough for us to follow his footsteps.

Lake Windermere is famously known as Britain's largest lake. Robbie gasps at its length and breadth, her admiration fuelled by memories of her water-starved country. I — living next to Lake Ontario, a body of water so large from one side the other is not visible, and it is one of the smallest of the five Great Lakes — am less impressed. I educate my dear sister: "It is an astonishing fact that Great Britain would fit snugly into the area taken up by all of the Great Lakes combined. In fact, you could pop Lake Windermere into a corner and still have a bit left over. I looked it up."

As our three airmen do, we drive through Windermere, along the edge of this large-but-small body of shimmering, misty water and come into Ambleside where we will stay. They pass through the town on the way to Grasmere, a spit up the road but much more of a tourist trap now than in 1944, and way more expensive. The fact that he mentions Ambleside is enough to justify our stay and the more modest fee doesn't hurt. Broadview, our B&B, one of a cluster of stern slate row houses, fronts the sidewalk of a narrow, busy road. Our dad and his mates, we are sure, drove by this very house and their very eyes took it in.

Robbie sidles the front wheel up onto pavement and waits nervously in the car, being rocked by traffic passing a whisker away, while I spring out to check us in and arrange parking. Once that's sorted, we are ushered into a room not much larger than a closet and furnished in an extraordinarily cluttered fashion. We have two single beds, foot to foot along one wall, a miniature chair stuffed in a corner, and a giant heavily carved, mirrored wardrobe that takes up half the room. We fear opening it and being sucked into Narnia. On top of this clunky object sits a foolish little T.V. viewable only by standing on the chair. A frightening collection of pillows and stuffed animals clutters the beds. "Humph," we say, inspecting this odd arrangement, home to us for the next three nights.

"It isn't even clean," Robbie announces in high dudgeon. "They need a dusting lesson."

We unpack a little, set out our toiletries, take off our shoes, make a cup of tea, put our feet up and relax. Biscuits have been furnished. We are here in one piece. It's not so bad.

Slate is an interesting building material and here it dominates. Broadview, like its neighbours, is made up of layered thin slabs. I find them forbidding and prickly looking, sullen grey even in sunlight, slickly black and sinister in the rain. There is no doubt that there is charm in these houses but, for me at least, it is muted. We wander up into the town for pizza in a little café that gives us a view of the village and its guardian mountain, whose steep sides rise up behind the houses. A sudden squall swoops in, bending the trees and splashing roads and building. We have been warned of these. It is over quickly and we walk home through drenched streets for an evening in our cluttered room going over the diary and our father's many postcards.

From his leave we have quite a stack collected by him to give his far away Nooney a taste of his adventures. She embraced his travels vicariously, looking up locations in the atlas, finding library books to give her background. None of these postcards is addressed or stamped, they are sent as a bunch in an envelope.

"I've never seen these." Robbie holds out two postcards that I have produced from my stash. "They are wonderful. Where did you get them?"

"I think they came in a collection of photos Mummy sent me a long time ago. I didn't realize you hadn't seen them. They were taken at Crag House in Grasmere. Don't they look happy!"

These are not commercial postcards but photos that have been printed up to be used as such. Each shows a group of people relaxing on the grass under overhanging trees. They are sunlit and idyllic and yes, everyone looks happy. On the back of the first Daddy has written: *Under the trees by the swimming pool at Grasmere. Left to right: A German wench staying with Mr. and Mrs. Smart, yours truly, Mike (standing), Alf (sitting), John (suitor of the German wench), Mrs. Smart and Kriss the faithful 'ound.* Of course we search for Daddy first. He is standing next to Mike, both of them looking toward John. Something funny has been said; they are laughing. The German wench appears unamused. Her presence is a puzzle among these fellows involved in bombing her country but there is no further explanation. After his description of the who's who of the photo he adds: *More evidence my pet of the gay life we aircrew lead.*

A little tongue in cheek. They have just come off a harrowing period of Operations. She knows what he has been through. She will be pleased to see him happy but also understands what lies ahead. And somewhere in that comment is also a nod to the fact that he is on vacation while she holds the orchard together and raises their children.

The other postcard is our favourite as we so rarely see candid shots of him. The three friends are chatting under the tree. Alf, the rear gunner, lies on the grass propped up on one elbow, smiling at his two fellow crewmembers. Daddy, in the middle, is hunkered down by the trunk of the tree, chuckling at something Alf is saying. Mike is leaning against the tree, hand on his knee, looking down, a grin on his face. They seem so comfortable together. We could drown in our father's smile; it is so relaxed and carefree. We know what is coming but we revel in this little oasis of happiness.

Their dress interests me. Alf wears a casual light jacket, but also a tie, Mike has a natty leather jacket and, unlike his mates, is tieless, Daddy is in his dress blues. His two friends, young and fancy free, cultivate a more varied wardrobe; there are women to impress. Daddy has no such need and, being a family man, has to watch his pennies. In the list of possessions left behind after his death there is no sign of any extra clothing for holidays or going out on the town. It is the most austere of wardrobes. He is well supplied with socks and has an extra pullover (and two Cranwell fronts, whatever they might be) but that's it.

On the reverse of this photo he has written: *The swimming pool is just behind us, obscured by the rocks and trees — brr but it was cold Nooney (We did go in too by gosh!).* Wearing their swimming trunks and carrying their clothes they climb the moraine hill behind Crag House where they are staying, and up the River Rothay to a waterfall beneath which lies a deep pool. It is icy and they do not stay in long, these Australians, not used to leaping into freezing water. I see them, laughing, egging each other on. Mr. Smart, their host, goes in first, showing the Colonials the way. Cold or not, it is now a matter of pride. In they go eyes plastered open with shock, breath sucked back into startled chests. Honour satisfied they hop out and dry off. And, there they are, hair combed, neatly dressed, enjoying the late August sunshine and having the moment captured by Mr. Smart.

The next morning as we stand at the gate of Crag House, we do not know all of this delightful detail; it is later supplied by Michael.

We know for sure this is where they stayed and we know there is a "pool" but we do not know what kind or where it is. Just the fact that Crag House, at the edge of the little village of Grasmere, still exists is golden to us.

Robbie had contacted the current owners, telling them our story and receiving a gracious reply. It is no longer a Guest House although it is possible to rent out a self-contained holiday apartment but, intrigued by our mission, they offer us a day or two as their guests. We are giddy at this chance until we realize that our dates will not work: they have a holiday planned for the time we are in the Lake District. Too bad. We must be happy to just look.

We have parked the car in a field up a lane beside the house, quite illegally we quickly realize, but we won't be long. I push gently at the gate at the bottom of a driveway leading through a glorious spring garden. Rhododendrons are in riotous bloom in a variety of colours from red to orange to apricot and everything in between. I long to give these perfect blooms a surreptitious pinch to make sure they are real. Yellow laburnums pour over the walls scattering saffron petals on the ground. I think of my winter barren garden in Canada and wince. "Oh to be in England now that April's here…" Well, May … but close enough.

"Ooo, I don't think we should go in," Robbie squeaks. "They aren't there you know."

"Oh come on! Between us we have travelled about 20,000 miles to be here. We have been reading and researching for months. He was here for Heaven's sake. It's one of the few places we can be sure about. We are going through this gate!"

We wander up the inclined drive to the house, wondering if the garden was as full of flowers when he was here in late August, a summer garden, roses perhaps. Built in 1855, we can see the stone inscription at the peak of the central gable, it is a gentleman's house. When it was built Wordsworth would have been around, worshipping the Lake District and fretting about the abomination of railway access to his shrine. It never happened. To this day, the only way to get into this area is by road.

Crag House, named for the barren hill that rises up behind it, is beautifully preserved. Built of soft grey stone and dripping with vines, it sits on a rise above the garden. Chimney pots sprout from the roof. There is a sturdy stone retaining wall and an open space for parking in front of the house. To one side is a little kitchen garden. We see some splendid lettuce and a Beatrix Potter, Mr. McGregor-style rabbit trap. White mullioned windows gleam. We peer in at the ground floor: a comfortable living room. Robbie is squirming with guilt at this trespassing although she is boldness itself in most situations. A glassed in vestibule bars us from peeping into the front hall.

At the side of the house there is another steep rise with a little path and steps leading up. Perhaps the pool Daddy mentions is up there? We find a flat area with a picnic table but no sign of swimming possibilities past or present. As we turn to go back down we look across at the house. We are at the level of the upstairs window, and a rather surprised face is peering out at us. Caught! Waving sheepishly, we indicate that we are coming back down.

The woman who meets us by the side of the house is not upset, just concerned for our welfare. "I thought you were lost." Out pours our story. She isn't the owner, who is a local and very successful artist and, indeed, away. But Vicky, and David (who pops out to see what is going on) the artist's friends, have rented the holiday apartment. "You must come in and have a cup of tea and tell us your story." And, boldness rewarded, we are in the building in which our father stayed.

The kitchen is a perfect — stone floor, Aga stove, scrubbed wooden table. We ask about the pool and David phones the owners who cannot help but are pleased we have made it. David is a commercial pilot and a fund of knowledge about the RAF. He tells us of a recent BBC documentary on the women pilots who flew for Ferry Command during the War. They had a little booklet with instructions for each plane. No matter what they were asked to fly, Wimpy, Halifax, Lancaster, Fairey Battle, Manchester, Spitfire ... there was no hesitation; they hopped aboard, consulted the handbook and away they went. Robbie is impressed and a little chagrined. "Just imagine them being able to do that and here am I stalling our hire car on every hill."

When Robbie trots off to the bathroom, Vicky leans across to me and says, "Your sister is lovely. She is so engaging and has the most wonderful face and smile." I agree, she is lovely, her face a map of a life fully embraced.

Vicky and David invite us to leave our car in front of the house, as parking in the town is impossible. We do, carefully closing the gate behind us, the gate we nearly did not go through.

Grasmere is a tourist's delight, its town centre tastefully preserved even as it houses shops selling postcards and Taiwanese souvenirs. Many of its old buildings would have been in place when Daddy, Mike, and Alf were here, when it was just a sleepy little village. One of his postcards, a view across the lake to Grasmere, with a tiny arrow indicating where they stayed, shows only a modest scattering of buildings: little to tempt three aircrew intent on a jolly night out. Their evenings are spent in Rothay, near Ambleside, with its offering of convivial pubs. Another postcard is a picture of Wordsworth's cottage. Perhaps we should visit it, but the inscription on the back makes us wonder if he bothered to go inside. He claims it is *not very inspiring to a lowbrow like myself* but then adds that its main interest for him lies in the fact that Sir Walter Scott used to come here to visit Wordsworth.

And now we remember that our parents loved not only Charles Dickens but also Sir Walter Scott. Good grief. My sister and I both read obsessively but Sir Walter, to us, is like munching sawdust. Yet here are our mother and father, two orchardists, soaking up not only Dickens but also the formidable Scott. Perhaps poetry is the sticking point, Wordsworth too daunting for our "lowbrow." Our father is, for this journey, the final arbiter of taste and he has given us a good enough reason to give Wordsworth's cottage a miss. We are free to find a relatively non-touristy café where we devour a couple of excellent meat pies.

Before we leave Grasmere it seems only right that we visit the gallery devoted to the work of the artist who now lives in Crag House. Even though we have not met her, we feel fond; after all she was willing to have us stay. Many of her prints are on display, pretty scenes and studies of local buildings. I turn to see what else this gallery has to offer and the breath is knocked out of me. There, in a little alcove, is the most wonderful picture of a Lancaster surrounded by cloud, backlit and gilded by the setting sun, heading east, crossing the coast, on its way to the enemy. I am in love. "You should buy it, definitely," Robbie says. "Fancy its being here; it seems meant to be." I part with a large sum of money, watch as it is rolled and placed in a protective tube, and we dance back to Crag House to collect the car.

***

Like spokes in a wheel the many long narrow bodies of water that give the Lake District its name fan out from the Cambrian mountains, swelling the rivers that flow down to nestle in the valleys. They may not be large by my new world standards, but they are exquisite. Daddy's favourite is Derwentwater. He tells his Nooney so on the back of a romantic postcard showing trees reflected in the tranquil waters, swans idling by the bank.

Our drive there unrolls more stunning scenery. We slip into Keswick, an old market town perched just north of Derwentwater. It is as picturesque as Grasmere but more real, less for show. Our three travellers pass through here; no details provided. We park and head for the edge of the lake through a light drizzle. There is a pebbly beach amply supplied with friendly ducks. The pewter and silver lake stretches away into the mist. It is easy to understand our father's fondness for it.

Further along the lake edge we spot old but carefully preserved wooden boats for hire. They line the little pier and some are pulled up on the pebbly strand. One of Daddy's postcards pictures a lake with wooden boats just like these. On the back Daddy declares that this is where they hired a boat to go fishing. Must be the place, we decide. Robbie tramps off across the crunchy beach, orange hat firmly clamped on her head and orange scarf flying, intent on getting the provenance of these vessels. She returns pumped with elation. "They definitely go back to the early forties, to the War." Trying not to let actual facts get in the way, we dash from boat to boat wondering if this is the one our trio occupied. If we knew that, if we could touch it! Oh, if only.

People flock to the Lake District for many reasons: the scenery of course, the timeless villages, hotels offering spas and gourmet food, the chance to troll tourist shops full of knick-knacks, but they also come to experience the great outdoors. Fishing, hiking, and climbing draw them now, as they did when Daddy and his mates were here. Robbie and I have no longing to tackle the high fells but our trio of airmen did and today's tasks include finding the mountain they scaled and standing at its base to marvel.

Helvellyn is the third highest fell in the Lake District, reached by a narrow path that winds up to, and across, a sharply pointed and steeply sloping ridge: the Striding Edge. This is what they choose to climb. You may be sure they were not supplied with the now *de rigueur* hiking boots, or backpacks stuffed with energy bars and Gatorade. They set off with what they have — Daddy in his RAF uniform — maybe a sandwich in wax paper stuffed in a pocket, or a biscuit or two. It is just a lark. His postcard, black and white and looking grim, shows a stark and perilous track. On the back he writes: *We climbed this, my pet — weren't we daring.* Then, in a pang of conscience, thinking of her at home, possibly wondering: "Isn't it enough that you go out to drop bombs while being peppered by flak, coned by searchlights, and shot at by German fighters? Do you need to go cavorting along mountain edges?" he adds to his note: *However it's not nearly as dangerous as it looks.*

Another postcard shows a monument at the summit that would certainly remind climbers of possible perils: Gough's monument. Gough, the inscription tells our intrepid trio, was an artist who went walking, fell off a cliff and his faithful dog stayed with his lifeless body for three months, keeping interested foxes and crows at bay so that, when it was discovered, the body was in one piece. Robbie fills me in on this scrap of history, remarking tartly that perhaps the dog should have had its name on the monument, not the perished Gough. Then she adds, "But perhaps not. He could have gone for help rather than just sitting there." Always two sides to such heroic moments.

Robbie believes that we passed a sign to Helvellyn the day before so we go in search of it driving along Thirlmeer, stopping to gaze at its inky surface. The sign eludes us and as we scan the steep fells on the other side of the lake, it is impossible to decide which is Helvellyn. At the foot of one of the higher peaks we spy a roadside pub, lucky because we are both in desperate need of a loo.

"We should go into the bar and ask which is Helvellyn."

"Yes. Maybe we should buy something. We did use the bathroom."

The fellow behind the counter is from Eastern Europe — nobody is local anymore, it seems. But he does know where Helvellyn is: right behind the pub. That solved, we order a pot of tea. Two chaps having a beer at one of the tables hear us asking after the mountain and soon we are sitting together chatting. They would be a little younger than we are, but not by much, and they are brothers. This strikes us as propitious symmetry. Even better, they are having a pint to celebrate having just climbed Helvellyn. More symmetry!

We tell them why we are interested. They are smart enough not to recommend we don hiking boots, get some rappelling gear and stride off. But they confirm something of interest. In the time that Daddy, Alf, and Mike did their climb they could not have started it from this side of the mountain. They would have gone up the Struggle to Patterdale. We have already passed that way so today we will not be walking in their footsteps but we can go to the beginning of the ascent on this side.

Our two friends at the pub tell us where the walk to the pass begins. We are to look out for Wythburn Church. A little way down the road, there it is hunkered down on the hillside, seeming to grow out of the earth. One of the windows set in the curved stone apse is so low that grass brushes the sill. The rest of the building, made of thick whitewashed stone, also hugs the ground. Unlike our dad, we want to see the inside. It is small and simple with rows of polished oak pews and a flagstone floor. Services are held rarely now, but it is left open for prayer or for shelter from the rain. Mossy gravestones tilt in the grassy graveyard dotted with clumps of fading daffodils. Wordsworth was here; he called it "a modest house of prayer." We climb the walkway that passes through the wall behind the church and we are at the beginning of the path to Helvellyn. Although this is not the route they would have taken, it feels right to be here.

Their leave is coming to an end as is our time following their footsteps. One last needful stop is Kendal; it is on the way and is featured on one of Daddy's postcards. It is famous for Kendal cakes touted as great snack to take out hiking; perhaps they were taken along on the Helvellyn climb. We are bound to try one and, when we do, rather wished we hadn't. As we drive through the town, nibbling dubiously on this cloying mixture of sugar and toothpaste, Robbie provides us with a truly inexplicable moment. "Oh there's the Woolpack," she cries pointing at a very old building. "Should we stop?"

Woolpack? What is she on about? I have no clue why the Woolpack should be of interest. Often I feel her grasp of details and her research is superior to mine so wait for enlightenment. Robbie tells me the travellers stayed there. Whitewashed, a model of Georgian symmetry, it is a handsome structure. On one side is an archway, tall enough to accommodate stagecoaches. Now it houses a Kentucky Fried Chicken. We gaze but don't stop. I confess to having no memory of

Daddy mentioning this place. Later, when we scour the diary we are puzzled to find that, in fact he didn't. It isn't until, months later when I meet Michael and he reads an entry about Kendal that I discover that this venerable inn had housed them for a night. How could Robbie be so sure of something she could not have known at the time? The certainty that we needed to stop and explore this place struck her as we drove by even though, until that moment, she had never heard of it. How can we explain the inexplicable? It happened and, even for such cynics as we are, its mystery is not unwelcome.

On the back of Daddy's postcard, the one that called us to drive through this town, he writes: *A very pleasant little country town with the war far away.* His thoughts are turning toward the base and all that waits for them there. The war is about to be very close once again; this is their last stop before they return to Spilsby. They will arrive late the following night.

The Second Dicky

Returning from their various leaves, refreshed and full of stories, the boys of the crew are reunited. The rascally Bruce is late returning after being picked up by the SPs in Nottingham. He is treated as a deserter until it is resolved as a mix up over military passes. While they are away life — and death — on the base has continued. Two crews are missing. One, Mellowship's, is a crew from their hut. Arthur's gloom is a little lifted by the bags of mail waiting for him.

And then it is back on Ops. On August 25 they are briefed for Konigsberg but the mission is scrubbed due to weather. The next night, August 26, exactly one month from their first Operation, mission reinstated, they join the bomber stream heading for Germany. What happens next will end their time together as a crew.

Over France, Michael starts to realize that something is seriously off. At first he thinks he has made a mistake, wondering, "What have I done?" Frantically he checks his calculations and his instruments but it gets worse. He calls up Stan, who is seated beside the pilot. Stan tries to talk to Bill and is quickly aware that they have a crisis on their hands. Bill has, to quote Michael, "gone funny, laughing, all over the place." Daddy writes that Bill is *delirious and then passes out*. He is pulled from his seat and our father cradles him until they get back to base.

Robbie and I have one burning question: with the pilot out of commission, how the Hell did they get home? Lancasters have no co-pilot. Once the pilot is injured, incapacitated or dead, there is no choice but to bail out. There may be a crewmember who could fly straight and level. Perhaps even get them to a safer place to bail out.

There are designated spots in the North Sea where it is possible to jettison the bomb load, clear of any allied shipping, making a return to base a less lethal proposition but, as we already know, landing these things is both difficult and dangerous ... not for amateurs. And, with Bill out of the picture, all they have is amateurs. Still, they get home. How?

It is not surprising that the second thing I ask Michael, after "How are you?" is "How did you land the plane on the night of Bill's breakdown?" I can see he is pleased. This elderly daughter of his friend is not some overwrought dingbat here to roll about in a welter of emotion. She wants to know the facts. He rubs his large, boney hands together in glee. "I'll tell you about that."

Once Bill is out of his seat decisions have to be made. Michael, the only other officer on board, takes over. There are, he tells us, very strict times for being over a target. These need to be followed to avoid being bombed from above, or accidentally bombing an airplane below. Hideous and pointless accidents often happen in spite of assigned times but avoiding them makes good sense. Going on to finish the raid is, therefore, out of the question. They will turn back. Right, but while this confab is in progress, who is flying the bloody plane? "Now," Michael grinning happily, goes on, "I'll tell you how we were saved. We were terribly lucky."

When a new crew arrives on base it is customary to send the pilot out on a raid with an experienced crew, says Michael, "to see what it was like, so he would know." Wise move. This newbie pilot comes as a passenger, standing by the pilot, watching and learning. At least one fellow in each of these neophyte crews about to be initiated into this nightmarish world, would come at it with some idea of what to expect; he "would know." This extra chap, a trained pilot, skipper of a sprog crew, was called a "second dicky." "And do you know," says Michael, close to vibrating with delight, "that night we had a second dicky on board." This young man finds himself suddenly promoted from observer to pilot. He brings them home.

Had he not, our story would be so much shorter. For although it is possible to survive bailing out either over land or in the North Sea, it is a poor bet. Perhaps they would have been able to deploy the dinghy had they opted for ditching in the sea. Perhaps they would have been picked up. Daddy would have radioed their location, it was still summer, not the killing dark and icy waves of winter. Maybe they would have survived. When Bill goes "funny" they are over French territory that is rapidly being reclaimed. They might have safely parachuted down, been taken in by a grateful French farmer and his family, offered baguettes and wine and sent home in style. If they had fallen into German hands, they could have been cheerfully greeted, as so many were, with, "For you the war is over," or they may have been summarily executed, Hitler's orders at that time. I cannot avoid wistfully thinking that nine months as a POW waiting for Mummy's letters and the Red Cross parcels, and then release and home, trumps what actually happens to him in the end.

The consequences of that night for these seven men we have become so attached to are huge. At first they hope Bill will pull through, be declared fit to fly, and they will go on adding up their Operations until they have completed a tour, and the magic thirty is reached. Cruelly, this particular night of stress and loss will not be counted as a mission. If you turn back because of mechanical or personnel failure — too bad.

Daddy and his crew remain together awaiting the verdict on Bill. He is in limbo, mooching around the camp unsure of his future, confused by what has happened. In Michael's kitchen, with more than six decades between us and these events, I tentatively wonder if there had been any warning signs of the unravelling of that night. "Nothing," says Michael, with unassailable certainty. "It came out of the blue. He never complained or ... we have no idea why it happened." I suppose we could leave it there — a man they had known, worked beside, faced death with, trusted to lead and command them, suddenly, with no warning at all, cracks. He "never complained," but then, none of them did. Everyone is afraid, of course. Only an idiot would not feel the leaden fear that goes with flying Ops. But you keep it to yourself. This is a crew of pragmatists. Many crews have special lucky items, carried in pockets, caressed in a certain way, placed just so in the cockpit, the stuffed toys, the lucky horseshoes, a particular WAAF driver, an order of entering the plane, the plane itself, all become touchstones. But for my father and his practical no-nonsense comrades, this is not their way. Michael insists that there was very little of this in 207 Squadron overall. "Very few people had mascots. Those that did, it meant everything to them, but we certainly never did."

Did they, I ask, sit around calculating their odds? How many in the squadron have made it to thirty Ops? How many are lost per raid? Which targets take the highest toll? Again, Michael is clear: not this group. "We never talked about it. You always knew it might be your last trip. But I never knew anyone who said: 'Oh my God, I'm on tonight. I'm going to die.' Never anything like that. You just went out and came back. And you said ... 'Oh, Joe's gone' ... it was always the other chap."

Isn't that how we all are? How do any of us cope knowing that death is waiting and inevitable? Out there, ready to pounce, are buses and lightning bolts with our names on them, restaurants keen to poison us, pianos ready to fall from windows, illnesses too numerous and virulent to contemplate. It would almost be sensible to stay quivering in bed, too afraid to face the day. But up we get, confident that these perils will pass us by and ensnare "the other chap." We will mourn for him but we will also feel a secret vindication, a touch of Schadenfreude; once more we have dodged the bullet. It is liberating to make a joke of death. There is nothing more hilarious than the annual Darwin Awards listing the horribly violent demise of fools who will now do the planet the favour of not procreating and passing on their dopey genes. Aha, we think, smirking happily at their fate, this is what happens to idiots. I am not an idiot. Perhaps I will live forever.

The boys of Bomber Command also find a shield in humour. Nobody "died." They "went for a Burton": just off down the road having a pint of Burton's Ale. Some "bought it," others, more brutally but with hard-boiled finality "got the chop." If they made it home roughed up by the flak, a "blood wagon" would scream down the runway Klaxons clanging. Aircraft mangled on the ground or disintegrating in the air were deemed to have "pranged," diminishing the menace by sounding incidental and rubber-bandish.

There is some comfort, for us, in this. It is hardly useful for men like our father to dwell on the odds, to mourn deeply every time a crew does not return. There is simply not enough energy. "We weren't callous," says Michael. "Of course, with Arthur, being a personal friend, that was different."

Ah yes. That is different. Think of Michael, this gentle man, young, full of life, a "comic strip," convincing himself that death would pass him by. How else could he have gone on? But when a close friend, a man he looks up to and admires, dies, he is devastated. He writes a misery-soaked letter to his mother. She, in turn, writes to our mother and so, all this time later, we find Michael and all that he has to tell us. But for most, the way to survive that kind of loss is to just get on with it. "If a chap in your hut was lost and he had a good bed, you'd immediately grab his bed: 'I'll have that.' I never knew anyone who brooded or was anxious." For most, that is how they survived.

Does Bill, older, somewhat of an enigma, perhaps allow his imagination too much freedom? If he had been able to speak his fears, as we in this confessional age do so freely, would he have sidestepped this breakdown? Such weak-kneed soul-searching is not encouraged. Men often find comfort in the arms of young WAAFs or local girls. Many weep there and confess their terror. But in the Mess among their peers it simply is not done. Men clearly unfit for raids, shaking uncontrollably or prone to rage, are observed with sympathy but help is rarely offered.

It isn't that the higher-ups are not aware of the enormous strain. It has always been part of the hazard of war. "Shell shock," it was called in the Great War. That's a pretty honest descriptor. The constant pounding of the guns, the mud and blood of the trenches, the ever present stink of death unravelled many. There was some understanding that a break might help and men were often moved back behind the lines to mend their shattered souls. If that failed and they ran from the guns, they were promptly executed. By World War II it was called "battle fatigue." Carrying a gentle hint of Victorian swooning, it sounded less serious, but of course wasn't. By the 1950s it had shifted to "Operational Exhaustion" and then, with Vietnam and later the implosion of the Middle East, we had PTSD — Post Traumatic Stress Disorder. Sometimes help is given, and sometimes understanding, but the stigma and the stain remain.

For those who have never faced what war requires and who lack imagination it's easy to dismiss this suffering as weakness of character. A man with his legs blown off is unequivocally a casualty of war; a man whose mind has snapped is more problematic. And, for those running the war, he is trouble. Studies were done, papers written, statistics kept; throughout the Great War and its horrifying sequel much ink was devoted to this. I would not be so cynical as to assert that nobody was much interested, in a human way, in the plight of those who crumbled under the strain, but I do think that the majority were not. What they were interested in was efficiency. Aircrew are enormously expensive to train. The reckoning that any one trained crew member in Bomber Command will repay his costly education by providing, on average, fourteen bombing raids is, to me, shocking. Such calculated waste is a punch to the heart.

Those directing the war machine ponder this cost and are very interested in keeping it as low as possible. They know full well these crews are sent out to do terrible things in unimaginable conditions. They know some will splinter. They know others may, after a few Ops, quite sensibly say, "Fuck this" and refuse to go. Should the rot set in, they fear these men, volunteers all, might, in worrying numbers, refuse to fly. Perhaps that would have happened but somehow we doubt it. We have read enough searingly honest autobiographies to know that most believe that they have come to do a job, that it has to be done, and that it is their duty to do it. Those in command know this too, but they cannot risk any crack in this edifice. They need to keep the planes flying.

A bullet to the head is an attention-getting deterrent in the army. A slightly more humane understanding of shell shock and the burgeoning interest in psychology between the wars make that solution less palatable. And anyway, the men of the RAF, all volunteers, could not be court-martialled. Even had they been conscripted, the British people have a pretty good idea of what faces those waves of planes growling over their heads at night, and, at least until the war ends, they see them as heroes. Firing squads would not be popular.

The more sensible commanders keep an eye out for signs of stress and make accommodations as far as possible. But, in the end, those making the decisions at High Wycombe give the orders as to where and when to bomb and how many to send. There is not much room for mollycoddling, as they might have called it.

Conclusions are reached about who might be susceptible to falling apart in some unseemly way. Those from "good families" raised with high moral character, it is assumed, will have the necessary backbone. It is hardly surprising that sons of the upper classes are commissioned with despatch and pointed in leadership directions. They are deemed to have the right stuff. They will be stalwart leaders with nerves of steel and unimpeachable courage. Problem solved. Some men are, they believe, just naturally genetically superior, a disturbing echo of Hitler's belief in eugenics. Of course, there is not a shred of evidence that it is possible to predict who will snap, no matter what the bloodline. As one outraged fellow on a website writes: "It is hard to call a man a coward who has volunteered for service, survived the horrors of training, and gone out on half a dozen Ops before folding. Who of us knows where our limit lies?"

The vague notions of "flying stress" or the more casual "flak happy" at least acknowledge that external forces are at work. Finally there is the officially sanctioned label, LMF: Lack of Moral Fibre. Such an old boys, public school, stiff upper lip ring to it. The man so labelled is missing some vital component that makes him a man. For young men who have joined the air force hoping to right a wrong, make a difference, stop a tyrant, and serve King and Country, to be so branded feels worse than death. Even for those who joined up to see the world, have an adventure, get away from home, or meet some girls, it is a cruel blow. They grow proud of their uniforms, are loyal to their crews, do not want to let them down. So, combine a culture of stoic fatalism with the degrading threat of LMF and you have a potent tool to keep men, even those at the end of their rope, going out into the dark over Europe to face everything the enemy can hurl at them.

Michael tells me, again with cheerful certainty, that LMF was not a factor in World War II. I'm glad he believes that. He says he never encounters somebody written off because of it. But many others do. In the worst cases, the squadron is called on parade and the wretched fellow who has been found wanting is marched out to face the brass. In my imagination it is raining. The parade ground is damp and puddled; a fine mist drifts from a gloomy sky. The night before somebody (a weeping WAAF perhaps) has collected the uniform of the man soon to be disgraced and carefully unpicked the stitching on his insignia: the chevrons on his upper arms, the wings on his chest ... whatever marks his rank and affiliation. These are then loosely sewn back in place. The disgraced airman is paraded in front of his band of brothers. In a moment of utter humiliation the insignia is dramatically torn from his uniform. The cunningly pre-planned loose stitching presumably prevents a Monty Python moment where the Wing Co, panting and grimacing, pins the man about to be shamed to the ground and, getting a good purchase with a knee on his chest, struggles manfully, but in vain, to rip the insignia off. That couldn't happen of course, though I rather wish it could. Whatever is lacking in the man being cast out, there is an equal lack in those who turn their backs on him.

Not all cases provoke such public drama. Often a man just disappears; busted to AC2, shipped off to a far-removed squadron, and told to mop out the latrines. Some welcome this: better than death. Rank also plays a part in determining consequences. While NCOs are demoted and assigned menial duties, officers are simply posted elsewhere with their privileges intact. Later in the war the notion of LMF is refined into four categories: LMF, Inefficiency, Misconduct, and Medical. Perhaps some understanding and humanity is creeping in. Or have the mucky-mucks taken note of how the Americans, those crass and rough-hewn ex-Colonials, are handling the Lack of Moral Fibre in their aircrews? Well, they aren't because that is not what it is called. A man exhibiting stress is seen to have a psychological problem and provided treatment. How very sane.

Now that I am making comparisons, here are other ways in which the Yanks are more nurturing. American aircrew are supplied with flak jackets and their casualty rates reflect this sensible decision. Their helmets actually offer protection for their New World heads. Metal plates behind their pilots' seats give them a better chance of getting the crew home. To be fair, Bomber Command starts out with a similar seat protection for its pilots but, in the summer of 1944, it is removed to save on weight. So now, if the pilot is wounded or killed and there is nobody to fly the plane, the entire crew could die and the plane be destroyed. No wonder these men sometimes feel themselves expendable in the eyes of those running the show. "Acceptable losses" — that's what they are. Cannon fodder. Statistics. The suicidal Charge of the Light Brigade, the men at Gallipoli clambering out of their trenches into the Turkish guns while the British Command take tea on the beach ... so it goes. Who, exactly, in all of this, is Lacking Moral Fibre?

Happily not our Bill. After a series of interviews with psychiatrists, he falls into the "medical" file. It will be close to a month before he knows what is in store for him. This leaves his crewmates in their own frustrating limbo. The cohesion of the crew now shattered, they become "odd bods" — men with no affiliation, to be picked up by a crew short a man due to illness, injury, or death. The comfort and protection of the men they have come to trust is gone.

Our father's diary reflects this untethering. He writes a lot — what else is there to do — but it is scattered and random, a lucky dip of bits and pieces. I find it hard to read. He is back to the pointless drifting of the goal-free month in Dumfries almost a year ago. Perhaps documenting this gives him some sense of control.

The weather gets some attention: *Gorgeous sunny cool day, just right for doing nothing, followed by morning tea at a farmhouse café.* And later: *cooling down, much rain and wind.* They develop a craze for snooker, drop it, and find a passion for darts. A dart board is liberated from the mess and set up so they can play in the hut: just them, away from other crews who are going somewhere. *Things have tightened up*, he tells us, but they manage to skirt the rules. He gets a haircut, they go to the movies, there is a night out to Skegness where *beer is scarce but the meal is grand.* Another night he sees a loose barrage balloon float across the base. He finds odd jobs to fill time. *Stan and Bruce arrive back from a jolly evening out, all over blood having pranged their bike in a ditch going forty miles per hour. They trot off to be patched up by the MO and are giggling themselves silly over the whole thing.*

Some of the boys are picked up for Operations. He records these, often with more detail than those he has taken part in in the past. Is he worried for them, cast out into unfamiliar territory? Cliff comes home *full of beans after being a spare bod on a raid to Konigsberg and an overnight diversion to Scotland*, although he is disgruntled at the sproggy crew he is called to fly with: *they are late to the target, fail to drop their bombs and jettison them in the Baltic.* Our Lime is missing the professionalism of his mates. Mike does an Op with Spragg's crew and is swept up in their nine day leave. Alf and Bruce temporarily join Johnny Middleton's crew. It is lucky for them that it is temporary: on the night of October 6 his plane is shot down over Germany. He and his crew are buried in Hamburg. Cliff for a time is with Wall's. Daddy mentions only one Op for himself — to Boulogne — but apart from that and a few briefings that come to nothing, he is at a loose end.

Feeling pulled apart, they go together to see the Wing Co, afraid they will be split up for good. This worried group of young men is assured that nothing will be done until Bill's fate is decided. This is cold comfort. Rumour has it that he will either be grounded, and then they will be scattered for certain, or will be sent to Coastal Command, taking with him those crew necessary.

In the meantime, Bill is given the job of link stooge — something to do with the dreaded Link Trainer. Perhaps the higher ups wonder if some purpose might help him more than time spent fretting in enforced idleness. He and Daddy take themselves to the pictures. In nine days he will hear from the medical board. So they wait and worry.

Arthur decides during this idle time, to put in for his Commission. Why now? The puzzle of who gets Commissions and when, will, I am now sure, remain forever unsolved. We read of men being commissioned at the end of training with not one Operation to their credit. Some do the requisite thirty Ops and are passed over. And there is everything in between. Class and education seemed to play a role earlier in the War. Michael, over tea in his "Greenacres" kitchen, can speak only of his experience; it is the same process as our father's. You submit your papers, have an interview, wait. It seems to be done on a whim.

Both Arthur and Alf give it a go as they are hanging about with their war more or less put on hold. Perhaps it is just something to pass the time. Of course it leads to a few nice things: pay goes up a bit — especially nice for a married man. You get a fancy new uniform — perhaps less scratchy than the Sergeants' blues — if you are shot down and captured you go to a better class of POW camp and receive nicer treatment, your quarters are often, though not always, more spacious, people salute you, you eat in a superior Mess — but likely the same food. And somewhere I read that you are issued with pyjamas.

With these inducements why is there not a constant line to the door of the Wing Co? In actual fact having a Commission makes little difference where it really matters: operations. First thing in the morning you get off a smart salute to your "superior" or accept one from your "inferior," whatever the case may be. After that, you are all in it together. Although it is easier to get a Commission as a pilot or a navigator, in some crews, a gunner might be Commissioned and his skipper not. In practice this is insignificant; once in crew mode, the skipper is the boss. Given that they all face the same peril, it does seem silly that they are not all commissioned. There is a move in that direction at one point but it drifts away. Too expensive, perhaps. As I said, a puzzle.

Daddy ambles off for his interview, application in hand. His ill-mannered superior finds the wording not to his liking, screws it up and tosses it in the waste paper basket. *Ignorant clod!* is our father's summation. We fall in love with this expression and make it our own. Pushy drivers on the roundabouts, annoying obstructionists at hotel desks, foolish boobies in the endless stories we tell each other — all fodder for our happy cries of "Ignorant clod." Most satisfying.

Later he tries again and the paperwork passes inspection. Now he waits to see various big nobs. There seems little urgency although he would like it settled before they are sent away from the base, a fate he fears may be ahead of them. When the interview comes he is told he must muster up a few more operations before a recommendation can be sent even though his lack of operations over this month long hiatus stems from the fact that there is no vacancy for a w/op in 207. Even sillier is the response to poor Alf, also in search of promotion. He is informed that he is too shy and invited to return in three weeks. Just what might occur in that small time frame to magically transform a bashful youth to a confident extrovert we cannot imagine. Neither of them is fretting about the commission, there are more worrying signposts in their futures.

On the other hand, the news from Europe is good: *Maginot and Gothic line pierced, Belgian frontier crossed and Russians racing toward Germany from the east.* Hopes of early victory fill the air, but all are treating it cautiously for fear their hopes may be premature. This is in early September. A week or so later he reports: *War prospects continue bright although the Allied armies on the Western Front have paused for breath on the Reich frontier, and Brest, Le Havre, Calais and Dunkirk still hold out.* They begin to think going home may be a possibility; perhaps the war will be over by Christmas. *Rumours are floating around that we will return to Australia immediately the European War is over.*

Some fun is contemplated on September 10, and I cannot help the thought that in four days I, the younger daughter at home in Australia, will turn three. I could be sad that he makes no mention of birthdays and anniversaries but I know all that is taken care of in his letters. He lives in two very different worlds, although they are by no means exclusive as this day shows. A little "do" is planned with Bill and Cliff. They set off to The Shades in Spilsby for a grand natter session. This happy time is interrupted by a *blonde, stout, repulsive female who insinuates herself into our midst. From then on I lost all interest in the proceedings and, after falling asleep several times, got up and took my leave.* Off he stumbles, slightly sozzled and, after attempting unsuccessfully to buy some fish and chips for the boys back in the hut, makes his way home. The contrast between this pushy broad and his pretty, slender, restrained, and far away wife surely fuels some of this repulsion. The next day in the hut he writes six aerograms to Nooney and confides miserably to his diary: *how I am missing that very lovely person.*

It is now late September, a long and frustrating month since Bill's implosion and finally he travels to London for the verdict. It is the worst: he is grounded for good — no more service flying of any sort. So even the relatively less agonizing option of Coastal Command is off the table. They will be absorbed into existing crews, with one exception: there is no spot for our father — *it is problematical what the future has in store for me.*

Still there is room for rejoicing on behalf of others. Two of the men in the missing crew have reached home and are safe. There is the possibility that another may have escaped but, he writes *all the rest of the crew are definitely dead.* We like this direct language. Yes, they are dead. They have not passed away, nor have they bought it, or got the chop, let alone gone for a Burton. They are simply, and definitively, dead. If he uses the slang of his fellow airmen when talking to them, and perhaps he does, he does not play around with the truth in his diary. What would that achieve after all?

And so, with Bill gone, and Mike definitely crewed up, they wait. Alf and Bruce, after suffering from head-shattering hangovers, swear off beer. This provides Daddy with companions for what he describes, tongue-in-cheekily, as *a number of respectable evenings in Skegness and Spilsby.* There are some rag-tag sports afternoons. But you can almost hear the disconsolate shuffling of his feet. *Ops on tonight and most of the crew are on — not me of course. Mitchell went on leave this morning so I took the afternoon off. There is nothing for me to do anyway.*

He notes, gloomily, the news that Spilsby is about to take in another squadron: 44 from Rhodesia. He fears such an influx will make it very crowded. It is a throwaway bit of information, just another annoyance in a world that has gone awry for him. But it is not unimportant. Of course he doesn't know it but he has just written something pitifully ironic.

How dispiriting to feel so useless, hanging about the hut, as others go out fighting to bring this dreadful thing to a close, to have it over by Christmas, as they hope. Then, because time has passed, they go on leave, all in different directions. Daddy fulfills a promise he has made to himself — a visit to his cousins, his mother's family in Bowermadden.

Disappointment, Triumph, Sorrow

Spilsby is our most weighty destination. Training over, Daddy begins operations here; he leaves from this base to go on leave in the Lake District, he returns and his crew is broken apart. And this is where he dies. As Michael says kindly, reading excerpts in his kitchen. "This is the nasty bit I'm afraid." And then, as the details of Daddy's death mount: "It's all very harrowing. Do you want me to go on?"

"Well," I respond, "we have to." As, of course, we do.

Spilsby, the town, which gives the base its name, is depressingly down at heel, shops boarded up, streets quiet, another victim of Britain's sagging economy. We find a room at the White Hart, an inn at the centre of town, chosen because it is pictured on one of Paddy's postcards to Nooney. He writes a goofy comment about the statue of Sir John Franklyn, which graces the town square: *This is a statue of the guy who discovered the North West passage. He was born in Spilsby. Funny how one learns. I always thought it was Spencer Tracy.*

Over supper in the White Hart dining room, we spread our binders and notebooks on the table plotting, between mouthfuls, our battle plan for the next few days. Lincolnshire, packed with operational bases during the war, offers an embarrassment of riches but, as always, our focus is on the world seen through the eyes our father and his friends.

"I hope we can find The Shades," I say, examining our wish list of places to see.

"Yes, it pops up a lot and we did find it on the internet. You wrote to them, right?"

"Never heard back. The website could be prehistoric. We should ask somebody local."

At that moment a pleasant looking fellow dining alone at the next table looks up and smiles at our clutter of plates and binders. Well, that's all the opening we need. He is, we are happy to hear, a local, and yes, he is familiar with The Shades. In fact he used to drink there many a time. It is a subtle difference: I long for him to say, "I drink there. Often. It is a favourite." Instead he tells is it is now a Chinese restaurant and has been one for at least eight years. We curse outdated websites and swallow our disappointment. But then our new friend gets involved in our story and sets us on a new path of discovery.

For months now we have been traipsing about the World Wide Web, not a highly intellectual process but often an inexplicable one. Over and over we have hopefully entered "Bomber Command," "207 Squadron," "Lancaster Bomber," trusting that this vaunted search engine will reveal all. And here we are, in a three hundred-year-old inn, not a computer in sight, chatting to an actual human being, and finding out that within an easy drive there is a treasure trove dedicated to all these things RAF: the Lincolnshire Aviation Heritage Centre of East Kirby. It is a labour of love curated by two brothers and we can meet them, this font of information tells us enthusiastically. He supplies us with directions and promises a world of revelation.

The next morning, after a quick and painless drive through the flat world of Lincolnshire, we are in front of a huge hangar housing the magnificent "Just Jane." This is, for both of us, our first Lancaster. It is some time before we can get out of the car. Her massive wing span, her olive brown skin, her solid wheels, her four great engines, her noble nose ... she is simply beautiful.

Under her wings and around the edges of the hangar is an impressive, if slightly chaotic, collection of Bomber Command memorabilia. Glass cases contain everything from posters to insignia, to personal stories, to bits and pieces of smashed aircraft. We find wireless sets, we see helmets, flying boots, and then we find the photo of Daddy's squadron. His picture is here. It is high up on a wall and hard to see but it is the actual photo, less grainy than our internet print-offs, more real.

We do not pursue the promise of a connection with the brothers who have created this, and to this day I do not know why. Sometimes we are bold; sometimes not. Perhaps we should have gone aboard "Just Jane" with her cheeky painting of a forties sex-pot on her fuselage. It is, we discover, possible to purchase a ride on her. She does not fly but she does rumble about the runway. We talk ourselves out of this treat. It is expensive and we allow this to sway us, which becomes yet another regret to add to our extensive collection.

Outside in the grounds are memorial trees with engraved markers at their feet. We find a name we know, a name mentioned in the diary: Middleton, who shared his hut and whose crew went missing. Daddy knew him and that is enough for us to stand and gaze for a moment at the plaque marking his passing.

"Next?" Robbie is all business. I consult our list. With The Shades as a known watering hole gone and reborn as a Chinese restaurant, the other favourite drinking spot is Skegness on the coast.

"Wolds." What a lovely word, like a sweet ball of custard on the tongue. Our father and his mates take buses, bum lifts, even bike the road to Skegness across these very Wolds. And they fly above them too, pointing to the North Sea and beyond. Stories of Lincolnshire's famed flatness ignore the subtle and lovely rolling Wolds. Underpinned by chalk, they break gently from Spilsby north and toward the coast. They are a walker's delight, we are told. They are also a soothing wonder to drive through. The morning is still young and it is a short trip.

The Wolds may be lovely; Skegness, where Arthur and his mates enjoyed the pubs and the beaches, is not. It was once a lively, possibly glamorous, resort, famous for its bracing air. It now staggers under the country's general decline. The town oozes disappointed expectations. Tacky arcades, tawdry restaurants wafting unappetizing smells, no sign of the sea from the main street, nowhere to park ... it is tempting to just chuck it and drive back to the White Hart.

At the Information Centre, one cramped room with a minimalist collection of pamphlets, evidence of more austerity, we find a friendly custodian, bored out of her head and eager to chat. In 1940 there was a rat plague, she tells us. Spilsby offered a bounty on rat tails. Although she is too young to have memories of airmen wandering from pub to pub or strolling along the beach, she has a friend who remembers dogfights over the coast and being told to look down as the Germans flew above so they would not see the whiteness of a face looking up.

Of course we must visit the pier. Well, we suppose we should. Neon signs offer enticements: Skegness Pier Amusements, Ten Pin Bowling, Casino. It is equal opportunity fun for Mums and Dads and Kids: slot machines, bowling, bumper cars, a mega-slide, a bouncy castle, games of chance, and prizes, prizes, prizes. There is a café, an ice cream kiosk and anything fried that your arteries could long for. At the end of all this is the actual pier, which goes out only a short way into the water but gives us, at last, a view of the beach and the sea. Off shore, grey and shadowy in the perpetual haze, is a huge wind farm. The arms turn and turn in brisk Skegness air. Then there is the beach where our father ambled, stooping occasionally to pick up and pocket a shell. At some point he also goes to Blackpool, it seems, as there are postcards from there. Perhaps he collects shells on that beach as well. One thing we do know is that he liked to pick up and keep shells, pretty things to take home to his wife and two little girls. English shells, a lovely curiosity from this time away from them.

On the list of the things that are returned to our mother, in that small cardboard box, months after the war is over, is the blandly noted item, "A sock full of shells." Returning from a day at Skegness (or Blackpool, or a walk on the beach at Whitley Bay) he empties his pockets, shakes out the sand, and carefully stows the shells he has harvested in a single sock. For Joanne, my oldest daughter, this is the sweetest thing to know about her long dead grandfather. "I wish we knew where they are," she says. "I wonder what happened to them." So do Robbie and I; where are they, those random memories?

We are much in his mind during this time. He sends a swag of postcards showing scenes of Skegness: *To Nooney, the most adorable person in the world, Paddy* and *To my darling Nooney, Paddy. To Wendy from her adoring Daddy.* Robbie's postcard, with a similar inscription to *Bobs*, shows a small sailboat bravely battling the vaunted bracing air. As Robbie ended up spending a large chunk of her life living aboard and sailing across two oceans this is delightfully apt. There is another one for both of us featuring the Skegness beach's donkey rides. Eight kids, faces split with laughter, each on a child-sized donkey are ambling across the sand. The pier is in the background. On the back is written, *To Wendy and Bobs from Daddy — wish you two had been there to ride on the donkeys.*

Skegness checked off our list, we drive back across the Wolds looking for All Saints Church of Great Steeping, home to monuments to both 207 and 44 Squadrons.

"Remember the rat?" says Robbie.

"Funny," I was just thinking about that. "Must be that lady talking about the rat plague."

"It rather puts everything we think we know in doubt. Was that what you were thinking?"

I nod and we fall silent contemplating the puzzle of memory.

We were very small, walking together down the path to the barn on our orchard. Next to this path a gutter ran, taking washing water away from the house — a nice spot for a rat to hang out. Suddenly one shot out of the ditch and ran up Robbie's leg, across her shoulders and escaped down her other side. A good deal of screaming ensued. Well, that's how I recall it anyway. Years after this terrifying encounter, when Robbie and I were in our teens, it came up. "Remember the rat that ran up your leg and across your back?" she asked me. "No," I was appalled, "it ran up you." Suddenly we had a mystery. There was a rat, we could agree on that, but just which sister did it career over? Both of us remember fiercely and with Technicolor clarity it was the other one who was trespassed upon. Clearly one of us was right and the other had simply passed this unpleasantness onto her sister. This is a Gordian knot that cannot be cut.

"Such a mad little moment," Robbie muses. "How can we trust anything we think we know?"

With that sobering thought, we pull up to the entry gate of Great Steeping's All Saints. A sign next to the gate tells us that services take place twice a month. We try the blue door, set oddly on the side of the building, like an afterthought. It is locked, and has an abandoned look. The yard has been recently mowed: a rough cut leaving drifts of grass along the walls and around the edges — landscaping at its most basic. I venture around the back of the church where blackberry bushes grow and a small area provides a nice spot for quick bladder relief. We are now, as you can see, utterly focused on our search and beyond shame. Even the woman in the house behind the church, who is hanging out her washing, fails to faze me. She is concentrated on her pegging and does not even glance my way.

Robbie is at the front gate with a pencil and notebook taking down the pastor's name: Reverend Coates, living in Spilsby with a handy phone number. We can contact him and hopefully see this memorial.

Possibly befuddled, possibly avoiding our inevitable date with Spilsby airfield and our father's death, we manage to fritter away what is left of the afternoon. I have a postal code for our next destination and feel confident that Fred will lead us through. And maybe that could have happened had I not plugged in the wrong numbers. By the time we stagger in, it is half an hour from closing. So, here we are at the Battle of Britain Memorial Flight at RAF Coningsby, the home of the only Lancaster that flies in Britain and one of only two in the world that fly.

"No point in going in, love," the kindly chap tells us. "Tours are over for the day."

"Oh," I am riddled with guilt. "What have we missed?"

As it turns out, not much really. The tour, full of technical stuff about the airplanes kept there, is not really our cup of tea. But the hall has a good display of artefacts and history of the RAF where we are taken by portraits of early airmen, blue bloods with slightly superior expressions, their silk scarves tossed nonchalantly over their aristocratic shoulders. They create the culture of stiff upper lip loyalty that marks the men of the RAF even if, as War demands increasing sacrifice, the men who volunteer are of more prosaic stock.

There is the gift shop to peruse. I find a small stuffed bear wearing a flying helmet, a leather Irving jacket with a fur collar and, underneath, a roll-neck sweater. He has goggles and khaki pants. He is made in Britain. And his tag says: "Something to be Cherished." How can I resist? As I pay, I chat with the lady at the desk, telling her a bit about our search and how silly we are to be late getting here. "Oh," she says, "if you can come back tomorrow, you can see the Lancaster take off."

"Truly!" Robbie cries.

Of course we will be back.

Re-invigorated we zip back to the White Hart to phone Cannon Coates who promises that he will meet us early next day and open the church. All Saints sits at the edge of what used to be Spilsby Airfield. It is important to see its monument to 207 and be reassured that all that happened here is not forgotten.

The next day offers disappointment, triumph, and sorrow. The White Hart breakfast supplies us with luncheon eggs and a couple of apples and we are sitting in front of All Saints awaiting Canon Coates at the chosen hour. We are eager to see the monument and to meet this kind guide.

He does not come. We pace, admire this odd little church once again until, after forty-five minutes it is clear he will not be meeting us. Robbie writes him a polite and understanding note. We certainly can't be snippy to the man who so readily agreed to do this for us, even if he is not here. Casting a slightly regretful backward glance at

All Saints, we drive back through Spilsby where, at the Canon's other church, a jolly fete is in progress, perhaps explaining the Cannon's absence. Country Fetes can be tricky things. Who know what might be happening in the cake-judging tent?

Disappointments are part of any trip and we roll with them quite well. The no-show Canon is a part of the adventure. And, anyway, we can, and do, find this missed memorial on line. It is a simple marble plaque with the 207 shield followed by a brief and moving account of 207's time at Spilsby. "From here the squadron's Lancaster bombers each with seven crewmen took the battle to the enemy mostly by night. Until 6th June 1944 this was the only way in which Great Britain could strike out from these shores in its own defence and in the cause of freedom." So, there it is, as they say, in a nutshell. It goes on to point out the carnage. In the two-year period that 207 was stationed here "511 men were killed. 104 of whom have no known grave ... 133 did not return from operations of whom 109 became Prisoners of War until May 1945 and 24 evaded capture."

There is a separate monument to 44 Squadron. Someday I may come back to this part of the world and visit the places whose doors were not open to us. But if I do not manage to do so, that it will be OK. The memorial plaque concludes with "LEST WE FORGET." We haven't.

"Iconic" is a word so over-employed that its meaning has leached away, but if it still has any currency, it can be applied with confidence to the Lancaster. Its silhouette, instantly recognizable, is etched into the imagination of those who lived through the war. Over seven thousand Lancasters were built. We are going to watch one of the two still flying, and because of its public appearances all over Britain, the most famous. Our visit to RAF Coningsby takes us to one of Bomber Command's most enduring memorials — this venerable kite — and, for us, the most moving.

Outside the airfield is a parking space, a good spot to watch the take-off. This isn't a show; they are merely getting ready to fly to Brighton to remind the world of what it owes. The Avro Lancaster, our special pet, flies with a Supermarine Spitfire and a Hawker Hurricane. These are fighter planes, tiny single seaters. They beat back the German fliers in the Battle of Britain and protected the Bomber stream heading across the North Sea or south over the Alps. "Spitties" swoop in to chase off a German fighter or stick close by to escort a wounded plane home.

We join a small group waiting to watch the take-off. One woman has a boyfriend who is part of the Lancaster crew. We tell our tale of course and I fetch the binder with Daddy's handsome face on its cover. A rather emotional lady insists on taking our photos as we hold his picture between us. Now we are getting weepy, too. The Lanc has appeared in the field behind the fence on the road across from us. It begins to warm up. Engines cough and hack, those game-changing Merlins we have heard so much about. There is taxiing and for a time we can't see her khaki mottled beauty. And then there is a howl as she hurls herself down the runway and is aloft. The sound is incredible — so unlike planes we are used to. There is such authority in her growling voice. I hear senior statement, vocal cords eroded by cigarettes and gin, rumbling hard-won wisdom and resolve. She is all that, and she is beautiful. It is no wonder those fly boys love her so.

The young woman whose boyfriend is aboard jumps about waving madly. I think because of her we get three low passes. How lucky for us. This lovely machine, with her dainty attendants, like sprightly ladies-in-waiting, fills the sky above us. What a slender and elegant body, what graceful up-tilted wings. Look at the line of the tail fins, and consider the power and menace as she swoops toward us head on. It is thrilling and heartbreaking. She is easy to love but we do not forget that she is built to destroy and that often she is destroyed in her turn. Then she and her companions wheel away to the south. By now we are both blubbing, scrambling into our handbags for Kleenex, and being patted kindly by the other watchers.

"Best thing yet," Robbie declares, through her tears. I sniffle in agreement, "Just perfect. Yes, it is."

It is time for lunch and we are searching for a thatched cottage simply because it is pictured on one of Daddy's postcards. To our amazement we find it. Located by the village of Langton (which we never do find) is the Round House, a cottage ornee (fancy language for an impossibly adorable cottage, the perfect home for a genial gnome). It was built in the early nineteenth century of whitewashed mud and stud with a thick overhanging thatch turning it into a delightful mushroom. Daddy, as we do, admires thatching and finds this example particularly arresting. We park across the road, settle ourselves on the nearside verge, a comfy grassy patch, and tuck into our lunch. A couple of cars roll by laughing and waving at two old dears munching apples and boiled eggs, nurturing their gentle grief, always talking of their father.

"Perhaps we should have made the time to go to Bowermadden," I worry, aware of how often we have been remiss.

"I don't think we could have," says Robbie. "It's a really long way, nearly to John O'Groats. And nobody who met him then is alive now...."

Family

Daddy's mother, Christine Mills, Nana to us, came from the most north-easterly corner of Scotland, close to John O'Groats. It is in the County of Caithness, the same county from which the Plowman clan hails. Some of that wild, flat and bleakly beautiful landscape with its bogs and moorland must surely have shaped our father and us. Even I have a tough core that can, when needed, override the drama queen and give me a bit of Scottish spine. Robbie is solid, our father stoic; the heritage shows.

Each Sunday, when we were children, my sister and I would walk to our father's family home, Balgargal, to spend the afternoon and early evening. If Mount Pleasant was poorly designed, this other ancestral home was simply mad. Our grandfather, whom we never knew, had, we were told proudly, designed it. The front door, entered, in my recollection, by nobody, led into the bedroom area. This is weirdly typical of Australian houses and means that guests marched past a row of closed doors before reaching the actual living quarters. There are so many silly things about the notion of making the most private part of the house public that I likely don't need to dwell on them. But in the case of this house it got even odder because the hallway through the sleeping quarters and past a door into the living room, suddenly debouched, with no warning, onto a wide, open verandah. Doors to the kitchen and dining room opened off this verandah and, round a corner or two, doors to our uncle's offices.

The common view of Australia is that it is bathed in perpetual sunshine. This is largely true, but there are exceptions. The small town of Orange is one such. Winters are chilly, snow falls, my stepfather's false teeth often froze in their glass on the bathroom shelf. It is cold. But here, at my father's childhood home, was a wide and inviting verandah looking out onto a rather chaotic flower garden bordered by a huge hedge, and completely open to the elements. Of course it was possible, on very bitter mornings to nip into the living room, from the corridor and pass through it to the dining room and then the warmth of the kitchen where porridge bubbled, but usually that was not done. One of the uncles actually slept on the verandah. The family dressed in their chilly rooms, braved the frigid hallway for a morning ablutions in the icy bathroom, scurried out onto the verandah taking in the frost-encrusted garden and made a dash for the cozy kitchen.

It was not a large house, but it was a full one. Two spinster aunts and two bachelor uncles, and of course, Nana, lived there. The uncles tended to the orchard; the aunts ran the house; they all fussed over Nana. We knew her to be precious and in need of cosseting. Conversations were punctuated with concerns over "Mummy's" comfort; is her tea too hot? too cold? Is she warm enough? Does she need a nap? As we called our mother Mummy and she was a bundle of energetic resolve this was a puzzle. Little Nana, with her white hair, neatly done up in a bun, and her wire-rimmed glasses, barely stirred. I loved her unreservedly although I never recall her, even once, speaking to me or even appearing to notice my existence. Robbie's experience was the same, enriched slightly by the memory of one conversation that haunts her still. Nana took a moment from marinating in her nest of blankets and shawls to tell her granddaughter that if she went to bed with wet hair she would wake in the morning paralysed. To this day Robbie will not put herself in such peril.

Children are generous with their love and she had ours. Clearly she was the centre of this welcoming and happy house. She had, to her astonishment at the age of forty-nine, found herself giving birth to the seventh of her children: our father. She was seventy-six when he died, over eighty when we made those Sunday visits. No wonder she wasn't reading us stories and playing tea-parties.

Daddy grew up with tales of his cousins still living in the Highlands. His visit on that last leave, although long postponed, is a happy one. He is met at the station. "Be ye Plewman?" At first he finds the accent hard to navigate but, by the end of his leave, is getting the hang of it. He grows fond of Peggy and Will. They take him to see his mother's birthplace. There is a muddy black and white photo of this visit. The house is a ruin: one wall with its gabled end, stands, connected precariously to the sidewall by an arched doorway. It is a crofter's hut made of stone, once stuccoed and whitewashed perhaps. Willie, the cousin, whose father was also born in this place, and his son Johnnie, stand in front of the hut, almost disappearing into its darkness. Daddy is silhouetted at the side, his hand on the wall as if to save it from any more decay. Not one of these men could have stepped through the doorway without bowing his head and crouching. The ground is strewn with stones, the sky is bleak. What Arthur makes of this ancestral home he does not say.

It may explain some things about his mother before she became the passive occupant of the rocking chair. She had emigrated with her first husband, who died on the way. Arriving in Australia, alone and bereft she needed to build a life for herself. There is a story of her crossing the Blue Mountains in a Cobb and Co coach and giving birth en route. This makes her Guinness Book of Records noteworthy — if it is true. Stories like that, true or not, grow from the notion that the main character is a person of some toughness. She raised seven children, she survived a second widowhood, and she was deeply loved. As her youngest son rests his hands on the stones of her birthplace he must be thinking of all of this.

It is only now that I wonder about Nana's homesickness and sadness. Were they her companions as she sat in the angle of the verandah, carefully shielded from drafts, swathed in life-saving crocheted blankets, rocking gently in her rocker and thinking her thoughts. Often the Presbyterian minister visited and they drank tea together and spoke to each other in Gaelic. She had lost a country, two husbands and a son. I wonder if she cherished the winter bleakness of that open verandah that her husband had fashioned. Did it take her back to the crofter's hut of her childhood; did it soften the ache for her vanished country and her missing men?

Daddy has left a cryptic list of highlights from this hastily recorded visit. He meets a minister and his young family, and he meets the Keiths, whose children do not clean their shoes on Sunday, which takes me back to those Balgargal again, where Sundays were framed by strict Presbyterian rules. This was a day of rest. Of course food had to be prepared but as much as possible was done the day before. My aunts sat on the verandah chatting and watching Robbie and me play with our visiting cousins. They could not use the time to darn socks, sew on buttons, turn sheets; this was considered work. Knitting was permitted but only if it produced something frivolous. Aunty Chrissie once knitted a pair of blue and white striped pyjamas for my teddy bear: so soft and detailed with tiny buttons, such a perfect fit. It was unexpected largesse in this careful household where wanting to have butter *and* cream with jam on the heavenly scones we had for afternoon tea was a sign of intemperance.

Daddy conjures the countryside of his mother's birth in a phrase: *Endless rain-flattened corn*, and the Spartan quality of life: *no baths*. But oh the food! He is back on a farm: fresh butter and eggs, huge servings of porridge. And there is Balgargal again: that wonderful porridge so sturdy it is possible, and a satisfying adventure, to eat a circle an inch or so in from the plate's edge making a wonderful milk-filled moat around the island in the centre, with its glittering castle mound of brown sugar. If I can find such resonance in these small hints of this visit, how much more at home he surely must have felt. It may be Spartan, cold and remote, but it is also family.

There is a second photo of this leave, possibly taken on the same outing as the visit to the ruin of his mother's home. He stands in front of a very compact car, by the back wheel. He is in uniform, cigarette in hand. He wears a half smile; he looks leaner and less relaxed. Willie, wearing a cloth cap and a benignly dour expression, stands by the front fender, also smoking. There is a rather large woolly dog in the foreground. Behind the car, to the horizon is a vast flatness. The notation on the back tells us that this photo was taken at Ha Durren.

We desperately want this to be the happiest of leaves, knowing in one month he will be dead. Peggy and Will think he somehow knows what's ahead. He talks and talks. The words tumble from him. He is not normally a chatterbox. But they sense desperation in this need to tell. We know these things because Robbie, when she lived in London, took the train up to the north of Scotland and visited Peggy and Will.

I am impressed by this visit. It was not on my wish list when I lived in Britain but it was for her. She remembers the simplicity of the life, the cold, the cramped pantry where the washing-up was done. They spoke fondly and with sorrow of their young cousin who seemed to know that his death was coming. Robbie's visit honours his last leave. Peggy and Will are gone but I know them a little now because of my sister, and Daddy's short packed notes.

And then the diary stops.

What Have We Done?

If we had not discovered Michael, the aching gap left when Daddy stopped writing would remain forever unfilled. And, even though Michael tells me a little, it will never be enough.

"Always smiling" is how Michael describes his friend Arthur. It seems true. Of course, in photos, we do tend to smile no matter our mood. But his are not "say cheese" grins; his smile washes across his face, crinkles his eyes, lights him up. Even in a formal portrait the smile, though less broad, fills his face. In the well-thumbed photos we have, his smiles are ever-present. There is one, possibly significant, exception.

Sixteen days after he stops writing his diary, October 26, 1944, the squadron is called together for the photo that has become our constant reference. It captures over 200 men and one lone woman. "Ah," says Michael, "Joyce, she was the Station Intelligence Officer. Very nice woman. An old maid she was but a very charming lady. That was Joyce."

The Ops board that day calls all crews and Big Wigs of 207 together for this photo. "Come on mate, let's go. It's show time." The Lancaster looms over its tiers of platforms and front row of seats. They climb into place, calling to friends. They stand or sit facing the camera, neat rows in uniform. At the far left end of the top row, underneath the hundred foot span of the Lancaster's wings, the opposite end to where Daddy is standing, there is a break in the symmetry. Except for this spot, all the men are posed, obediently facing forward, intent on the camera. At that far end two men are turned away, profiles, almost backs of heads, presented to the photographer. In the neat breakdown of the picture, where groups of ten or so men are, where possible, identified, this section has an explanatory note: these men are worried about their skipper. He is late and they want him in the photo; they need to be together.

To us, this moment of crew unity simply emphasizes the fracturing of our father's crew. Daddy, Cliff, and Stan are together in the back row framed by the port engines, Alf is further down by the aircraft's nose, Michael below him in the second row, Bruce in the front row, a small man as suits a gunner, his mo now happily grown back. Bill is, of course, now gone, though where to we do not know. Normally they would have stood proudly together for this important moment. The fact that Daddy stands with two of the old gang tells something about loyalties and friendships that are still strong. But they are no longer a crew. They have been split up and reassigned. Is this the reason for his sad face and empty eyes?

For he does look bereft. For all the times my eyes have flown to the men in the back row standing between the two mighty engines, searching for my father's face, it is a while before I realize that, in this moment, he is not smiling. Tiny as this picture is, it is very clear. This is not the fellow we are used to. Two deep furrows mark his cheeks. His eyes look hollow. He seems thinner. Even in the photo by the car in Scotland he looked leaner, less robust. Something has shifted. And, with no diary, how do we find out what that is?

Michael's diary for the missing month reveals no angst. It is gently domestic, punctuated by mentions of Ops. Early in October, in a carefully documented culinary coup, Daddy and Bruce "scrounge some eggs from a neighbouring farm." They settle down by the fire in the hut to enjoy a feast of boiled eggs, toast, butter, Horlicks, and condensed milk. It is sixty-seven years since that night, yet the unaccustomed luxury of fresh farm eggs and the memory of friends round the fire in the hut is still bright. "That was good," Michael says, as if it were only a day or so ago.

One night they take the train to Skegness, have a meal and go for a slope — that's a drink. On another night Michael and Daddy play crib "for a late hour and a small stake." "Yeah, we played a lot of crib. Arthur was good at that. He usually beat me." Food is lovingly recorded: Alf volunteers his tins of tomato soup and spaghetti, which, with toast from the Mess, are worth noting. Another night they enjoy the remains of a chicken. And one morning Arthur arrives at noon to wake Michael so they can go for lunch.

There is nothing in all of this to indicate that our father is miserable, but he would not have confided such feelings. It isn't their way. Still, it is hard to ignore that sombre face, so different from everything we know of him and every photo before. And there is that nagging story of his constant talking in Bowermadden and Peggy's feeling that he believes he is going to die.

He has been assigned to a crew by the time this photo is taken; flying with Sparkes. There is some hint, we learn from one of our mother's few confidences, that he worries about this. He thinks his skipper might have a drinking problem. She believes that may have been a contributing factor in the fiery crash that last night. We know now that it wasn't. And anyway, after eight hours in the air and a successful bombing run, unless he is sipping from a clandestine flask, poor Sparkes could not have been even remotely inebriated enough to be a problem. But, if Daddy does not trust this man or feels less safe flying with his new crew, justified or not, this could help to explain those empty eyes.

***

Among the things he sent to Mummy is a pretty card, tied with a ribbon and with verse in flowing script. He finds it in some shop, perhaps in Spilsby or while wandering around Skegness, and instantly knows it is perfect. On the front of the card is a pastel sketch of a man walking a country road leading two draught horses, sturdy brown fellows with white blazes and creamy feathering spilling over their feet. Leafy trees, a very English scene, shade the path but, if you don't look too closely, those trees might almost be eucalypts; one horse at least is a close cousin to our farm horse, Toby. It must have spoken so powerfully to him, that image of a man going home after a job well done. The verse would break your heart.

To Greet You — at the end of the day

Through the quiet evening hour one hears
A cheerful rhythmic sound
And on the sunlit road appears
A ploughman homeward bound

He's heading for the Heart's Content
I wish this day for you
A home made fair with love and joy
And friendship deep and true.

He cannot wait to get back to the camp, find a stamp and send it off. On the facing page he writes, *To my Nooney, may the day when I am coming home to you again be very soon, Your Paddy*. It is not so long since he confided in his diary just how much he is missing that lovely person. The more I know the harder it is for me to think of what is to come. He is so often at camp churning out letters, hoping for better weather tomorrow, missing home while the young fellows are out on a tear. Still, I can't help thinking that he may be happier than they; he knows what his life holds, he has made his decisions, he knows he is loved. They are all still looking for all of that; frightened of dying with life so unexplored.

When does our mother receive this loving and carefully chosen card? Perhaps it is just before he dies. Does it inform or create that vivid dream: "on a sunlit road ... a ploughman homeward bound?" Mail is slow. Likely she does not get it until after his death. Imagine the pain that brings.

No longer confident that he can count on his crewmates, Arthur is desperately homesick and fearing he will not make it to the end of his tour; more than enough to give him that lean and sombre look. But there may be something else, a question we have avoided for much of this journey. How does he feel about what he is doing? It is a simple enough question but the answer is fraught. War turns young men into killers; how do you live with that? How does he?

Wilful blindness is not an option for us and so we return to the controversy about Bomber Command. We know about Dresden but somehow think it a fair trade for Coventry, not only in our minds but in the minds of sensible historians. It is satisfying to growl, "Well, they started it," and they did. But ... saturation bombing, flattening cities as a quid pro quo...? I had been proud to say that my father served in Bomber Command. To my mind Coastal or Ferry Command sounded slightly effeminate. They aren't smashing Hitler, winning the war: that's what Bomber Command, with its noble motto, rendered in plain English, its meaning not concealed by Jesuitical Latin, "Strike Hard Strike Sure," is about. And then we begin to read and wonder, and gag, at the whiff of sulphur, the moral squirming, the sputtering outrage. These questions, which have no easy answers, trouble us in our search; they dog us still. They are — as perhaps they were for our father — a permanent bruise.

Butch Harris believes that reducing Germany's cities to rubble is the fastest, the best, perhaps the only, way to win the war. He is not alone. In July 1941 Churchill thunders, for all the world to hear, a promise that my father and his fellows in Bomber Command are bound to carry out: "From now on we shall bomb Germany on an ever-increasing scale, month by month, year by year, until the Nazi regime has either been exterminated by us — or better still — torn to pieces by the German people themselves." And, whatever revisionism they may indulge in after the war, the majority of the British people, clinging to their little island, with Nazi Germany staring them down across the Channel, and with no way to strike back except through Bomber Command, think this is a jolly good idea.

Before I leave for England on our quest, I visit my family dentist, George, who fled Czechoslovakia in his early twenties, first working in Holland and then in Canada. He carries these experiences lightly, or so I believed. As he pokes about in my mouth, he tells me a story. When he was three his little village, a place of no military value or interest although occupied by the Germans, is inexplicably bombed by the Allies. As the bombers are returning from an operation to the east and passing over his village, a German soldier opens fire on them. This is, of course, stupid and futile. Given that it is late November 1944, it must be clear to the German on the ground that their war is being lost. Perhaps his blasting away, just for a moment, gives this frustrated soldier a sense of control. One of those bombers, RAF as the Americans did not do night raids, taking exception to being fired at, turns back. For some reason there is still a bomb on board. It is unloaded onto George's innocent village.

"You don't forget something like that," he murmurs as he pauses, allowing me to spit in a handy funnel. The windows of the house shatter inward, showering splintered glass over his small brother sleeping in his crib. His mother brushes the shards off her baby, scoops him up, grabs little George's hand, and they run. The street outside is full of roiling dust, debris, and screaming neighbours. Holding onto one another, not sure what is happening, fearful another bomb will fall, they scramble through the smoke, over bricks that used to be their homes.

George tells this without rancour, but it does not reflect well on the crew of that plane. What do they write in their logbooks, I wonder. Are they shame-faced? Do they agree to keep it quiet or are they proud of their spite, proud to have stuck it to Jerry?

Every airman keeps a logbook but we have not found our father's. Wherever it is, we crave whatever light it might shine. As we know him to be far from expansive, perhaps that light would be dim. Still, it might help to explain the month of silence and those haunting eyes. Lacking his logbook, I pore over *Bomber Command War Diaries*, a tome packed with agony, glory, and shame. Almost every book we have read calls on this resource. And it is impressive. It is the most comprehensive record of wartime raids and will help us know something of that missing month. Group 5 is our focus; it includes 207. If Group 5 is mentioned then there is a chance that 207 is flying that night, and maybe our father is as well — not piercingly accurate but a good start. For the absent month I search for raids involving Group 5.

The diary, up until his last leave, records each sortie: the date, the time, the place, the target. It is that last one, the target, that mostly interests us. To our relief, each raid he records is a clear military target. Is this, we wonder, also the case for the raids he flew in the month before he died, the raids not recorded? Sometimes the answer is a clear "yes." Walcheren is pounded five times: its seawall twice, gun positions three times; the Dortmund-Ems and Mitelland canals are attacked and a synthetic oil plant at Gelsenkirchen is targeted. At this stage of the war accuracy has vastly improved. In spite of this, bombs still miss and civilians die in flaming towns. Even when they are spot-on lives are lost. It would be naive to think otherwise; war is messy.

The propaganda film, *Target for Tonight*, made in the early days of the War, paints a jolly picture of the RAF fly boys leaping into their bombers in a cloud of "cheerio old chap" banter, sallying forth to drop rather benign looking bombs on the deserving Hun with laser-like accuracy and, after a mildly pulse-raising spot of bother, sliding home in triumph, hair barely ruffled. It makes everyone feel good, but it is a lie. In the early days, bombs frequently land miles from the target, exploding harmlessly in fields or wiping out militarily insignificant families. The attrition rate for the crews is horrendous; the damage minimal. But slowly, accuracy improves. Pathfinder Force emerges to pinpoint routes and targets with flares; Master Bombers oversee and co-ordinate; navigation and weather prediction evolve. By the time our Dad and his mates are bombing they have a really good chance of hitting the target and, as long as the target is a flying bomb facility, a rail yard, a chemical factory, or anything whose destruction advances the war effort and brings peace closer, they can feel real pride in what they are doing.

But what if targets are less clear? What are they being ordered to do then? Because of the missing logbook, we cannot know what raids Daddy is sent on in the period between his return from leave in Scotland and the day that troubling photo is taken, but there are a number of unsettling possibilities. In a clearly stated directive, Harris is ordered to "demonstrate to the enemy the overwhelming superiority of the Allied Air Force," within the shortest time and with maximum force they will hurl all they have at "objectives in the densely populated Ruhr." This is just the kind of directive Harris likes. So, when the Ops board is revealed on October 14, 1944, two days before the photo is taken, the crews mustered in the briefing room, are not told to find and destroy targets of military interest, they are simply directed to obliterate a city. "The object is to exterminate Duisburg for good and all," an airman who took part in the daylight raid writes in his diary.

How does it feel to be given such orders? How does it feel to carry them out? Many try to aim at factories if possible, easier in daylight to see what you are doing, and what you have done. The night both Duisburg and Brunswick are targeted cities and their occupants are destroyed. Families, not combatants.

It seems very likely that our father is involved in one of these raids. He certainly knows about them. Each raid his courage is tested, but now, perhaps, his honour is as well. What is he part of? What is he doing to women like his Nooney and children like us? We are on his mind more now. We have the postcards that he has sent home, addressed to us, loving messages on the back. He came here to protect us and a way of life he wanted us to have. Now he is wondering what ugliness he has been asked to commit. Perhaps he wonders if he is still worthy of those he is trying to shield.

If he is having a crisis of conscience, he is not alone. The men who fly the planes and release the bombs are not unaware of what is happening on the ground and many are deeply conflicted. Some simply refuse to look. Others go home to their families after the War, pierced with regret. Others take the view that they are simply giving back what Germany has dished out. For all, their job is to bring this war to an end; then the killing can stop.

Daddy's letters to our mother might have revealed his feelings about this, but they are gone. His good friend, Michael, shows some discomfort when the topic is raised even though I bring it up with the deference and respect I believe he deserves. "It wasn't as bad," he says, "as they made out. Well, some of them anyway." There was no indiscriminate bombing. "And in my time we didn't bomb cities just for the sake of it. Often factories would be in the cities so they would cop it, naturally. But we didn't just go to knock down houses like the Germans did." Still, he admits that Harris's "We'll get 'em, serves 'em right: they sowed the wind now they are going to reap the whirlwind" wasn't, as he puts it, with his typical understatement, "much of an idea."

There is in this little speech, disquiet, but not guilt. He believes sincerely that they are as ethical as is possible given their task. I hope he is right and that I am wrong about the sadness in our father's eyes in that photo. Perhaps he held Michael's view of things. I do not wish him regret or shame.

As the war staggers to its end and first the brass and then the general population begin to absorb the photos of what has been done to Germany, there is a horrified intake of breath. Churchill as far back as 1943 had wondered aloud, "Are we beasts?" but could see no other way. The people of Britain are now feeling his discomfort. In the mangled streets of cities reduced to rubble are the dead. These are people who looked not unlike themselves; they come from the same stock. Sprawled bodies of women, twisted and ugly in death wear the same house dresses and shapeless coats as the mums and grandmas of their English villages; the unseemliness of hiked up frocks reveal familiar stocking tops on plump legs; the wicker baby carriage toppled on its side looks just like the one in the High Street, the crushed towns are those they used to visit on holidays.

What have we done? They want to know. And of course they want no responsibility in all of this. Churchill's political nature asserts itself: he needs to distance himself. He joins the paroxysm of revulsion sweeping his land, as the news that bombs flatten buildings and kill people, suddenly dawns on them, and he turns on these young men. He does not even acknowledge their contribution in his victory speech, a victory largely due to them. No medals are struck for the heroes of Bomber Command, no national monument undertaken by the government.

Without a handy bottle of wine to ease us through, my sister and I contemplate our sad-faced father and all those who fought in Bomber Command — the things they were called to do, and the guilt they were made to bear — we feel the insult, the neglect, and the self-righteous ignorance. The Afrikaans have an expression about a fierce storm, "It's raining old women with clubs." It is more than apt. Old women are tough; add clubs and they are formidable. We are old and we are armed with fury and we are pissed. Those men of Bomber Command were, we believe, good men. They did what was asked of them, they did it with courage, they did it night after night — many thousands of them died in a battle against what can only be described as evil — and most of all, they did it for us.

Heartbreak

In Great Steeping, the village close to the Spilsby base, our trail runs cold. Where is this abandoned airfield that rendered us fatherless? We pull off onto a side road, park under a stand of lush trees and look about for aid. We are on the edge of a schoolyard where pink-cheeked children are enjoying recess. We watch them fondly until it occurs to us that a car containing two ogling adults parked next to a playground might well give somebody fits. Already one of the teachers is striding purposefully toward us. We hastily move the car and seek directions from a tweedy chap out walking his dog. Happily he knows a thing or two and sends us in the right direction.

By the side of a dusty country road lined by scrubby trees, the flat Lincolnshire farmland melting into a pale sky, we park the car. In the distance, what is left of RAF Base Spilsby crouches at the edge of a ploughed expanse. The runway has been torn up and the aggregate used for the Humber Bridge. There are some buildings still standing but most have gone. Bits of original living quarters are extant but on private land. It simply looks dismal. We are getting close to the saddest part of our journey. The debate about whether to drive toward the abandoned Avro hangar is a short one. We will be content with finding the Spilsby Airfield Memorial that will, we hope, be a balm for the wound of general indifference. We have heard rumours of plans for a splendid monument to be built in London; it will trumpet the glory of men like our father. Perhaps it will make amends to the men of Bomber Command; even better if it starts a more balanced assessment of their worth. In the meantime, where is the promised recognition of 207?

It would be a mistake for us to be too self-righteous. We two well-meaning, kind and loving daughters have managed to seal off our minds and imaginations from knowledge and understanding of our father for most of our adult lives. We flew above this part of our history, catching glimpses through the clouds, never flying low. I'm not suggesting that we avoided knowing him, but our carelessness for all those years now fills us with guilt and some shame. There were two solitudes in the house where we grew up: our mother's very private loss and her daughters' inability to gently probe. The sin of omission is ours as well.

Back in the car, we drive slowly along the road and then, there it is. The website bills it as "one of the best — if not the best — airfield memorial in Lincolnshire." It is pleasant but a long way from grand: a gravelled space, curved brick walls at each back corner, like encircling arms, neat right angle walls at the front edge, a monument in muted grey granite in the middle. It invites us to walk up to this monument, dedicated to "All the Men and Women who served at this airfield," his squadron, 207, the one he and Mike drove to with reluctance and then learned to love, the base where he operated from July 17 to November 11, 1944. Just shy of four months, such a little time. In the centre of the monument is 207's shield: a winged lion, statant: standing firm. Their motto, Semper Paratus — Always Prepared — has a sensible, practical ring that would have pleased our father.

There is no mention of 44 Squadron; the one Daddy worries will cause over-crowding. Made up largely of Rhodesian airmen, like 207, it was formed in the Great War, disbanded and then re-formed for a second round. Its shield features an elephant, symbol of a powerful attack. Its motto is Fulmina Regis Justa, "The King's Thunderbolts are Righteous." Yes, we think, they are, and it seems a pity that they get no mention in this low-key roadside memorial. For us, they are significant.

There is an information board off to the side containing a map of the airfield with the typical triangulated runways. There is also a history of the 207's time here. At War's end they bring POWs home from Europe in Operation Exodus and ground crew are flown on a "Cook's

Tour" over Germany to view what, together, they have wrought. We don't hear a lot about ground crew: those who service and repair the planes to keep them flying, the armourers who load them with bombs, the runway personnel, those who see them off and wait for their return. They and the factory workers who build the planes and the bombs and, of course everyone in the line of command, make all this happen. They take a share in the glory; should they also split the blame?

They also face their share of danger. Of the three notable incidents written up on the information board, the first concerns the men who deal with the bombs. In April of 1944, three months before Daddy and his mates get there, a crew is disarming a 1,000 pound bomb in a shed when it explodes, killing ten armourers. The bodies of three are never found. They have no graves; there is nothing to bury. The explosion damages airfield buildings and some in neighbouring communities. Later that year, November 1, when Daddy and Mike are there, comes a second incident involving a Lancaster swinging violently out of control on take-off. It smashes into four planes causing an inferno that destroys the Lancaster and three Halifaxes.

And now with the third event, we come to what Michael calls "the nasty bit." Although Robbie and I had, for so long, harboured rather vague notions about our father's death, by the time we reach this notice board, we are aware of what happened. It is no longer just a generic "fiery crash"; it doesn't involve an error by a squiffy pilot; nobody is romantically "shot down over Germany." It is, we think, sadder than any of these. It reminds us of the cruel joke that ended everything for Snowy Traeger. Dumb luck. That's all.

***

As raids go, that November 11, 1944, night attack on Harburg, its target the Rhenania-Ossag oil refinery, is relatively easy. They come in west of Hamburg, surprisingly lightly defended. Over the target the flak is moderate and only about twelve searchlights are operating.

Seven Lancasters are lost in the raid. Michael, flying with his new crew, reports seeing two go down. On the way home, between the Friesians and Heligoland, they come in for more flak from both places and from flak ships. Michael tells us, "Several scarecrows went up." In an aside he explains that these are "anti-aircraft stuff." I'm not about to argue with this gentle, hospitable veteran about how he sees his war experience, but he is, in fact, very likely wrong about this.

Morale is always a worry for the men running things at High Wycombe. Can't have crew going into a funk when they are surrounded by flaming aircraft plunging from the sky. So they come up with a mythical German weapon: the scarecrow. Planted rumour carries the news: Jerry is sending up explosions that look like the flaming wreckage of aircraft shot from the sky. They do it, the airmen are told, to put you off, to break you down. In fact, as far as we can discover, what they are seeing are not German-staged explosions to mimic crippled and burning aircraft but actual aircraft shot out of the sky. Once scarecrows are concocted, these dazzling pyrotechnics no longer represent seven good men, fighting alongside you, being blown to pieces, but simply a silly German trick. Very wily, those High Wycombe chaps.

The raid over, Daddy and crew are heading home toward the black line of the English coast, behind it a welcoming and friendly dark: the base, a bacon and egg breakfast, a warm bed, safety. Of course it is never over until it's over. No letting the guard down. A fighter could have followed them back, ready to strike. Still, home is in sight; they can have a coffee, look forward to a cigarette and blessed sleep. And he has been granted his commission, two days before. He hasn't gone for his uniform upgrade; he does not own the Officer's hat. But he is warmed by that satisfaction.

As they near the base, the towers of Lincoln Cathedral piercing the night sky to the west, he allows himself to relax a little. "Well, one more down. I wonder how Mike made out. He's on tonight. Perhaps we can get in a game of crib." They close in on the base, are given clearance to enter the funnels to land: "Pancake. Pancake." Ahead is a convergent line of ground lights laid out to direct them safely, to funnel them to the runway. All around are aircraft, circling and waiting for the go-ahead. The pilot lines up and begins the descent. Out in the dark over the farmland, also waiting for a signal, is a Lancaster from 44 Squadron with seven tired men thinking the same thoughts as Daddy and his crewmates. "Pancake. Pancake," they are told. They have been given the order to enter the funnels at exactly the same time as our father's plane.

***

"Doesn't that sum it up," says Robbie as we turn from the story of our father's death, pinned behind glass on a notice board by the side of a narrow dirt road. She is referring to the WAAF's introduction to this history of Spilsby, "Life on a Bomber Station was made of moments of feverish activity and breathless excitement, followed by suspense and, all too often, heartbreak."

Robbie has a card in her well-stocked handbag. We find a pen and she writes a note for any who might care to know. She tells who we are, why we are here, and who we are remembering. The scrubby growth by the roadside offers nothing in the way of flowers for a memorial so we take photos. Robbie continues to be horrified by how inappropriately cheerful she looks in these pictures, but we are, at this point, not so much sad as winded. It is odd to be here, to see his last raid written up in black and white, to be next to the remains of the runway. We shed no tears. We bundle back into the car intent on finishing this sad chapter with a search for the crash site.

Our father died "over Bratoft" according to the official records. Driving through the flat farmland and skinny back roads, the car brushing against hedges, occasionally shrinking into them to let another car go by, we find ourselves inexplicably guided by Fred, to a church set in an overgrown yard in the middle of nowhere. A farmhouse tops the trees some distance off but otherwise we are, on a sunny Friday morning parked at the gate of a venerable place of worship seemingly un-anchored by any community. We clamber out, lock the car, open the little metal gate in the churchyard fence and walk up the stone path to the door. The entryway is a covered porch with an elaborate mesh gate, installed to keep birds from nesting in the rafters.

We have no expectation that the church will be open but the heavy door yields to us and, as we enter, we hear women's voices. A mother and daughter are doing the flowers for the Sunday service. The mother is busy in a side chapel, her daughter attending to the main altar and their cheerful voices skip back and forth: family, local gossip, doings of the week. At first they take us for tourists and proudly point out the church's claim to fame: a painting rendered on a piece of timber from a ship that sailed with the Armada before foundering, being salvaged, and then decorated. This treasure is placed high on the back wall, high enough to deter thieves now that the Parish is aware of its provenance and value.

When we tell them why we have come to Bratoft they down their tools and stand with us by the small side chapel wondering if they can add more information. There is a man in his eighties living nearby, he might know something. They could try to get in touch with him? Thankful as we are for such an offer, we feel that this little encounter will serve.

The mother would be in her eighties too. She has a recurring dream that goes back to her childhood and the war. Her mother is bundling her up to hide her in a cupboard because the Germans are coming. She hears them at the door. And then, she laughs dismissively, they turn into Red Indians. "Silly, really, but it terrified me. It still does." When I say that I hope our visit does not resurrect this dream for her, she shrugs this away. Perhaps our story has added another layer to this dream. Perhaps it has robbed it of some of its menace.

This little slice of gentle country exists largely because of the terrible and brave acts of the men in our story. Two women can snip and trim and artfully arrange their collection of flowers, picked from their own gardens, on the altar and in the chapel, for the small and probably dwindling congregation to gather and raise creaky voices in songs of thanks. Surely a portion of gratitude is owed to the men on our minds that day in that church. The way of life those airman knew in Lincolnshire more than six decades ago was likely not so very different from what we are seeing today. They understood what they were risking and what that risk was aiming to preserve.

As we say our thanks and goodbyes and leave the church we look up into the spring sky. Above us and very close to where we are, early on a dark November morning in 1944, after eight hours of flying, after successfully avoiding the probing network of searchlights, the flak, and the German fighters, after unloading their bombs, after turning home in relief, after crossing the North Sea and the English coast with the lights of the airfield in sight, with thoughts of a quick debriefing, breakfast and a blessed sleep, a horrible mistake is about to be made. Two Lancasters, those beautiful and deadly giants, one from 44 Squadron and one from 207 Squadron, are directed, at the same time, into the funnel of lights leading to the runway at Spilsby Airfield. In a grinding, ripping, splintering collision those two aircraft carrying a total of fourteen men, all young, all loved, smash into each other and disintegrate. Debris rains down; the noise must have been heard for miles. This old church is a witness. Its two women, peacefully doing the flowers, alive and well and happy, have deep roots here. It is more than fitting that we have found them today.

Michael is also a witness. He reads solemnly from the entry he made after returning to his hut that evening: "While in the circuit over base we saw two kites collide in the funnels. I instantly thought of Arthur and Alf, both on tonight." Two more planes nearly suffer the same fate but are "given a red and sent round again." In the fields beyond the runway they can see the glow of the wrecked kites. "In the debriefing room we learned that Sparks had collided with a 44 bod." So Daddy's apprehension about 44 Squadron's arrival and possible crowding comes horribly true — but certainly not in the way he imagined.

In the end it is that simple. A mistake is made and fourteen men, with families and futures, die. Somewhere, possibly dead now herself, there is a WAAF who, on duty that night, makes this catastrophic error: she directs two planes to line in up the funnels and to land at the same time. She likely knows many of the men who die; she has spent this war trying to keep them safe. She watches in horror as the fire engines scream out to douse the burning planes and the ambulances move in the retrieve the dead. Curled up in her bunk in the early morning, staring into the dark, she is wracked with misery and guilt. At one time I wanted to know her name; not to lay blame, simply to add her to the list of damage caused by this dreadfulness. She has to go on, living with her mistake. It is almost worse than dying.

The men prefer WAAFs in the control towers; they say they are clearer. They like to hear a woman's voice guide them in; it feels like home. Nooney, who would for our father be conjured up by the voice guiding them in, never knows that this is how her Paddy dies. It is long after the war before such details are released. It would not have helped morale to know that such errors are possible.

Michael believes it was a "good prang," that they are killed instantly and do not suffer. He finds some solace there. That night he writes in his diary: "The chopper descended on Arthur, the most upright, sincere and honest chap I have ever met. It will be a terrible blow for Enid and the children. Having successfully carried out a raid and to be killed in your own funnels is a terrible tragedy."

Michael doesn't know, and I don't tell him, that this isn't a case of pilot error. I wonder now why I do not explain this. Perhaps I feel it is not my place to change the way he had seen things all these years. These are his memories. Leave them be.

Following an inquiry, the protocol for entering the funnels is modified; now the planes enter on a time sequence. All of Bomber Command adopts this. Well, that's something.

Sorrow

After Spilsby and Bratoft and the Lancaster any notion that we might skip Cambridge is gone. It is not a place he visited or ever saw, but he is buried here. I have seen the grave before; Robbie has not. She worries it might be a bother for me to make a second visit. No, I think we should and see it together and, swiftly, so does she.

East Anglia brings us more quaint villages and gently rolling farmland. Britain is too picturesque and fertile for its own good. Rhododendrons march in purple splendour across the green hills and Queen Anne's Lace forms a buttery hedge along the country lanes.

We arrive in Cambridge latish in the afternoon. The ancient streets, lined with one glorious building after another, are crowded with students on their bicycles, their wicker baskets full of books. Our B&B, the "Cam," is easy to remember and reasonably priced. Finding it and getting safely parked is an ordeal that leaves us tired and cranky. And we are hungry. A long walk past dignified Victorian terraces takes us to a barnlike restaurant with bare wooden tables and a New Age vibe. The squash soup is silky and satisfying; the homemade bread a yeasty wonder.

With our final cup of tea for the day in the teeny front bedroom of the Cam, we pull out the binders once more. Robbie has pictures of the funeral taken by some kind person and mailed to our mother. Poor Mummy. She hears from Wynnis Madigan, Michael's mother, that an Australian conducts the service. Perhaps that helps.

Four days after her dream, the telegram appears. It is agony to imagine that moment. Enid, who may never be called Nooney again, is in the garden by the side of the house when she looks down the driveway and sees her mother crossing the ramp aided by the Methodist Minister. They make their way up that same path that her dream Paddy had walked. They have come by sulky, leaving it on the road as the horse cannot cross the ramp. Mummy lays her trowel down, stands, and smooths her hands on her apron. She knows why they are here. She knows what they are coming to tell her.

The puzzle is why they are there at all. One of the last things the men of Bomber Command do before leaving on an operation is to designate who is to be informed if they do not return. It seems that Daddy wants no intermediary. We have a copy of the telegram. "Personal: Mrs. E. R. Plowman ... Deeply regret to inform you..." It outlines the accident, telling her when and where and how. It does not tell her why. We cannot imagine such news arriving in the hands of a stranger or being delivered by phone. It is equally hard to imagine our father naming Jimmy, his obstructive, self-absorbed mother-in-law, as the one to break the news. He writes to her during the war as a duty. He is polite. In his diary he refers to her as "Mrs. Ern," which we find funny (Ern is our grandfather) and a tad disrespectful. He would not have given her the delicate job of delivering this blow to his Nooney. So why, if she isn't the chosen messenger, is she coming up the path, telegram in hand, a minster at her side?

Orange is a small town, everybody knows everybody. When the telegram arrives there is consternation in the Post Office. That poor girl with two little kids. Who will be the messenger? How can we soften the blow? We could call her mother! What a good idea. She'll know what to do. And it is done. Jimmy is called, goes to town, fetches the telegram and the minister, and they trot the sulky along the leafy road to the laneway, tether the horse, struggle across the awkward iron bars of the ramp, and walk toward the stricken young woman in her garden.

This is November 15. The next day is his funeral; allowing for the time difference, he is actually buried on the day she receives the news.

I suppose she works that out for herself unless she is, like me, completely mystified by datelines and time differences. I hope so. How much harder it is to mourn a man you have not seen buried. Even worse to know that he is in the cold ground before you know he is dead. And there is more that she never knows. Michael tells me something I do not expect. Arthur, he is told, is "fairly well smashed up" but the MO is going to patch him up and they can go and see him. "But I don't think we ever did." There is a body, one able to be "patched up" for viewing, for saying goodbyes.

Often there isn't much to bury at those funerals where men have died in crashes — think of the stories of the dead tail gunners' turrets being hosed out after a raid. Sometimes remains are divided up among coffins so there will be something to bury, in others rocks or earth are added so the pallbearers will not find themselves lifting an empty box. We find some solace in the thought of a body, still whole and ready to be placed in the ground of the country he died defending.

Death, for the boys of Bomber Command, does not always look like death for the Army boys. The men who wade though the surf on the beaches of Normandy, then fight house by house reclaiming Europe, have their noses rubbed in death at its most graphic. The blood-stained water and the floating bodies, the man beside you blown to pieces, the mangled limbs, the spilling guts — these are their companions and haunt their dreams. It is not like that for the Bomber boys. A kite next to them is hit. One of the crew reports it. The Navigator makes a note. If men are seen bailing out, parachutes deployed, that is recorded too. This information is relayed at debriefing as the squadron waits to see who got home and who didn't. Casualties are chalked on the board in the crew room. Until names are listed, death is arm's-length. If men in the hut are missing the MPs arrive promptly to take away their possessions. It is important to stop the crews who have survived the night from brooding. Out of sight, out of mind.

Knowing this, it does not surprise us that Mike, Alf, Bruce, and Stan decide against a viewing. Doing what they do each night will not be made easier for having seen what can result. But perhaps when it is a friend that has got the chop it might help to have a body to bid farewell.

Would our mother have found comfort in seeing her Paddy one last time? Unlike her confused younger daughter, she didn't harbour delusions that he was wandering around Germany and would someday reappear. But, until you have stood in the presence of the dead, how can you ever be sure that death is real? How can you say goodbye?

In that box of possessions arriving after the war are four items labelled "damaged": a watch, a comb, a cigarette lighter, and a notebook. At first I wonder if our father was a careless fellow who did not take care of his things. Then I realize that these items were with him when his plane crashed. Our mother would have taken them from the box and reached the same conclusion. Perhaps these battered and burned things that had been his helped make it real for her.

Years ago, not long after our moment of intimate confidence in the restaurant on the Arno, when we were in the UK together, she disappeared for a day, returning with no explanation. I did not press. I believe she went to Cambridge and stood at the foot of his grave. Her mourning was private and deeply personal, not for sharing.

Once you remarry, or so my dictionary informs me, you are no longer a widow. I wonder about that. Until she dies my mother wears the engagement and wedding ring given to her by Paddy. My stepfather's wedding gift is an expensive diamond and platinum watch. A mistake, really: watches simply stop on my mother's wrist. She never wears them. The extravagant diamond job is slipped on for special occasions but it is never actually ticking.

"Widow" is a sad and lonely word. The sound of wind in winter trees. It comes from "alone" or "separated." And that is achingly true but it does not stop being true just because she has remarried. Part of her is alone forever. The person left behind, who was a lover, a companion, a friend, a soulmate, is frozen in a past life. At the moment those two planes collide, that part of her dies. She is a mother, a daughter, a sister, a friend, but she ceases to be a cherished Nooney.

There should be a ghostly graveyard somewhere with solemn marble headstones marking the end of women created by love, for they die just as surely as their men. Their lives do not just take a different road. They end. In the days that follow the wrenching loss there is mourning for the death of the women they have been as well as for the love they have lost. They have to reinvent themselves, to be born again as something quite different.

In those weeks after the arrival of that telegram she leans on her elbows and peers at her face in the mirror, asking her reflection, "Who am I now? I am not who I was. What has replaced the old me?" It seems it should be marked on her, like a livid brand, this loss. But, no. It is the same face. Thinner perhaps but not transformed. She is here; there is no choice. She stares back at her stricken self. "Stricken," past participle of strike. She has been struck, like a child who has just touched a hot stove in that second when he turns his face to you in disbelief. That blank, and yes, stricken look, the second before the face crumples in a howl of anguish. She is in that place between pain and collapse. Stricken. Struck. Unexpectedly, unfairly, cruelly, part of her has been lopped off.

Dutchy, our father's good friend, comes back after the war to fulfill his pact with his two friends. For Ern's parents, as we know, he heals a squeaking windmill, and then he goes to see Mummy and us. At her funeral, many years later, he is chosen to give the eulogy. I have his notes for this speech. He arrived at the neat little bungalow, he tells the congregation, to find a bright, vivacious woman, attractive, and totally in control. He came to offer his support and she ended up comforting him. He sums up her busy and purposeful life: she worked for Legacy, was President of the Home and School, had a lovingly tended garden, kept a spotless house, supported and loved her many friends. She had, he says, an intense interest in everything and was remarkably well informed.

Dutchy kept in touch with her after the war, inviting her to Sydney to stay with his family. There she met another Arthur, Arthur Chiswell, Dutchy's uncle, the man who would become our stepfather. Dutchy married, had children and, when he retired, moved to Orange and became an orchardist himself. He took an interest in us, Arthur's two daughters, but, once again hobbled by some sense of our father as a topic too tender to speak of, we didn't sit him down and find out what he had to tell. My middle daughter, Megan, of a new generation and in no way hobbled, on a visit to Australia, wandered with him through his orchard where he answered all her questions. We know more about him because of her and some of the things he told her have found their way into this story. In so many ways he was more than faithful to his pact.

My indomitable mother marched on through her grief, pushing it aside, not allowing it to have sway over her. I saw her cry only twice. These two memories, both from the time before she remarried, are so vivid because seeing a crack in her calm and capable façade was rare and unnerving.

I was playing under the hedge separating what we called the "clothes paddock," the area where she hung out the washing, from the orchard. She didn't see me as she struggled through the trees from behind our outdoor dunny, carrying a brimming and foul-smelling pail full of our waste. She had already prepared a hole to receive the maggoty contents and a shovel stood by ready to move the pile of earth and bury this noisome burden. She had to do this chore regularly, but this time, as she hauled this mess, two-handed, trying not to slop anything on her clothes, she was weeping, choked despairing sobs. I was transfixed but knew enough to stay put. This was private; she would not like an audience.

Then there was a night when I couldn't sleep. I could hear the sewing machine chattering away in the kitchen and went to see what Mummy was doing. Some sort of fancy dress event was coming up and she was making costumes for Robbie and me. On the table was a jewelled palette of red, green, orange, and blue crepe paper.

Mummy was busy pleating, pinning, and sewing this gloriousness into two long skirts, one for each of us. I was so enchanted that it was a moment before I realized that she was crying. There was no hiding what I'd seen this time. I asked what was wrong and, uncharacteristically, she told me. It is the only time I remember her speaking of money; we were certainly poor in those years but Robbie and I never felt it. We sailed through life convinced we were royalty. Mummy did not burden us with any of her worries, least of all this one. But that night she confessed through her tears that she was crying because she hadn't the money to buy real fabric to make these skirts. Crepe paper was all she could manage. I told her it was beautiful, we would love them, and took myself to bed.

We were brought up to keep emotions to ourselves, pretty hard for my overwrought self. One day, when I had let fly about something in front of guests having tea in our garden, I was taken into the house and given a stern lecture. I remember nothing about who was there or what exactly I had said and done, but I remember what she said: "We keep our feelings to ourselves. We don't parade them in front of others."

Determined to keep her grief private, unable to share it, she never gave herself permission to mourn. It got her in the end. No drug, no treatment could shift the black shawl of depression. She was, as a last resort, moved to the local mental hospital and given shock treatment. It didn't help but she did have an enjoyable stay, telling my sister brightly that she has met such interesting people. She was convalescing at a seniors' home when she died. They found her on the floor of the hospital room; she died alone, trying to crawl toward the light of the corridor. Her heart had given out. As Dutchy said in his eulogy, "she burned too brightly."

***

As we pore over the photographs of our father's funeral, knee to knee in our cozy little room in the Cam, we have no idea who attends or how it unfolds. In these pictures we see three coffins draped in Union Jacks. One is Daddy's, the second the bomb aimer from his crew, the third from the 44 Squadron. They arrive in squared-off hearses flanked on each side by uniformed men, three to a side. Young and solemn, they march slowly, double-breasted greatcoats buttoned against the November chill. Following the hearse are three more men, also uniformed; one is very tall. They pass rows of white crosses on one side, a flag at half-staff on the other. In a third picture our father's coffin is being carefully lowered by the six who walked with it. The three followers, including the tall chap, watch, heads bowed.

We decide that a rather handsome chap, the only one of the three bearing witnesses not wearing an officer's cap, is likely Cliff. This is based on close examination of his tiny face in the squadron picture. How nice to think he might be at the funeral. It is some time before we discover that that would not have been possible.

Dear Cliff. He is so young. He loves his parents and runs home to them at every chance. At first our father worries this escape artist might be the weak link in their chain but he becomes solid and a good friend. In early October, Cliff says goodbye to his old crew. He has been assigned to 617 Squadron, home of the Dam Busters, housed at Woodhall Spa, where he will enjoy superior accommodations. This likely makes little impression; friends matter more than the hut you occupy. He is in no hurry to go and, Michael tells us, manages to miss the transport. This frees him to go off with Stan for a slope in Thursby. Mike has one last laugh at Lime who has managed to pack his kit bag with his torch at the bottom still switched on. He has to pull everything out and repack. Such a teenager ... with less than a month to live.

Among our father's things sent home after the war, there is a letter addressed to Cliff. We will never know the contents of that letter: likely a chatty update on doings at 207 and interest in how things are for his old bomb-aimer. He does not know he was killed on Ops on November 6, their deaths separated by just five days.

The original crew, now scattered — Bill gone, Alf, Stan, Mike, and Bruce placed with other crews — must briefly ponder the stats: two dead, five still kicking. Better odds than the average: statistically almost half will die. Of course, in the case of Daddy's second crew, it is one hundred percent. But this is better not dwelt on.

So, Cliff is not at his funeral although we do not know that as we thumb through our binders in preparation for our visit to the Borough Cemetery. But Michael, discovered so much later, is. He is the tall man in the picture. He walks behind the hearse, stands beside the grave.

As Michael reads, in his surprisingly strong voice, a world of riches opens. He knows, respects, and loves this father we are seeking. They have chosen to join the same crew; they have trained and flown together. They have taken leaves, gone drinking, and sat talking late into the night together. They have shared a hut and a friendship, and faced death together. Michael has seen his firm friend die and he has accompanied him to his final rest in English soil. It is a marvel to have found him, our King Tut's tomb and all its treasures.

There is no wake for Arthur, no shiny lacquered casket with a satin lining, no gathering family and friends. But it is a procedure of great dignity all the same. Michael goes to his superiors asking if he may have time off to be at Arthur's funeral. Permission granted, it is now his task to travel with his friend's coffin.

He presses his uniform, rounds up an officer's cap for Arthur's casket. Our father is so new to this status that he does not yet have the gear to go with it. Michael takes on the two-day task of accompanying our father in his last journey: from Spilsby to Cambridge. There are tickets for him, and for the body. He and the others, accompanying men who have died with our father, are briefed as to their duties and whom to contact at Jesus College in Cambridge. How do they sleep that night, these young men performing such a sad task?

By 11:15 the next morning they are being driven to the station mortuary through an honour guard of twenty Erks, ground crew, here to aid and to mourn. They load seven coffins draped in Union Jacks onto a flatbed truck. Three of these are bound for Cambridge. Michael and the others step back and salute the biers before climbing into the transport and following the truck with its unhappy burden to the station at Thursby. The coffins are loaded on trucks, one for each destination as men who had flown together and died together are scattered.

We never discover just how a particular war cemetery is determined for those who die in the UK. For the British born, a place close to home is chosen. Sometimes denomination plays a part. Otherwise the choice seems random. Cambridge is a lovely spot; we have no quarrel with this resting place.

It is not an easy journey. In his diary, Michael's misery is expressed in uncharacteristic impatience. After the trucks are loaded they fill in the time before leaving for Peterborough with tea in the refreshment room. Their next stop is Ely where they have a three-hour wait. More time-filling: scrambled powdered eggs and fried tomatoes on toast at Woodcock's café followed by a trip to the pictures. And yes, our meticulous diarist actually records the name of the café. Robbie and I, when we read this, swoon in admiration. Michael finds the wait and the inefficiency a splinter in his sad young soul. "The platforms are crowded with people all asking everybody else which is which train to where, when do you change, where does it go. Nobody has a clue and the station staff is extraordinarily taciturn. Even mute. If by hitting on some happy phrase by chance, you may draw remark, which is at once abrupt, barked sideways at a milk can or mail van, unintelligible and rude. After repeating ourselves a dozen times we found out where the train drew in." Tired, bereft, bearing the heavy responsibility of delivering such cargo, it is the only time we heard frustration from our young and resilient Michael. It does him proud, I think.

But the trials of this day are not over. Cambridge when they arrive, at 10:30 that night, is dark and freezing and nobody is expecting them or their cargo. Jesus College hastily arranges billets and there is scurrying to deal with the airmen who rest in their much travelled coffins. Michael and the other officer he is with are whisked to the Officer's mess for some hastily prepared "bung" sandwiches. Translated, this means fairly grim, but food of any kind is welcome along with a drink from the bar and a blazing fire. As is often the way, the other member of the party, a mere sergeant, has wandered off to bed, no sustenance, bung or otherwise, offered. But he is not forgotten by his colleagues; a sandwich is made, and despatched along with a cup of coffee.

The funeral is set for eleven the next morning. After breakfast, Michael takes his lively curiosity for a stroll around the college. Then it is time: "Hearse arrived, bearers at each side. Slow march to the grave. Stood by while the padre conducted the services at the end of which we saluted while the Last Post was played, and then Reveille. When the coffins were lowered we turned, stood in front of each grave, saluted, and turned away." By 7:30 that night he is back at camp.

Michael closes his diary and looks up, a little damp about the eyes. "So, that's how it went. It was all very sad."

***

After a good night's rest and a definitely un-bung breakfast — the poached eggs are superb — in the minimalist dining room of the Cam, we set out to find the Borough Cemetery, first making a total hash of buying flowers to lay on our father's grave. We'd noted a florist on the way back from our evening meal the night before, but can we find it again? Cursing our addled heads, we circle and peer, desperate for the elusive source of floral tributes. Finally we spot it on a distant corner that involves crossing lanes of traffic and squeezing into a hatbox-sized parking space in front of the store. I emerge triumphant with a potted azalea. Setting her jaw, Robbie backs out into a stream of cars crankily negotiating the Cambridge rush hour. I program Fred for the cemetery where we park and, clutching our flowers and our Kleenex, head for the main building.

Robbie admits to being slightly unhinged by our harried search for floral tributes. "Perhaps we should find a toilet. Who knows how far we'll have to walk or how long we'll be here. We need a pre-emptive strike. I don't think I can handle any more stress right now."

I can hear Robbie in the adjacent stall rattling around. "What fresh Hell is this?" she demands indignantly. She is in a stall with no toilet paper. Mine, I quickly discover, offers a similar disappointment. Passing the Kleenex box under the partition I moan theatrically, "How can they do this to the bereaved?" Robbie begins to giggle. We emerge and head for the Cemetery Office, stifling our inappropriate mirth.

A chap called Alexander is assigned to guide us to the grave and takes our mission on with alarming verve, Googling our father's RAF history and eagerly telling us information we already know. We pass a fenced area and he spies two Commonwealth Graves fellows. He waves them over and we ask one of our vexing questions: Who chooses the inscription? What is the process? We know that a simple wooden cross marked those graves during the war. The austerely elegant Portland stone markers came later, in the fifties. Mummy had remarried and had a son by the time the letter arrives asking her to choose the words for Paddy's headstone. What a sad and lonely decision. We are told that a book of suggested inscriptions is provided but when I ask can we see it, they shrug their regret: they do not have a copy nor do they know if any still exist.

Some years ago, when Marion, our youngest daughter was eighteen, she travelled to England with her father and me. We visited Cambridge, went for a punt on the Cam, to Evensong at King's College and, almost as an afterthought, to visit my father's grave. Marion insisted we stop and pick up flowers. She could not imagine her own father dead; she could not imagine a life without her father in it. And for me, the father that I had kept quietly far back in my mind was pushed to the fore. After standing for a time gazing at the inscription we began to wander among the rows of graves. Marion did the math. "God," she muttered, "I can't believe it. Most of these guys were eighteen or nineteen. They were my age and they are dead." Even her grandfather, dead at twenty-seven, was a shock. She had everything ahead of her but for them it was a brick wall. All those stolen lives were breaking her heart.

It is hard to find anything positive in such a waste. I have always found the Remembrance Day refrain: "They shall grow not old, as we that are left grow old: Age shall not weary them, nor the years condemn," slightly irritating. It is a bit insulting to make a virtue of untimely death. As I sail into my seventies, well aware that I am running out of racecourse room, no matter how weary I might feel, no matter the wrinkles and the occasional ache, I would not want it otherwise. I cannot, for the life of me, feel that my father would swap an early death for decades with Nooney and his girls. I can't think that any one of those men in that cemetery would agree to a similar bargain.

Robbie and I lay our flowers in the same spot that Marion had lain hers all those years ago. The inscription chosen by our mother reads: "His Love and Courage Remembered Forever." We are trying to make a truth of that.

Alexander, our impromptu guide and enthusiastic purveyor of inaccuracies, first tells us that the stones are replaced every three years. Portland stone is very soft. Perhaps a foolish choice for eternal memorials as that would make this one the twentieth stone. Then he gallops over to correct himself: they are replaced every *twenty* years. So this is the third. It is in lovely condition and certainly not the one Tony and Marion and I would have seen. I am suspicious that the inscription is slightly different. This can happen, Alexander tells us. The stones are engraved in France and sometimes errors are made. If I can show that a change has been made, the stone will be instantly replaced. I cannot be sure and so leave it be.

Next to our father lies John Albert Baker, the bomb aimer in his second crew. They have much in common: he is also twenty-seven and from New South Wales. We don't know if he is married. We don't know if he leaves children.

Robbie is prowling the rows of graves, reading out other inscriptions. Some we admire. The very best is simply "Beloved." It says all that needs to be said. Others, spouting pious and smarmy self-satisfaction that these are the chosen ones and have gone to a better place, drive her to distraction. She flies into a comical mini-frenzy.

"I could spit on your silly graves," she rages.

"Oh my. Perhaps spitting is a bit extreme, especially as we are currently knee-deep in war heroes."

Considering that the relatives pick the inscriptions, it is they who should be more properly the objects of her scorn. The allowed inscription is sixty-six letters (spaces counting as a letter) and there is a charge for each extra letter. The meandering message on the grave that provokes my sister's ire is well over this limit. She finds some satisfaction in knowing that they got a bill for their folly.

I reserve my contempt for an inscription declaring: "Good innings. Well played." I glare at this offence. "Really, what kinds of British-Public-School-Playing-Fields-of-Eton-crap have we here? Let's pretend that flying sorties to Germany is just a jolly game. You make me puke." Robbie's turn to point out that vomiting on the remains of war heroes would not be good form either.

On this benign sunny day in this groomed and revered place, no matter how snippy we might be about some of the words on the rows and rows of pale headstones, at bottom we know each person laid to rest here has a story; each one represents a life given, a life lost.

Alexander redeems himself for his inaccuracies by telling us one of these histories. A particular grave is visited each year by the same man. This goes on for years. He arrives alone, pays his respects, leaves. Eventually his daughter comes with him. After years of being a distant and moody father, he has finally talked to her of his pain and, as he visits the grave, his daughter tells his story to Alexander. On a night this haunted man can never forget, the Ops board shows his crew is up for a raid. There is a full moon; it is suicidal. He declares his intention to refuse. His friend cheerfully volunteers to take his place. The aircraft does not return. All are lost. His instincts were right but there is no joy in such a survival. A pall of guilt descends. Each year he goes to pay his respects to the man who died in his place. His daughter finally understands why her father is difficult, angry, taciturn, unable to love. There are many ways to die in a war; this is just one of them.

With a sense of fulfilment we return to Daddy's grave to run our hands one last time over the gentle curve of the warm stone. We have traced our father's life from volunteering, through training, to battle, and death. Now we have seen where he rests.

No Certainties

Soon we have to say goodbye to each other and fly to our far-from-each-other homes.

"We must have at least one Devonshire Tea," I announce as we drive through country villages on the way to the airport. Robbie is agreeable. And there, right in front of us, is the very thing. We are plied with tea, satisfied by fat scones, clotted cream and homemade strawberry jam in a cozy, pleasantly crowded tearoom, our table by a large window where we can people-watch as we mull over our journey. We are in a pensive mood.

"How much do we really know, after all this?" Robbie says. "How much do we know about what he was like, that farm boy who hid in the outhouse to read? Then went away to war and got himself killed."

"I know. But we have learned a bit."

"And we will keep searching."

"Yes," I say, "we will. I think until we die."

We let that thought lie for a bit, idly watching the passing parade of pallid Brits.

"Look at that chap," says Robbie, "he's so tall and thin and pale." Dressed in a black suit, he strides by, beaky nose leading, shoulders hunched. "I think Cruikshank drew him. Look how thin his legs are."

"Megan calls them 'lucky legs.' Do you know why?"

"No. Why?" Robbie perks up.

"Lucky they don't snap off and go straight up his arse."

Much adolescent snorting follows before we slip back into pondering our father. I wonder aloud how our lives would have been different if he had not been killed.

If ... We are not giving multiple paths in any one life. It is the puzzle, the pain, and the glory of being human. Once those two planes met and exploded over the village of Bratoft that November morning in 1944, for us, one plot line ended abruptly. But the "if" still hangs there.

What if he had come home at war's end? What if he had completed a tour unscathed and, during his last months in England, slipped easily into the role of instructor, had not missed, as many of them did, the adrenaline rush of operations, the mateship of being part of a crew? What if he had enjoyed more leaves, explored more corners of England, cemented new friendships and one day, after a victory parade or one last armistice pub crawl, had boarded a troopship and returned to Australia to be met by a wife and two daughters, a couple of years older than when they last saw him, but excited and grateful for his return? What if it had all turned out so neatly and satisfactorily? What then?

Of course our lives, Robbie's and mine, would have been very different. We would have had a father. We would surely have been shaped by that. Perhaps our life choices would have been different. Our mother would not have lived the rest of her life working to conceal the stone in her heart and finally slipping into a black depression and dying too early because she had lost what gave her breath.

We continue to nibble our cream and jam smothered scones while taking comfort, on this slightly chilly day, in the steam rising from our tea. One of England's great strengths is making a really, really hot cup of tea, lawsuits be damned.

Another Dickensian beanpole strides by, another Lucky Legs, his long toothpick shanks sheathed in black pants, his sharp, pink-tinged nose to the fore, his shoulders hunched. Robbie observes him dispassionately. "There's his brother," she remarks blandly. "Look."

This strikes me as hilarious. Our contemplative mood broken, we gather our belongings, leave a generous tip and make our way back to the car. We have lingered as long as is safe. Our goodbyes are coming soon. We live 12,000 miles apart and we are in our seventies. There are no certainties.

But it does not stop us talking and talking as we drive. So much to be said, even now. "Remember, remember," we say over and over, reliving these two weeks. And Robbie has more stories of her multiple family and friends all cherished and each detail precious. There is a hair-raising moment when she cuts off a fellow on a motorbike. In fact she does not even see him. He shakes his fist at us as we speed away. "What if he got my license number," she moans when she realizes what she has done, and spends the next twenty miles expecting klaxons and flashing lights. She is also convinced that she has stripped the gears. I believe they are made of sterner stuff and we return the car without incident. And then we are aboard a bus together headed for the terminal. I will be dropped off to catch the Hoppa and she will head into London to St. Pancras and a train to visit her friend. We natter frantically, making the most of this last journey together when it is cut short and we are suddenly parted. Robbie, we are told kindly, must get off, I will go on. We thought we would have time to wait together.

"Goodbye, dear sister," she says as we hug awkwardly around luggage. "This was wonderful. I am so happy we did it."

"Me too. We have fun together."

"Yes, we do."

"Don't you dare die," I am crying.

"You either," she says her eyes bright with tears.

And then she is walking away toward the terminal, her orange scarf lifted by the wind, her orange hat askew: my lovely sister.

Tears

Some months after our trip, I spend the morning rearranging the binder. Robbie has sent me a copy of Daddy's medical, conducted when he first signed up, and I need to add it to this bulging catalogue of our search. It is amazing to both of us that this long ago document was archived and made available. And it has solved a small mystery: Daddy's eyes were, we are told, grey. "Now," Robbie asks tartly, "who has grey eyes." It does seem a bit dubious until I find myself mesmerized by the eyes of one of my grandsons. They take me back to the blanketing mist hanging above the gentle Wolds of Lincolnshire. Miraculously, this small boy's eyes carry both his great-grandfather and the world where he died.

Robbie sends me an email with the subject line "Tears." She weeps easily now, she tells me, and often. It's the same with me. Something has been dislodged in us. Something has shifted. I tell a friend of these foolish wellings. He is puzzled. How can I miss what I have never known? It isn't that; I'm not missing somebody I remember. I was only two when I last saw him and have no mental image to call up for comfort. He was never a person I *used* to know and love. But now, because of this pilgrimage to places where he was, through our reading and re-reading of his diary, our parsing of each word on his postcards, our intense scrutiny of his few photos, we have made him flesh and blood, have come to know and to love him. And now there is a hole where a real person, a father and a friend, could have been. Lost and now found so that he can be mourned.

We lost our father twice: first to a cruel, unnecessary accident and second to our own carelessness and a timid deference for our mother's buried grief. By the end of our journey together he is both alive to us and newly torn from us. We are able to weep for what we have lost and for him: a young, open-hearted, honest fellow who left his family, had a glorious and terrible adventure, and never came home.

Epilogue

"Did you see the video of the Lancaster flying over the memorial?"

"Yes, and the poppies dropping..."

"Lovely!" Robbie sighs.

My darker side asserts itself: "It was very moving but ... a little unnerving. For a moment it looked like blood pouring out of the Lancaster."

"Oh." I can hear her processing. It's all in the perception. Those Lancasters brought both hope and despair. "I'd never thought about blood." Now I am sorry I planted that in her head.

We are on the phone, months after our trip, luxuriating in the opening of the Bomber Command War Memorial in Green Park, London. Our hunger for recognition has been fed. Some might argue that it is too late, but it is certainly not too little. Made from Portland stone, the monument has suitable grandeur and dignity. Inside, flanked by Ionic columns, are the bronze statues of seven men. At nine feet tall and standing on a massive marble base, they are powerful. They are also deeply moving. The sculptor has avoided the macho images of war, so often found on memorials. He has shown a crew just home from a raid. They are barely upright and clearly exhausted. Faces are drawn, one looks up to the sky, searching for planes still to land, another bows his head, shoulders slumped slightly. They have just been to Hell and back. They have not had time to register that they have beaten the odds one more time. They are not triumphant; they are not vainglorious; they take no joy in having their foot on the neck of the foe; they are simply knackered.

This honesty is carried into the meticulous detail of their flying suits, parachutes, Mae Wests, webbing ... all their gear. It is so real you imagine you can hear them sigh. It is so right. It is simply brilliant. And it is about time.

Robbie recovers from my blood comment. "I read somewhere that there was one petal for each of the 55,000 who died. Just think, one of those big fat petals was for our father." He was remembered and honoured. We wrap ourselves in the comfort of that thought.

Later, I read somewhere else that a million petals were dropped. Given the vast red veil that drifted across the sky as the Lanc made its glorious pass above the memorial, a million seems more reasonable. Who knows? Once again we are hearing contradictions. This happened only weeks ago and already other versions are appearing. How did we ever think we could discover, at a distance of over seventy years, our father, fully real to us? We have, all things considered, done pretty well. There were petals; they were glorious and possibly sinister. Do we have to know exactly how many?

Bibliography

Bishop, Patrick, *Bomber Boys: Fighting Back 1940-1945* (London: Harper Press, 2007).

Burleigh, Michael, *Moral Combat* (New York: Harper Perennial, 2011).

Charlwood, Don, *Journeys into Night* (Burwood, Victoria, Australia: Burgewood Books, 1991).

——, *Marching as to War* (Hawthorn, Victoria, Australia: Hudson, 1990).

——, *No Moon Tonight* (Manchester: Goodall, 2000).

Enright, Michael, *Flyers Far Away* (New South Wales: Logueville Books, 2009).

Frank, Anne, *The Diary of a Young Girl* (New York: Pocket Books, 1952).

Gillies, Midge, *Amy Johnson: Queen of the Air* (London: Phoenix, 2004).

Gray, Philip, *Ghosts of Targets Past* (London: Grub Street, 2009).

Gunston, Bill, ed., *So Many* (Toronto: Macmillan Canada, 1995).

Hecks, Karl, *Bombing 1939-45: The Air Offensive against Land Targets in World War II* (USA: Robert Hale, 1990).

Hessel, Peter, *The Mystery of Frankenberg's Canadian Airman* (Toronto: Lorimer, 2005).

Hewer, Howard, *In for a Penny in for a Pound* (New York: Stoddart, 2000).

Lewis, Bruce, *Aircrew* (London: Cassell, 1991).

McCaffery, Dan, *Dad's War* (Toronto: Lorimer, 2004).

Middlebrook, Martin and Chris Everitt, *The Bomber Command War Diaries* (Hinkley, UK: Midland Publishing, 2011).

Moorehead, Caroline, *A Train in Winter* (Toronto: Vintage Canada, 2012).

Ondaatje, Michael, *Divisadero* (Toronto: McClelland and Stewart, 2007).

Radell, Rick and Mike Vines, *Lancaster: A Bombing Legend* (London: Osprey Publishing, 1993).

Rees, Peter, *Lancaster Men* (Crows Nest, NSW: Allen and Unwin, 2013).

Rolfe, Mel, *Looking into Hell* (London: Cassell, 1995).

Taylor, James and Martin Davidson, *Bomber Crew* (London: Hodder and Stoughton, 2004).

Wilson, Kevin, *Bomber Boys* (London: Cassell, 2006).

——, *Men of Air* (London: Orion Books, 2007).

Yates, Harry, *Luck and a Lancaster* (Ramsbury, UK: Airlife Publishing, 2001).

Films & DVDs

RAF Bomber Command, Allegro Corporation (2007).

Target for Tonight, Imperial War Museum (1941).

The Valour and the Horror, Koch Vision, National Film Board of Canada (1992).

Acknowledgements

Memoirs are tricky. They deal with real events and real people. They demand kindness and accuracy. Any failure in either of these domains is mine alone.

Help and encouragement came from many people:

My husband, Tony, whose loss hurts every day, for coming to the UK with me to meet Michael and for his gentle and genuine interest in my search.

My family: daughters Joanne, Megan, and Marion, who made me think I could do this. Son-in-law Bill, who shared his expertise. Jenni for her enthusiasm.

Michael Madigan: generous in his sharing and so missed.

Tony Adams: a noble veteran and now a friend.

Diana Fitzgerald Bryden, Lee Parpart and Jane Warren, my wise and respectful editors.

The Humber School of Writing, Karen Connelly and the Inklings, for support and laughter.

Guelph's treasure, The Bookshelf, whose Green Room is set aside each Monday morning as a space for writers, providing coffee, quiet and a distraction-free haven. Thank you.

And, of course, Robbie, who shared this journey and was my first reader, who laughed and cried and made me believe I could get it done.

CPSIA information can be obtained
at www.ICGtesting.com
Printed in the USA
BVHW030510230920
589426BV00001B/5